EXPOSED

Frank Connolly is an investigative journalist and author who lives in Dublin. His work with *The Sunday Business Post* contributed to the establishment of tribunals of inquiry into planning and police corruption in Ireland. He has published a number of bestselling non-fiction books, including *Tom Gilmartin: The Man Who Brought Down a Taoiseach* (2014), *NAMA-Land* (2017), *United Nation: The Case for Integrating Ireland* (2022) and *The Christy Moore Songbook* (1984). He has also published a novel set against the background of the Dublin bombings in 1974, *A Conspiracy of Lies* (2019).

EXPOSED

SCANDALS THAT ROCKED THE IRISH STATE

FRANK CONNOLLY

MERRION PRESS

First published in 2026 by
Merrion Press
10 George's Street
Newbridge
Co. Kildare
Ireland
www.merrionpress.ie

978 1 78537 602 3 (Paper)
978 1 78537 603 0 (eBook)

A CIP catalogue record for this book is available from the British Library.

Text typeset in Minion Pro 11.5/17 pt and

Cover design by Fiachra McCarthy

Merrion Press is a member of Publishing Ireland.

To the victims of ruthless power and live-streamed genocide and all those who continue to seek truth, justice and freedom in these dark and dangerous times.

CONTENTS

PART III

Prologue

AFTER A LONG HOT DAY HELPING voters to the polling stations, Bertie Ahern was looking forward to a cold pint. At the bar of The Goose Tavern in north Dublin, he joined his team in sinking the first of the night. It was general election day, Friday, 6 June 1997, and he had a good chance of becoming taoiseach, the political leader of the country, following the count the next day. From the bar, he nodded and beckoned me over. I said it looked like he was going to win and form a government. Cautious but quietly confident, he said he hoped so.

He wanted to know more about a story I had been investigating for *The Sunday Business Post* over recent months and years. It involved Ray Burke, a prominent member of his front bench and likely Cabinet minister in what would be Ahern's first government as taoiseach. It concerned an alleged payment of up to £80,000 to Burke by two businessmen eight years earlier, during the 1989 general election.

I told 'the Bert', as he was known to his circle of friends and political mates, that if he wanted to know more, he should take a trip out to Sutton, some three miles away, to meet Jim Gogarty, the man who claimed to have witnessed the bribe. I told him that Gogarty had a room full of files to back up his story.

'I won't have a fucking Michael Lowry in my Cabinet,' said Ahern.

Lowry was a Fine Gael minister in the outgoing coalition government who had resigned from office in November 1996 following allegations that he accepted improper donations. He was later embroiled in a series of controversies relating to large and improper payments and other benefits that the Moriarty Tribunal found him to have received from two of the country's richest men, Ben Dunne and Denis O'Brien. By June 1997, he was a pariah, and a symbol of the political and corporate corruption that Ahern had so often decried on his long and winding road to power.

Nothing in our brief conversation would have surprised Ahern, as prior to the election I had spoken at length to his party strategist and handler, the legendary P.J. Mara, about the financial contributions made to Burke during the June 1989 general election campaign. Mara confirmed 'off the record' to me that Burke may have received 'political donations' at the time, but he denied there was anything improper about the circumstances and warned that if I published otherwise it could lead to unfortunate consequences for *The Sunday Business Post*. Over previous months, Burke and his press handler had denied that he received any payments in return for political favours and threatened legal action if we said anything to the contrary.

Following our brief engagement in The Goose Tavern, I was left with the impression that Ahern knew a lot more than he let on but had wanted to hear what I was prepared to divulge. There was no doubt in my mind that the 'most skilful, the most devious, and the most cunning of them all', as Charles Haughey once described Ahern, would be a formidable and dangerous adversary for anyone who crossed him. But I was prepared to take that risk. After all, that was my job.

Introduction

FROM THE LATE 1980S, THE IRISH establishment and successive governments were rocked by a series of political scandals that started with Charles J. Haughey's term as taoiseach and continued to the resignation of Bertie Ahern from that role in 2008. They were tumultuous times, during much of which I was working as a journalist with *The Sunday Business Post* (1993–2002), *Ireland on Sunday* (2002–4), *Village* magazine (2006–7) and *The Irish Mail on Sunday* (2007–8). The investigations I carried out, along with my colleagues, would lead to the establishment of two tribunals of inquiry and expose the corrupt practices that characterised the leadership and actions of the mainly Fianna Fáil-led governments over those twenty years.

The fallout from what went on during those years is still being felt today, particularly in the shortage and cost of housing. It was this, along with the key role played by Michael Lowry in the formation of the coalition government following the general election of November 2024, that inspired me to write this book. A former Fine Gael minister, Lowry was a central focus of the 'Tribunal of Inquiry into certain Payments to Politicians and Related Matters' (commonly known as the Moriarty Tribunal), which was established in September 1997 to investigate payments made to him and to Charles Haughey by prominent businessmen, including Ben Dunne. In 2011, Fianna Fáil leader and later Taoiseach Micheál Martin called for Lowry's resignation and his removal from political life, following publication of the findings of the Moriarty Tribunal. Yet in 2025 the same Micheál Martin accepted the support of Lowry and other regional independent TDs to form a coalition government with them and Fine Gael. So, it seemed like an appropriate time to revisit what had happened during those times from my particular and unique perspective.

This book follows my investigations into corruption allegations and how they resulted in the resignation and disgrace of a series of senior politicians, including Ray Burke, Pádraig Flynn, Liam Lawlor and, eventually, Bertie Ahern, as well as uncovering their benefactors in the business community. The seeds of the banking and property collapse of 2008 were sown in the policies pursued by successive governments that fed the boom-and-bust economic cycle. They were nurtured by the improper and self-serving relationships between developers, builders, bankers and the politicians and parties they financed and supported. Their misdeeds were enabled by the failure of those responsible for the regulation of the banking, corporate, political and policing authorities. The book also examines how members of the Garda Síochána engaged in criminal behaviour that led to a series of wrongful arrests, harassment and abuse of citizens across a north-western division of the force in the 1990s.

It is my aim with this book to inform readers about illicit business practices and poor governance that have enriched the few, widened inequality and failed to provide the infrastructure, climate protection measures and public services that citizens are entitled to expect from their government. To do so, I concentrate on my investigations into planning and Garda corruption in the 1990s and 2000s, during which time I worked with many excellent journalists, editors, production and other staff in various newspapers and media organisations. In Ireland, a generation has been denied the right to decent, secure and affordable homes due to the State's failure. The roots of today's housing crisis stem from the negligence and greed of those powerful political and business interests who are the subject of this book. The words of Ciara Mary-Alice

Thompson (CMAT), in her song 'Euro-Country', capture the human cost of this corruption:

> All the big boys, all the Berties
> All the envelopes, yeah, they hurt me
> I was 12 when the das started killing themselves all
> around me
> And it was normal, building houses
> That stay empty even now, yeah
> And no one says it out loud but I know it can be better if
> we hound it.

I hope that this work will help to explain how and why so much pain was inflicted on so many, and in some small way help to ensure that the 'big boys' do not always win.

PART I

Chapter One

Will We, Fuck!

JIM GOGARTY, FROM KELLS IN COUNTY Meath, was a former chairman and managing director of Joseph Murphy Structural Engineers (JMSE) based in Santry, Dublin. He left the company following a bitter row with his employer. Born in 1917, he served in the Garda Síochána reserve in the 1940s, before training as an engineer and working in construction. For over twenty years, he was a loyal enforcer for Joe Murphy senior, a tough operator from Kerry, who made big money with his brother John in Britain's post-war construction boom.

Gogarty spent his final years in the company in a fierce battle with Murphy, trying to get what he believed was his due in promised pension entitlements. When an advertisement was published in *The Irish Times* in 1995 offering a reward for anyone who could provide information leading to a criminal conviction for planning corruption, he seized the opportunity. The reward of £10,000 was posted by Newry solicitor Kevin Neary on behalf of environmentalists and lawyers Michael Smith and Colm MacEochaidh, who were members of An Taisce, the heritage protection group. They were frustrated at what they considered to be widescale corruption involving public officials, politicians and businessmen in planning and zoning decisions across the country.

They were not disappointed. A total of fifty-five complainants came forward, including Gogarty, the seventy-eight-year-old then living in Sutton in north Dublin.

The first news story relating to the complaints sent to Neary was printed by *The Sunday Business Post* on 9 July 1995 and written by reporter Marion McKeone, who gave a brief outline of Gogarty's complaint, which had been provided to her by the two lawyers but without meeting the source.[1] She told me that Ray Burke was the politician involved. I wanted to follow up on the story, as I had previously investigated Burke in relation to planning and zoning controversies for *Magill* magazine in the late 1980s. McKeone introduced me to Smith and MacEochaidh, and, through them, I made direct contact with Gogarty. We agreed to meet in the Newry offices of solicitors Donnelly Neary & Donnelly, where he set out the conditions attached to any future co-operation.

Gogarty told me he had previously been let down by journalists who had abused his trust and, on occasion, misrepresented the facts he presented to them. It took a while to convince him that I would not publish any material he provided to me without his consent, and for him to accept that anything I did reveal would have to be verified and supported by documentation. During an hour-long discussion, he disclosed enough to convince me that he had a story to tell that implicated Burke, Gogarty's former employers and builder Michael Bailey in a blatant act of bribery and corruption.

It took a number of meetings at Gogarty's home for me to acquire a deeper understanding of his complaints and of his character. A cantankerous man at times, he was angry and understandably bitter, mostly against his former employers, but also against those in political and media circles, as well as in the police, who had failed to act on his complaints and to deal with the threats and intimidation to which he was subjected in his efforts to secure his pension rights. He also had an impish sense of humour, was self-deprecating and fully aware that he was, at the very least, partially complicit in the act of bribery he witnessed in Burke's home.

On 13 August 1995, I reported further details of the complaints sent to Neary in a piece that asserted 'a coalition politician and three former

Fianna Fáil office holders are among those accused of accepting payoffs in exchange for assisting with land rezoning applications in Dublin'.[2] The coalition politician was a prominent member of Fine Gael, the largest party of the 'Rainbow' government that included the Labour Party and Democratic Left. 'While the complaints do not exclusively concern land rezonings in Dublin, the most prominent politicians implicated are from constituencies in the capital, where most of the planning controversies of recent years have taken place,' the story continued.

Kevin Neary had told me that some of the replies to the advertisement were 'very credible' and would probably stand up in court, and that the sponsors of the reward wanted then Minister for Justice Nora Owen to instruct the attorney general 'to consider how best immunity from prosecution might be facilitated for those offering information on corruption'.

In order to reassure Gogarty about my intentions to pursue his claims energetically, the *Post* published a further story on 3 September stating, somewhat presciently, that the 'Corruption exposures may need inquiry'. This followed discussions with Smith and MacEochaidh, who were seeking an independent investigation, and with the Dublin North-East Labour Party TD Tommy Broughan, who took an active interest in the corruption allegations and met with myself and Gogarty, one of his constituents.

Gogarty was in poor health and lived with his wife, Anna, with whom he had raised seven children in Shielmartin Road in Sutton, north Dublin. Anna was friendly, hospitable and patiently supportive of her husband when we met at their home, which was close to Howth Head with a view over Dublin Bay. A large front room contained a table covered with boxes full of documents relating to Gogarty's years of employment as chairman and managing director of JMSE. His anger with his former boss and company founder, Joseph Murphy senior, was evident and based largely on his grievances over the manner in which his pension arrangements had been handled by the firm. His main concern was how Anna, some twenty years younger than him, would manage after his death.

He wanted the full truth of his alleged mistreatment by Murphy senior over his pension and other entitlements to be exposed. He described threats and intimidation suffered at the hands of Joseph Murphy junior, who succeeded his father as managing director of the company. Gogarty claimed that these were not properly investigated by the gardaí. Crucially, he also recounted how he witnessed Ray Burke being bribed in 1989 and had retained evidence of fraud, breaches of currency regulations and tax evasion by Murphy senior and his companies, which, he maintained, were part of the culture at JMSE.

After examining and discussing these records at his home, I put it to Gogarty that the best way to ensure that his financial concerns were addressed and his mistreatment by his former employers properly investigated was through exposing the political corruption he witnessed in the home of the politician. I cautioned that it could take many months to achieve results, not least due to the potential legal obstacles we would face from Burke, the Murphys and other politicians and public servants who were implicated in the wrongdoing.

Gradually, and with the benefit of a sharp memory, Gogarty outlined in meticulous detail the circumstances surrounding the meeting in Burke's home in Swords, Dublin, in June 1989, during which the politician was given two envelopes containing a total of £80,000. Also present, he said, were Joseph Murphy junior and Michael Bailey of building firm Bovale Developments. The money was paid to Burke in exchange for his assistance with the rezoning of lands in north Dublin.

Gogarty had been asked by Murphy senior to go to Burke's home in his capacity as chairman of JMSE and 'to keep an eye' on his son. Bailey drove them from Santry to Swords in his dark grey Mercedes. On the way, Gogarty asked him whether they would get a receipt for the payment from the politician. 'Will we, fuck!' was the colourful reply from the builder.

Mick Bailey hailed from Roscommon, and, with his brother Tom, started work in Dublin as a bricklayer, going on to create a successful house-building business. The name of their firm, Bovale Developments, was derived from their homeplace Boho and Tom's wife's townland of Glenvale, also in Roscommon. By 1996, Bovale Developments was building up to 150 semi-detached houses a year, mainly in the Swords area, with an annual turnover of £10 million. A big man, rough and ready, and with hands like shovels, Mick Bailey courted public officials, politicians, bankers and anyone else who could advance the interests of his construction company. He owned a large home in Batterstown, County Meath, and several racehorses, and he rode out with the Ward Union Hunt. He famously celebrated a bet that scooped him £50,000 at Cheltenham by jumping into the winner's enclosure, where he kissed the Queen Mother and was promptly seized by the police.[3] Bailey was a member of Burke's constituency organisation and a generous contributor to Fianna Fáil.

A year before this meeting with Burke, at Murphy senior's request, Gogarty had negotiated the sale of JMSE land at Forest Road in Swords with Bailey. In early 1989, Murphy senior told Gogarty he wanted to sell off the remainder of the company's land bank in north Dublin and he approached Bailey once again. Murphy was anxious to dispose of the land urgently due to an internal company dispute, but he wanted to maximise its value before he did so. This would require 'political support', which Bailey could deliver. In the weeks before Burke was approached by Bailey, a deal was hammered out. It was agreed that Bovale would either buy all the land or take a 50 per cent stake in it if Bailey could 'procure' its rezoning from agricultural to residential use, thus multiplying its value before the sale. A letter to this effect, providing details of every plot and folio in the 720-acre land bank, was drawn up by Bailey in advance of the meeting with Burke.

The payments to the powerful politician in north Dublin were intended to smooth the path to the ultimate rezoning of the lands for large-scale housing development. When they arrived at Briargate, the large, detached house on the Malahide Road in Swords where Burke lived, Gogarty had a copy of the document containing the proposal agreed with Bailey and the location of the lands, which stretched across a large part of the politician's Dublin constituency.

During the meeting, Bailey and Murphy junior each handed the politician an envelope which, as agreed, contained sums of £40,000. In the case of Murphy junior, it was £30,000 in cash and a cheque for £10,000. According to Gogarty, he had been at a meeting at the JMSE offices in Santry earlier in the day when the cash contribution for Burke was counted and placed in the envelope along with the cheque. Frank Reynolds, another director of the firm, was involved in gathering the money.

Burke accepted both envelopes, which he placed in a drawer. When Gogarty offered him the document containing the details and location of the lands, Burke replied that he had already received a copy from Bailey. A busy man, he was in a hurry to end the meeting. It was only a week or so before the general election, and he had a lot of homes to canvass and hands to shake. He mentioned that he had a television interview to do and ushered his generous donors out the door in quick time.

Over subsequent meetings at his home, Gogarty gave me access to extensive documentation concerning his involvement with JMSE and payments made to others by the company. Among the recipients was George Redmond, the powerful assistant city and county manager for the greater Dublin area. If proven, Gogarty's claims had the potential to open a Pandora's box of planning irregularities in the expanding city and expose the role of elected councillors and TDs, as well as local authority officials, in suspect planning and rezoning decisions. The failure to enforce accepted standards and regulations would have a direct impact on the quality of life for hundreds of thousands of urban dwellers.

Inevitably, Gogarty's version of events would be disputed by the other parties he named, but, for now, it was a story as big as anything the *Post* had printed since the paper was first published in 1989, the same year as the substantial handover in Burke's house took place. Over the following months, we reported on Gogarty's claims without naming him, his former employers or the politician. Gogarty was not inclined to come forward publicly at this time.

On 31 March 1996, a lead article provided detail on the payments made in Burke's home in June 1989. It described how 'a source' told the *Post* that he was present when a senior politician was given 'cash and cheques' to the value of £40,000 during 1989, and that a property developer handed over an equivalent sum to the politician on the same occasion. The story went on to highlight the source's claim that he was subjected to threatening phone calls, attacks and intimidation at his home, which the gardaí had failed to investigate properly. His solicitors confirmed that they had sent details of the allegations to Minister for Justice Nora Owen, a Fine Gael TD for the same north Dublin constituency that Burke represented.

On the same page it was reported how JMSE had provided crucial materials for the controversial nuclear power plant at Sellafield, on the west coast of England.[4] Only those who knew the details of the alleged payments to Burke referred to in the lead story would have realised the significance of that detail. The decision to run the two apparently unrelated reports together was intended to increase the pressure on Burke and Fianna Fáil, as well as JMSE, in relation to the growing political controversy, without facing legal action. The result was that the *Post* was sent letters by solicitors representing Burke and JMSE warning the paper not to identify their clients in any reporting or it would face defamation proceedings.

In response to the article, then Minister for Labour Bertie Ahern commented that the reported allegations of planning payoffs should be dealt with by the Garda authorities, while senior Fianna Fáil sources insisted that the party would 'forcefully deal with any of its members who are shown to be implicated in any political corruption.'[5] These remarks were published in a follow-up article in the *Post* alongside fresh allegations of irregular payments to Burke from a separate, unnamed source. They resulted from a call to me from Jim Geraghty, a former Fianna Fáil councillor in Dublin County Council, who had served during Burke's two terms as chairman of the council in 1985 and 1986. He claimed that he had witnessed cash payments to Burke on two separate occasions.

From Rush in north Dublin, Geraghty had been among those who came forward with information to the Newry solicitor a year earlier, and, after months of discussion, he agreed to make a signed affidavit for the *Post* containing his sensational claims before they were aired on 7 April 1996. He did not want to be identified in the article for fear of recrimination against himself, his family and his business, or even to be described as a former public representative.

Headed 'Fianna Fáil will deal forcefully with corruption', the article reminded readers of the allegation by Gogarty that Burke (both unnamed) was handed £80,000 in exchange for assistance with the rezoning of hundreds of acres of land in north Dublin, which 'would be achieved over a period of years at a cost to the developers of £1,000 an acre in payoffs.' Readers were informed that, 'The developer who organised the meeting indicated that the politician was anxious to get the money urgently to cover election costs. The payments were partly intended to cover the payment to other named councillors who would support the zoning motions, he says.' The article then described how Geraghty, who was not known to Gogarty, witnessed two payments to the politician in Burke's office in Dublin County Council on O'Connell Street in the city centre:

> I was with [name excluded] when this man came in. He had a carrier bag with him and he left it on the table. I walked out. When I left, I realised that I had left my briefcase behind me. I went back into the office. The guy had the bag opened. I saw bundles of cash, Irish currency, in it. The man with the bag had his back to me. As I walked in, he said: 'There is 60 grand there.'

Geraghty first thought it may have been a development contribution but then realised that such payments are made to the relevant department of the local authority. This was not the only such payment he witnessed:

> On another occasion I was with [Burke's name excluded] and somebody came in, a man, with a plastic bag which he handed to [name excluded] and said: 'There is what we agreed on. Do you want to check it?' [Name excluded] said: 'No, it is ok.' You could see the notes through the bag although there would not have been as much there as on the other occasion. That time the bag was practically full, stuffed with notes. It is only in later years that I began to realise that I had probably witnessed two irregularities.

The following week another story expanded on the involvement of JMSE in the supply of materials for nuclear installations in Britain. A State property controlled by the Office of Public Works in Dublin was used to store steel for the company, which was intended for the Sellafield plant during the 1980s. Sellafield was previously called Windscale, but the name had been changed following a disastrous fire at the plant in the late 1950s that had carried radioactive material across the Irish Sea, subsequently blamed for causing cancer clusters along the north-east coast of Ireland.

In late spring 1996, I met with senior executives of JMSE at their offices in Santry, who denied knowledge of any political payments to Ray

Burke. Burke himself maintained a self-enforced silence, despite a series of questions from the *Post* relating to the Gogarty allegation. It was not the first time that the north Dublin politician had been embroiled in allegations of bribery, and he had developed a thick skin when it came to adverse media attention.

Burke grew up in a house attached to St Ita's psychiatric hospital in Portrane, County Dublin, where his father worked as a nurse, while also serving as a TD. P.J. 'Paddy' Burke came from farming stock in Kilmeena, near Westport in County Mayo, and he was first elected to the Dáil in 1943, the year his son Raphael was born. Paddy Burke, known as the 'Bishop' due to the number of funerals he attended in his north Dublin constituency, was still a serving Fianna Fáil TD and councillor when Ray was first elected to Dublin County Council in 1967. By this time, the younger Burke, then just twenty-four, had set up his own estate agency, PJ Burke (Sales) Ltd, named after his father.

On Paddy Burke's retirement in 1973, his seat passed to his son following that year's general election. Ray inherited the friends and acquaintances his father had nurtured during his five decades as a TD, including many from the west of Ireland. The Burkes were joined at the hip to Tom Brennan and Joe McGowan, whose company, Brennan & McGowan, was among the most successful housebuilders across Dublin county and beyond. Ray Burke's estate agency sold the houses that Brennan & McGowan built across north Dublin, earning some £85,000, over £1,000 a month, between 1972 and 1982 from commission on the sales. Brennan & McGowan raised an estimated £150,000 in finance for 'Mr Burke and Fianna Fáil' between 1972 and 1984, although it appears that little, if any of it went into the party coffers.[6]

In 1974, Oak Park, a company which Brennan & McGowan part-owned, purchased two acres of land in Swords for £7,000. The land was acquired from Joseph Coleman, a patient and ward of court in St Ita's, where Paddy Burke was employed. Coleman later died in St Brendan's psychiatric hospital in Dublin. Brennan & McGowan built the large house 'Briargate' on the site, which was gifted to Burke by his father as a wedding present, although it was not registered in his name until many years later. Questions were raised in the late 1970s and 1980s about Burke's acquisition of this house, along with other unusual financial dealings with the builders, which became the subject of a Garda investigation. Burke admitted that he was questioned on a number of occasions by gardaí about his relationship with Brennan & McGowan, as well as certain zoning decisions he supported, but he dismissed allegations of improper behaviour out of hand. However, they never went away.

In 1987, I had interviewed him for *Magill* about some of the controversial votes and his appointment of his close advisor, Tony Lambert, and other associates to An Bord Pleanála, the planning appeals board, when he was minister for environment some years earlier. Now, almost ten years later I was on his trail again.

Chapter Two

Sheik Down

BERTIE AHERN WAS FAMILIAR WITH THE controversies surrounding Ray Burke over their years in politics, including one that erupted just eighteen months before the 1997 general election. As minister for justice in the government formed by Charles Haughey following the 1989 election, Burke had been responsible for the administration of the Passport for Investment (PFI) scheme, which allowed non-nationals to obtain an Irish passport in return for a substantial financial investment in the country. In late December 1995, I exposed Burke's controversial role in the award of eleven such passports to a Saudi millionaire and banker, his family and a friend.[1]

On a Saturday morning in December 1990, Burke issued eleven Irish passports to Sheik Khalid bin Mahfouz in return for a promised investment of £20 million in the State. The documents were signed by Burke at his home in Swords before they were presented the next day to Sheik Mahfouz by Haughey during a lavish dinner in the Shelbourne Hotel in Dublin. Burke ignored the requirements under the PFI programme that recipients should live in Ireland for a period before they were entitled to benefit from the scheme.

Sheik Mahfouz had purchased Glenmore House, Clonee, County Meath, several months earlier, but he didn't visit the address once before he collected the passports from Haughey after arriving in Dublin in his private jet. The passports were issued by Burke before the naturalisation certificates were signed, which was another breach of the requirements under the PFI legislation. A requirement to swear fidelity to the State, which was normally made before naturalisation was granted, was also waived, apparently because it might have conflicted with the Sheik's obligations to his own country.

In the week after Christmas 1995, the original documents that led to Burke granting the passports to the Sheik, several of his family members and a Pakistani citizen, Haroon Rashid Kahlon, were provided to me by a senior figure familiar with the application. The documents established that Burke did not comply with the correct procedures when he authorised the passports. Over the following weeks and months, the *Post* ran a number of stories which followed the money trail and the dispersal of a large chunk of the promised £20 million paid by the Sheik to various companies and their owners, some of them with strong connections to Fianna Fáil, and to Haughey in particular.[2]

In 1990 Khalid bin Mahfouz controlled 20 per cent of the shares and was a board member of the Bank of Credit and Commerce International (BCCI). The bank, established in Pakistan, was under investigation by US authorities for alleged fraud involving deposits of hundreds of millions in dollar loans to the National Commerce Bank of Saudi Arabia, owned by the Sheik's family. The collapse of BCCI and the Sheik's wish to avoid arrest were believed to be behind his application for Irish passports for his family and Pakistani advisor. He and Kahlon were later indicted in the US and paid $245 million in fines in a 1992 settlement of the charges against them.

It emerged that the main beneficiaries of the Sheik's investment were associates of Haughey, including millionaires John Magnier and J.P. McManus. Their company, Leisure Holdings, secured £4 million, a generous portion of the funds. Denis Brosnan, then chairman of the Kerry Group, publicly defended the manner in which the funds were allocated to Leisure Holdings, which he also chaired. The company later merged with UK company Barchester Healthcare, in which Magnier, McManus and Dermot Desmond, financier and friend of Haughey, were the major shareholders.[3]

Other beneficiaries of reported £3 million investments from the fund were Kerry Airport and a company owned by Noel C. Duggan, owner of the Millstreet horse riding and entertainment complex in west Cork.[4] Duggan denied any involvement with the PFI scheme, but in 1992 Kahlon emerged as an alternate director of Millstreet Equestrian Services, a company owned by the Cork businessman and Fianna Fáil supporter. The funds provided by the Sheik were administered by Pat Kenny, an accountant with Deloitte & Touche and a tax adviser to Haughey.

In 1992, Haughey was replaced by Albert Reynolds as Fianna Fáil leader and taoiseach, during the so-called 'country and western' coup in the party, which followed a raft of financial scandals surrounding the 'boss', as he was referred to by his party underlings. Burke was among those removed from Cabinet by the new taoiseach. In November 1994, Reynolds himself was forced to resign, following a row with his coalition partners in the Labour Party over his appointment of Attorney General Harry Whelehan as president of the High Court. Labour leader Dick Spring saw Whelehan as too conservative for the position, due to Whelehan's decision as attorney general in 1992 to apply for an injunction, later overturned, to prevent a teenage girl leaving the country for an abortion, in what became known as the X case. Reynolds refused to revoke the High Court appointment but fell on his sword when it emerged that Whelehan had failed to take action in relation to an extradition application from Northern Ireland for the paedophile priest Brendan Smyth, which had gathered dust in the attorney general's office for seven months.

Bertie Ahern was an architect of the debacle and the main beneficiary when he was selected as the new Fianna Fáil leader, but his hopes of taking over as taoiseach were dashed after Labour formed a new government with Fine Gael and the Democratic Left, dubbed the Rainbow Coalition. Ahern became leader of the opposition and brought Burke back into the fold as his spokesperson for foreign affairs.

When I obtained details of his role in the PFI scandal in late December 1995, Burke was positioned as a key figure in Ahern's circle, and his political star seemed destined to rise as the party headed towards a general election and back to power. In a profile of the politician, the *Post* detailed previous controversies that Burke had survived over his long career, including the manner in which he had acquired his home.[5] His role in the allocation of the passports in December 1990 became the subject of a government investigation in 1997 after the *Post* published that story.[6]

Ahern said little or nothing about the passport controversy as it unfolded and was apparently unfazed by the bribery allegations surrounding one of his closest allies. At the Fianna Fáil Ard-Fheis in April 1996, he had warned that the party would 'deal forcefully with corruption' of any sort, but his comments were in response to speculation concerning large amounts of money that Haughey received from benefactors while in office.[7] He was, however, also aware of a growing unease among his party colleagues in relation to repeated suggestions in the *Post* from early 1996 of payments made to an as yet unnamed senior serving politician.

Sensitivity about allegations of corruption became particularly acute after Judge Brian McCracken set up an investigation into reports of large contributions made by retailer Ben Dunne to Haughey and former Fine Gael communications minister Michael Lowry. This was instigated by the Fine Gael-led government in February 1997, just months in advance of an expected election. Lowry's role in his department awarding a hugely lucrative second mobile phone licence to businessman Denis O'Brien had also been the subject of intense political and media attention following the former minister's resignation in late 1996.

As a former Fianna Fáil party treasurer, Ahern was fully conscious of the internal rows surrounding large donations made to some senior party figures that did not always find their way into the appropriate bank accounts. His appointment of Burke as foreign affairs spokesman in early 1995 reflected his view that, as befitted his 'tough guy' image, Burke would not recoil from taking a hard line in the party's dealings with Sinn Féin when required during suspected peace negotiations in the North. It also illustrated the close relations between the two men. Ahern's decision to bring Burke into government was, therefore, unsurprising, but it represented a clear political gamble by the party leader, particularly once the investigation into the passport scandal began.

While Ahern and Burke prepared for the 1997 election, I was spending many hours at Gogarty's home in Sutton, poring over a trove of papers and files documenting his years working at JMSE and hearing of his perceived betrayal by Joseph Murphy senior. He recounted how he saved Murphy's companies and trusts within the JMSE group from potential ruin after they were, in his view, mismanaged by Liam Conroy, the former JMSE chief executive. I also spoke to Joe Murphy junior and Michael Bailey, who repeated their denials of any payments made to Burke.

By the 1980s Joe Murphy senior was living in Guernsey, and much of his accumulated wealth was hidden in offshore trusts outside the grasp of the British or Irish revenue services. Gogarty had run the Irish operations of the JMSE group as managing director for a number of years before he retired in 1982, aged sixty-five. He remained on as chairman, with Conroy moving in as chief executive of the Irish and British operations the following year, but relations between the two were fractious. In May 1988, Murphy senior agreed with a proposal from Conroy to ask Gogarty to step down but then changed his mind. This followed a letter from Gogarty setting out a litany of failings by Conroy, which, he wrote, threatened the very existence of the companies and trusts that Murphy senior had built over decades. Gogarty had kept records of a multitude of company documents, minutes of board meetings and contracts, which, he believed, could expose the company to criminal charges of fraud and lead to Murphy's trusts in the Channel Islands being dismantled. The letter warned Murphy that the businesses in the UK and Ireland were being handled in 'a careless, negligent and reckless manner as to indicate that in a very short time the entire organisation will come crashing down'.

As a result, Murphy senior and his twenty-six-year-old son, Joseph Murphy junior, moved against Conroy, who responded with legal action for wrongful and unfair dismissal. Following bitter and protracted High Court proceedings in 1989, during which Conroy submitted a lengthy and extremely damaging affidavit about the Murphys, a settlement was reached in August 1990. As part of the deal, it was agreed that the document would never be revealed by Conroy. Gogarty retained a copy of this sensitive affidavit, as well as many other compromising documents, which he was now prepared to use in his efforts to make Murphy senior fulfil his promise of a pension of some £500,000 and other benefits to maintain Anna and their children in comfort when he died.

While the detail of the deterioration in Gogarty's relationship with his former employer was fascinating in many respects, it was not enough, in my view, to convince the gardaí or the wider public that his case deserved any more attention than many others with similar grievances. His complaints to the gardaí of intimidation and threats against him by Murphy junior did not lead to criminal charges.

Gogarty began to accept that it would be in his best interests to make the meeting in Burke's house in June 1989 the hook on which to hang his wider complaints against his former employers. His son, Eamon, helped to persuade him that this approach could yield better results, and we agreed to push the story further by revealing as much as possible, without naming him until he was given the legal protections he sought. He was understandably concerned that, without a guarantee of immunity from prosecution, he could be charged with bribery if he went public prematurely with the information about his meeting with Burke in June 1989. Meanwhile, JMSE and Michael Bailey continued to deny that they had paid any monies to Burke and, like the politician, repeatedly threatened legal action if anything otherwise was suggested by the *Post*.

By this point, details from the judicial and other investigations into Lowry and Haughey were beginning to emerge, most dramatically in the case of the former taoiseach when journalist Sam Smyth reported on an alleged £1.1 million payment to an unnamed politician in the *Irish Independent*. Without mentioning Haughey's name, Ahern was forced to respond and, at the party's annual Ard-Fheis in April 1997, he insisted, for the second year running, that he would not permit anyone associated with corruption to represent Fianna Fáil. 'No one is welcome in this party if they betray the public trust,' Ahern thundered. 'I say this and mean this with every fibre of my body.'[8]

While it was widely understood that the focus of his comment was his former leader and mentor, the chatter at the party conference was as much about Burke and the potential danger the whiff of corruption around their foreign affairs spokesperson might pose for the party's prospects in an election only months away. The forthcoming contest was also not far from our minds when it was decided by the *Post* to publish an updated version of the claims by Gogarty, once again without naming, for legal reasons, any of the individuals involved.

On 4 May 1997, it was reported in the *Post* how the 'former company director who has made serious allegations of planning corruption against a Fianna Fáil politician has indicated that he will make a formal signed complaint if he is granted immunity from prosecution.'[9] The article went on to repeat the earlier claim by Gogarty that he was present 'when £80,000 was paid over to the politician who had promised to get a large tract of land rezoned.' Noting that the two men alleged to have made the payments were denying the allegations, the article incorrectly stated that the money was paid in two separate cheques, an error remedied in subsequent reports.

One of the reasons Gogarty agreed to this article being published was that other media reports, prompted by political sources, wrongly suggested that his motive in coming forward was to extract money from his antagonists. Fianna Fáil sources privately briefed that he was using the police investigation to get money from the Murphys and did not intend to make a formal complaint.

Correcting this narrative, solicitor Kevin Neary confirmed to the *Post* that he had told the gardaí that Gogarty was 'prepared to drop a separate civil action against his former employer and owner of the company if his complaints are investigated fully by the authorities'. The paper also reported that 'Garda inquiries were initiated several weeks ago after a series of questions were put to the Minister for Justice', while Neary said that Gogarty was prepared to make a formal complaint: 'A decision on immunity has to be made before he signs a complaint but it is not true to say that he was refusing to make a formal complaint to the Garda.' The article reported a confirmation by Minister for Justice Nora Owen that 'immunity was a matter for the DPP [Director of Public Prosecutions]'.[10]

Other media were now being briefed on the context of our investigation, and this added to pressure on the *Post* to run with as much detail as legally permitted, with the imminent election adding to the urgency. The widening media interest conferred added legitimacy to our work and to Gogarty's allegations, even if they portrayed our source as a grumpy old man with a vengeance. The dogs on the street knew that Burke was the politician at the heart of our story, and it was only a matter of time before he was publicly named.

The tensions within Fianna Fáil were evident in the tone adopted by the party's director of elections, P.J. Mara, in a heated phone conversation with me just weeks before polling day. He suggested that Burke may have received political donations in 1989, but he warned that to attribute another motive to any payments the politician received would be libellous and defamatory. As a former advisor to Haughey, Mara was used to deflecting allegations of financial improprieties and was not averse to threatening hell and high water if they were published. He and Burke's spokesperson also made it clear that the *Post* would be sued if we named Burke in connection with bribery and corruption, and a succession of legal missives were thrown at the newspaper to underline the threats.

When the votes were counted on the day after the election on 6 June 1997, Ray Burke was the first TD to be elected. The celebrations did not last long.

Chapter Three

Climbing Trees

ON 26 JUNE 1997 RAY BURKE was appointed minister for foreign affairs without any serious investigation into the allegations against him by the new taoiseach. Bertie Ahern's apparent determination not to 'have a fucking Michael Lowry in my Cabinet' echoed in my mind as I watched him lose the battle with his conscience. He formed a government with the Progressive Democrats, whose leader, Mary Harney, was more concerned with the potential destabilisation of any new administration as a consequence of the alleged payments to Haughey than she seemed to be about the rumours swirling around Burke.

While Ahern defended the appointment and professed to know little about the detail of the corruption allegations floated in *The Sunday Business Post*, the new taoiseach knew enough to tell Burke soon after the election that Gogarty was going to be granted immunity from prosecution if he co-operated with Garda inquiries. Notwithstanding this significant concession to Gogarty, he insisted that he could find no obstacle to his appointment of Burke to his Cabinet. 'I've been just about up every tree in North County Dublin chasing all kinds of things' in pursuit of the truth surrounding the payment allegations, he said in response to questions following Burke's inclusion in his Cabinet.[1]

It was a calculated risk on his part, as the road to peace negotiations in the North was now cleared with the election of Tony Blair and the Labour Party to government in the UK in early May and an expected resumption of the Irish Republican Army (IRA) ceasefire. In his role as minister for foreign affairs, Burke would have a crucial role to play in preparing the way for a historic settlement to the conflict. However, Ahern's confidence that the controversy would quickly blow over was misplaced. Even as he was parading his new Cabinet before the president at Áras an Uachtaráin, his own press team was briefing the media that Burke was the politician at the centre of the storm unleashed by the *Post*'s revelations. The party was insisting that the new minister received the payments as legitimate political donations during the 1989 election campaign. This interpretation of the payments allowed Ahern to justify Burke's appointment, but it also went a considerable way towards vindicating Gogarty's allegations.

The *Sunday Tribune* was the first to name Burke as the politician involved, when it reported that Fianna Fáil sources identified Michael Bailey of Bovale Developments as the sole donor of a £30,000 payment to the minister before the election in June 1989.[2] The story was inaccurate and incomplete, but it allowed the newspaper to put Burke in the frame as the subject of the payments controversy on which the *Post* had been reporting for almost two years.

Considerable confusion ensued when Bailey immediately denied the claim that he gave Burke the sum of £30,000. Contradicting the spin in the *Tribune*, he told the *Post* that he was present in Burke's home in June 1989 when 'a representative of Joseph Murphy Structural Engineers' handed a large sum of money in 'bundles of cash' to Burke. Bailey insisted that the most he ever gave Burke in a single election campaign was £1,000. He said that he had been a member of the St Margaret's Cumann of Fianna Fáil in Burke's constituency since 1977 and was a regular visitor to the politician's home.

At this point it had not been revealed that, in late June 1997, Dermot Ahern had been sent to London by his party leader and namesake to ask Joe Murphy junior about his company's dealings with Burke. He returned home with Murphy junior's adamant denial that JMSE gave money to Burke in 1989. Burke was appointed to Cabinet a day later.

Within weeks *The Irish Times* was reporting that it had been confirmed to Dermot Ahern that JMSE had, in fact, made a sizeable contribution to Burke's election campaign in 1989. Bertie Ahern then stated publicly, in July 1997, that he was satisfied about the circumstances surrounding a donation of £30,000 by a building firm to Burke: 'There is no question in my mind that it was a political donation under the law as it was in 1989 and there were no favours asked or done in the context of it,' the Taoiseach said, without naming the company involved. To compound the mystery, party sources were briefing that Burke had passed on £10,000 of the 'donation' to party headquarters at the time.[3]

It seemed that an attempt to circle the wagons was underway with the vague story that Burke had received a political donation, a portion of which had been passed on to the party. However, Fianna Fáil could not clearly confirm the exact amount of the payment, whether it was paid in cash or by cheque, and where or by whom it was handed over to Burke.

In the meantime, JMSE and Bailey confirmed other aspects of Gogarty's story, including that they were jointly involved in developing more than 700 acres of land in north Dublin. They confirmed the land was owned by JMSE before it was sold to Bovale. It had been rezoned when the previous government granted a lucrative tax designation[4] on large tracts of the lands in early 1997, Fianna Fáil confirmed.

Efforts to kill the Burke story by claiming the payment was a legitimate donation, downplaying the rezoning aspect of the land deal and dragging the Fine Gael-led administration into a confusing cocktail of misinformation were unsuccessful. The payments controversy soon mushroomed into a full-blown political scandal. For more than eighteen months, JMSE, Murphy junior and Bailey had denied knowledge of any payment to Burke in 1989 and any meeting involving their company executives and the property developer in the politician's home. By the government's own admissions, these denials were now exposed as lies, and my long-running investigation and the stories the *Post* had published, despite numerous threats of legal action, were vindicated.

It was a rocky start to Bertie Ahern's first term as taoiseach and things were about to get a lot rockier. His minority government, with its seventy-seven Fianna Fáil and four Progressive Democrat TDs, was only possible with the assistance of four independent deputies, so it was vulnerable from the outset. The Burke revelations and the likely fallout from the imminent McCracken Tribunal report into payments to Haughey and Lowry threatened to undermine the administration within weeks of its formation.

Mary Harney was between a rock and a hard place, as her weak election result, after losing six of the Progressive Democrats' ten seats, meant she had no choice but to stick with Ahern or face political oblivion. She was given some details of Gogarty's claims by her party colleague, Michael McDowell TD, who was among the politicians Gogarty had contacted before I first met him in the summer of 1995. He had told McDowell about the threats made against him by Murphy junior and how the gardaí had failed to deal with his complaints, along with other details of his row with his former employers. Harney was also informed by a director of JMSE, Gay Grehan, about an alleged payment of £60,000 to Burke in connection with the north Dublin land. Grehan was aware of the questions put by the *Post* to JMSE in 1995 and 1996, and of the discussion among company executives during which different sums were discussed. Soon after he became aware of the allegation, he made contact with Harney through his wife, Mary, who was a member of the Progressive Democrats and a former candidate for the party in County Louth, but the politician paid little heed to the information.

The ongoing summer recess gave the government some relief from parliamentary scrutiny and media interrogation over the growing scandal, but it did not slow the *Post*'s investigation into the perplexing explanations from the government on the matter. Burke's attempt to tidy up the mess only saw him dig a deeper hole for himself. On 7 August 1997, the besieged politician issued a statement in which he contradicted the details of the *Tribune* story as regards the source of the donation but confirmed that he had received a 'totally unsolicited political contribution' of £30,000 from Gogarty. He confirmed that Bailey was also present when he accepted the money in his home in June 1989. Insisting that he had done nothing illegal, unethical or improper, Burke said that he 'did not do any favours for or make any representations to anyone on behalf of JMSE'. He did not mention the presence of Joseph Murphy junior, or that he had received a detailed file on the lands in north Dublin, which the company and Bailey were seeking to have rezoned. He claimed that he was the victim of a 'vicious campaign of rumour and innuendo'.[5]

Burke did the media a favour when he named Gogarty as his tormentor, thereby removing a potential legal obstacle to the *Post* publishing further details of the allegations following months of threats from the minister's handlers and lawyers. This also helped to convince Gogarty that it was time to go on the record with his first exclusive interview. He felt compelled to respond to Burke's claim that he was engaged in a vendetta against the politician and was relieved that, after months of being dismissed as a mendacious villain and a 'headcase' by Fianna Fáil sources, his claims were now being taken seriously.

In an article published in the *Post* on 10 August, Gogarty said, 'I am not involved in any vendetta. I am trying to vindicate my good name and see that my complaints were properly investigated.' He described how he counted the cash sum of £30,000 before it was given to Burke. He recounted how another large envelope, purportedly containing £40,000 in cash, was handed over to Burke in the living room of his home in Swords. The story continued:

> This is the first time Gogarty has spoken in public concerning this matter ... He explains how JMSE and the builder Michael Bailey, who was also present when the payment was made to Burke, were at the time exploring possible joint ventures on 720 acres of land in north Dublin.
>
> Gogarty denies Burke's claim last week that he was the only executive from JMSE at Burke's home when the payment was made and insists that Joseph Murphy junior was also present.
>
> 'At the meeting in Burke's house I gave the envelope to Joe Murphy junior. I had checked the amount. Another director collected the money. He could only get £30,000 in cash so Joe junior told me to get a cheque (made out) to cash. The other director got a cheque and I signed the cheque with him. My understanding was that Bailey was matching the amount. Bailey handed over an envelope which was somewhat bigger than the one I had.'

Gogarty also challenged a claim that Bailey had made to me some weeks earlier, when the latter alleged that he had personally put a cheque for £50,000 into the pocket of the former JMSE chairman in 1990. Bailey told me this was in return for Gogarty's assistance with his attempted purchase of a JMSE-owned property on Baggot Street in Dublin. The property was sold by public auction in 1989. Bailey said he cancelled the 'post-dated cheque' after he failed to acquire the property. This was disputed by Gogarty, who told the *Post*:

> Shortly afterwards Bailey asked to meet me. We met in the Skylon hotel. He was concerned with the proceedings I had taken against JMSE. He said he didn't want to get (Ray) Burke dragged in. I couldn't give a commitment. He put a cheque in my pocket for £50,000 which I still have uncashed. It was dated September 30 [1990] and the meeting took place a couple of days earlier.

The disputed cheque, he said, was intended to buy his silence about the Burke payment, and it would prove to be another valuable weapon in Gogarty's armoury. Gogarty also confirmed that, over previous months, he had provided documentary proof of his claims to Garda investigators led by Detective Inspector John McElligott, and had handed over a mass of files to the gardaí relating to JMSE's business. He then outlined the problems he faced after his retirement, claiming:

> JMSE would not finalise his pension arrangements in 1990 after he refused to sign a set of company accounts. He has claimed that he was subjected to intimidating phone calls. One abusive call from Joe Murphy junior, during which the London-based owner of JMSE issued threats against Gogarty because of his refusal to drop legal proceedings against JMSE, was intercepted by local gardai [*sic*] from Raheny station in Dublin. No prosecution was ever brought.

The report revealed that, two weeks before publication of the article, Gogarty had been offered immunity from prosecution by the DPP in return for his continued co-operation. 'He had also initiated a civil action against his former employers in which the details of the incident at Burke's home in 1989 have been repeated by way of affidavit,' it continued.

Gogarty revealed significant details of the discussions with Bailey on the development and potential sale of the 720 acres of land owned by JMSE in north Dublin, which were worth some £16 million in 1990 without zoning. He described how Joe Murphy senior refused to agree to a planned 50/50 equity deal with Bailey in 1989. Negotiations over the future of the 720 acres resumed between Murphy and Bailey in August 1990.

Bailey's role was to assist with procuring the required rezoning and planning permissions as outlined in the detailed proposal to JMSE, which Gogarty had retained. This document set out the context for the involvement of and payment to Burke and, potentially, other politicians and officials, whose approval was required to complete the lucrative housing development planned for his constituency. After weeks of dissembling and misinformation by the other parties involved, the lengthy interview clarified the circumstances surrounding the meeting in Burke's house and the amount paid to the politician.

In a later editorial in the *Post*, my editor and *Post* co-owner Damien Kiberd argued that Gogarty would not make up a figure of £40,000 as 'an allegation that Burke received £30,000 would be just as strong', there being no moral or ethical difference between the two amounts. Referring to Burke, Kiberd wrote: '[H]e says that the representative of JMSE just walked into his house and gave him £30,000. North Dublin is by all accounts a remarkable place. For at roughly the same time Ben Dunne was walking into the home of Burke's mentor Charles Haughey after a golf outing at Baltray and handing him bank drafts totalling £210,000.'[6] Kiberd was referring to details of Dunne's generosity to Haughey then emerging from the McCracken Tribunal. Dunne had told the inquiry that he just happened to have the three bank drafts in his pocket when he dropped into Haughey at Kinsealy on his way home after a golf outing one afternoon in the late 1980s or early 1990s. He felt sorry for Haughey, who looked a little depressed, so he gave him the drafts and said, 'Look, that is for yourself,' to which the Taoiseach replied, 'Thank you, big fella.'[7]

The exchange would not have seen the light of day if it had not been for Dunne's public meltdown on the seventeenth-floor balcony of a five-star hotel in Orlando, Florida, in February 1992. After a cocaine and booze-fuelled night with a call girl from Escorts in a Flash, Dunne appeared in his boxers shouting, 'Leave me alone, leave me alone,' to onlookers below. Coincidentally, they included Bono, who was staying with U2 in the hotel that night.

Dunne was arrested but avoided jail time in the US. However, he was ousted from his role as head of the supermarket group, and the details of his payment to Haughey came out in the wake of the company's internal ructions. It turned out the gift from the retailer to Haughey in his home, along with another million or more, was possibly linked to the politician's help in getting a Dunnes Stores tax liability reduced by the Revenue from £38 million to £16 million. The huge sums given to Haughey were banked offshore by his financial adviser, Des Traynor, including in the Guinness & Mahon bank in the Cayman Islands, where hundreds of Ireland's wealthy elite stored their money in the 1970s and 1980s. Apparently, Ireland's most powerful politician did not have a bank account in his own name for many years. In what may have been more than a coincidence, the offices of BCCI bank part-owned by Sheik Mahfouz, who had been handed passports by Haughey after they were authorised by Burke in December 1990, were based in the same location as Guinness & Mahon in George Town, the Cayman capital. The Cayman-based subsidiary of BCCI, International Credit and Investment Company, known as the 'bank within a bank', acted as a mechanism for the parent's massive and global fraud operations.[8]

When his report into Haughey and Lowry was finalised, in late August 1997, just seven months after the inquiry was established by the Rainbow Coalition government, Judge Brian McCracken confirmed what many already knew – Haughey had received substantial sums of over £1 million from Dunne. The judge found that Lowry had received almost £500,000 in various payments from Dunne, designed to help the politician evade tax owed by his refrigeration business. Other benefits Lowry received included Dunne paying over £390,000 for the renovation and extension of his home at Holycross, Tipperary. 'The Tribunal,' concluded Judge McCracken, 'considers it quite unacceptable that Mr Charles Haughey, or indeed any member of the Oireachtas, should receive personal gifts of this nature, particularly from prominent businessmen within the State.'

In the wake of the McCracken findings and report, the government announced that it would establish another tribunal of inquiry, to be chaired by Judge Michael Moriarty, with a remit to investigate further improper payments to Haughey and Lowry.

If the emergence of these details of Haughey's financial fortunes were not damaging enough for Fianna Fáil, Gogarty's revelations about Burke caused consternation within and between the government parties. Fianna Fáil had confirmed that it had received £10,000 from Burke out of the money he received from JMSE in 1989 as 'an election contribution', but it could not provide any documentary evidence to substantiate the payment. As reported in the *Post* later in August, 'the treasurer of the Dublin North Fianna Fáil Comhairle Dáil Ceantair, Michael Brady, a brother-in-law of Burke, said he would not comment on any election contributions or disclose details of party accounts'. The paper also confirmed 'that Inspector John Harrington of Raheny Garda station had been asked to investigate other claims of threats and harassment by Joe Murphy junior made by Gogarty relating to the period between 1992 and 1994 when he lived in Sutton, Co. Dublin'.[9]

Reeling from the McCracken Tribunal revelations, Ahern's government was still struggling to get on its feet as the Burke controversy escalated, while the minister battled unsuccessfully to get ahead of the unfolding story. Gogarty was now close to signing a formal statement for Superintendent McElligott on foot of a guarantee of immunity. The net was closing in on the Minister for Foreign Affairs, yet he continued to bluff and bluster while clinging on to power.

Chapter Four

Lines in the Sand

RAY BURKE'S WOES WERE COMPOUNDED WHEN it was reported in September 1997 in the *Post* that he had sought funds from the investments made by Sheik Bin Mahfouz in exchange for the eleven passports which the former minister for justice processed in late 1990. Burke confirmed that, in 1991, at his request, his friend and constituency manager Tony Lambert asked Pat Kenny of Deloitte & Touche, who was managing the Sheik's 'investment', to provide financial assistance for Prime Print, a company based in Burke's Dublin North constituency. Burke told the *Post* that he was contacted by the Swords-based company which, he said, was 'in major financial difficulties which threatened the company and the jobs of its employees' and that he approached 'De Loitte Touche who I understood had funds available for investment in Irish businesses.'[1] In the event, the monies were not secured and the company was sold.

Days after this article was published, Burke stood up in the Dáil to defend his honour and reputation in relation to what was being said about the JMSE and Bailey payments:

> I am taking the opportunity to state unequivocally that I have done nothing illegal, unethical or improper. I find myself the victim of a campaign of calumny and abuse. It is totally unacceptable that this matter should be allowed to continue to fulfil an agenda which has nothing to do with election contributions or any other aspect of

> reasonable or reasoned political debate in public life. If any further untruths are published about me, I will take all necessary steps to vindicate my good name and reputation.[2]

The defiant minister confirmed that he took a £30,000 payment from Jim Gogarty at a meeting in his home in June 1989. He asserted that the only other person present was Michael Bailey of Bovale Developments, denying reports in the *Post* that Joe Murphy junior was also there:

> In light of allegations made subsequent to my statement of 7 August last, I confirm that Mr. Joseph Murphy junior of JMSE was not present at my meeting with Mr. Gogarty and Mr. Bailey. I did not meet Mr. Joseph Murphy junior during or in connection with the 1989 general election campaign. Mr. Gogarty, who was the managing director of JMSE, was the only executive of that company present.

He claimed he took the money in two large envelopes but did not count it until Gogarty and Bailey had left. He said he gave £10,000 to Fianna Fáil's head office and £7,000 to his constituency organisation, while retaining £13,000 for campaign expenses, some of which he lodged in his personal bank account. He claimed to have 'no recollection of the denominations' of the money and said the question of why he was given the donation should be addressed to Gogarty. He insisted that no favours were requested by Gogarty or Bovale, or offered by himself, during the 'brief discussion' at his home, but accepted that '[w]ith the benefit of hindsight it is clear that in accepting this contribution, even in good faith, I exposed myself to the risk of being the subject matter of malicious allegations of the type now being made.' He said he had no knowledge of any relationship between Bovale and the Murphys.

Of his strange encounter with Gogarty, Burke said, 'I thanked the person concerned and he wished me well.' He could not explain why a man he had never previously met handed him an unsolicited donation for £30,000, much of which ended up in his personal bank account:

> My understanding is that the making of this contribution came about as follows. Mr. Gogarty indicated to Mr. Bailey that JMSE wished to make a contribution to my election fund. Mr. Bailey brought Mr. Gogarty to my home and, during a brief meeting, Mr. Gogarty confirmed that JMSE wished to make a political contribution to me. The contribution was entirely in cash. Prior to leaving with Mr. Bailey, Mr. Gogarty wished me well in the election.

Elaborating on his statement of the previous August after his name was first published in connection with the Gogarty allegations, he continued:

> I did not receive £40,000 from Mr. Bailey or Bovale Developments Limited on that or any other occasion. I did not receive any personal contributions from Mr. Bailey either before, during or after the 1989 general election, although I have established that over the years Mr. Bailey made a number of contributions to the Fianna Fáil organisation in my constituency on such occasions as race nights and so on.

Answering questions during the one and a half hour Dáil session, Burke described the £30,000 payment as the largest he had ever received but refused to discuss any other contributions made to him during the 1989 election campaign. He did mention that he had taken out an overdraft of £35,000 on 4 August 1989 to cover the cost of building tennis courts for his two daughters and purchasing a car for his wife. He also claimed that he had no offshore bank accounts and, specifically, that he had none in the Isle of Man.

Responding to a question by Independent TD for Donegal Tom Gildea, who asked whether Burke had received 'any moneys when he granted MMDS [multichannel multipoint distribution service] licences during his period as Minister for Communications under the Haughey-led Government,' the minister simply replied, 'No.' Asked by Fine Gael TD Jim O'Keeffe whether he had lodged monies in overseas bank accounts, '[s]ince the receipt of the money in cash in 1989', Burke replied:

> I have already answered questions regarding my accounts and I do not intend to give further answers in that regard. I have bared my soul to the House today and I find the Deputy's question offensive in the extreme at this stage. In fairness to the members of the House, I have tried to be fair, reasonable and up front with information. I have no overseas bank account.

In the course of his address and replies to questions, he referred to me on three occasions, noting that I was the journalist who had written so much in my 'usual complimentary terms' about the acquisition of his house in Swords. He told the Dáil that the matter had been the subject of a Garda investigation, and he railed against a line in my profile of him in the *Post* in February 1996 which asserted that the house was purchased 'from an inmate of the mental hospital at Portrane, Co. Dublin' by his father, explaining:

> My father worked as a nurse in the hospital in Portrane until the mid-1950s. He had come from a humble background in the west of Ireland – I am proud of his background as I am proud of mine. The assertion in that article was a complete and utter lie. I did not take an action against the newspaper because I have never taken one since I entered this House despite the things they have said about me. I have with me the Land Registry documentation relating to my home which clearly shows that, far from being bought from a hospital patient under his care, the house and site was transferred

> to me and I bought it in a normal commercial transaction from Oak Park Developments Limited. The house was built in the normal commercial manner. I was doing business with that company. That transaction, along with others, was the subject of a Garda investigation in 1974. I did not so much resent the attacks on myself – in this business one learns to live with them although they do not get easier. However, I am glad to have the opportunity on behalf of my family and my father, who died in 1985, to clarify the record in that regard.

The minister became emotional when he recalled how his late father had been dragged into the controversy. As I watched from the press gallery, Burke pulled out a handkerchief to dry his tears as he called out his media tormentor. After he finished, I was assailed by one reporter and a couple of Fianna Fáil TDs for the hurtful tone and nature of my journalistic assault on the distressed politician. I politely rejected their criticism and suggested they check the facts.

Outside the Dáil, Burke told the waiting media scrum that he had now 'drawn a line in the sand' on the matter. The problem with lines in sand is that they are soon washed away, and so it was with this case. Burke had entered a number of statements into the official Dáil record that would, in time, come back to haunt him, including his insistence that he did not have an offshore account and that the Gogarty 'donation' was the largest he received during the 1989 election campaign.[3]

A key part of Burke's denials and his claims about the reason for the June 1989 meeting would be undermined when Gogarty produced a copy of the detailed schedule, with folio numbers, of the lands in north Dublin that were the subject of the negotiations between Bailey and JMSE. Gogarty, in his capacity as managing director of JMSE, was a director of several companies that owned individual tracts of land outlined in the schedule. Gogarty said he had offered a copy of the schedule of lands to Burke during their encounter in the minister's home, only to be told Bailey had already given Burke a copy, which cast doubt on Burke's claim that 'at no time during our meeting were any favours sought or given'. The document specifically referred to the portions of land that required rezoning and planning, which could only be achieved in the urgent timescale required by the Murphys with the assistance of an influential politician, in this case Bailey's inside man and local TD Burke.

Gogarty then revealed a letter from Bailey to JMSE that included a request for 'a 50 per cent share in the ownership of the said lands in exchange for procuring planning permission and building by-law approval'. The letter was sent to Gogarty just days before the meeting in Burke's home, the *Post* revealed in late September.[4] Earlier in the month, *Magill* magazine had also published an extract from this letter, which added to the pressure on Burke and Bertie Ahern. *Magill* editor John Ryan got sight of the document after he met Gogarty's son, Eamon, at a wedding in Dublin. The letter added to the growing evidence that the payment to Burke directly related to the procurement of planning permission from the local authority over which he had significant and proven influence.

In response to Burke's emotional defence of his father's reputation in the Dáil, the *Post* published further details on the registration and ownership of his home in Swords.[5] Burke told the Dáil in his 10 September statement that he had acquired the property from Oak Park Developments, for whom he acted as a sales agent in the early 1970s. He moved into the house in 1974, yet it was not registered in his name until 1994. It was reported that the owner of the land since 1936 had been Joseph Coleman, 'a long-term patient in the mental hospital at Portrane … Coleman died some years ago in St Brendan's Psychiatric Hospital.' According to land registry documents, Oak Park Developments, owned by builders Brennan & McGowan at the time, had been listed as the owner of the land since April 1972, following its acquisition from Coleman, who was a ward of court.

As Burke had told the Dáil, his relationship with Oak Park was the subject of a Garda inquiry when he moved into the house. At the time of this article's release, Oak Park Developments was 'registered at the offices of accountancy firm, Oliver Freaney & Co., Northumberland Road, Dublin'. Freaney & Co. was also in the news in September 1997 because one of its partners, Noel Fox, had given evidence to the McCracken Tribunal concerning payments made by Ben Dunne, one of its former clients, to Haughey. Fox was later censured by the Institute of Chartered Accountants in connection with Oliver Freaney & Co.'s work for the retailer.[6]

Just hours after the *Post* hit the streets on 28 September, Ahern went on the RTÉ *This Week* programme to announce that a new tribunal was to be established to examine possible corruption in planning processes in Dublin. After some wrangling between government and the opposition over the terms of reference, the first version of which managed to avoid mentioning Ray Burke's name or the monies he had received in June 1989, they were altered to include potential payments to elected representatives by Bovale and JMSE.

As Emily O'Reilly commented in the *Post* in early October, Bertie Ahern was blessed that the election had been called in June and not later in the year. 'Had Haughey been summoned to the witness box at that point, had his damning testimony and eventual acknowledgement of the receipt of £1.3 million from Ben Dunne, come into the public arena, Fianna Fáil could have been fatally damaged. The loss of even a handful of seats would have deprived them of power,' she wrote.[7] In the light of the Burke disclosures, the misery inflicted on the party and its leader would have been far greater.

In the same edition of the newspaper, I noted how the cost of standing by Ray Burke was 'taking its toll on the Taoiseach':

> After adamantly refusing to put the Burke affair into the Moriarty tribunal, Ahern was forced into a humiliating climbdown when

> he conceded a new tribunal into allegations of corruption in the planning process in Dublin. There was a further U-turn when he was forced to accept that the new inquiry would also specifically examine the £30,000 payment which Burke received in June 1989.
>
> In the process, the Fianna Fáil leader has defied the description of him by his former leader Charles Haughey as the most cunning, most devious, most ruthless of them all. While the Taoiseach had claimed that his support for Burke is dictated by loyalty, and a belief that one is innocent until proven guilty can explain his actions, others suspect a more complex agenda.
>
> In his immortal words, Bertie was chasing up every tree in north Dublin following up the Burke allegations but to no avail. It was an unfortunate analogy as it recalled the famous incident when Burke had a row of trees planted in an unfinished housing estate shortly before an election only to have them removed the day after (and following the defeat of his preferred candidate). It was doubly unfortunate as it led to the inevitable question as to why he had not climbed the tree at Jim Gogarty's home … not too far from Bertie's own house on Griffith Avenue.
>
> Burke's belated and reluctant agreement to address the Dáil and answer an hour of questions was followed by a determination not to get sucked into the new tribunal investigating payments to Charles Haughey and Michael Lowry.[8]

Now, however, Ahern and his party had to endure the prospect of not one but two tribunals of inquiry into payments to Haughey, Burke and perhaps other senior figures down the road.

To make matters worse, the fall-out from the Gogarty revelations coincided with the release of an official report into Burke's approval of the eleven passports given to Sheik Khalid bin Mahfouz. The inquiry carried out by senior Department of Justice official Dermot Cole concluded that there had been a 'serious breach of statutory regulations under Section 17 of the Irish Nationality and Citizenship Act, (1956)'. He found, among other breaches, that 'the correct forms were not used for the applications and information on some documents was in conflict with others: statutory regulations were broken in the manner in which naturalisation certificates were signed by Burke at his home on the night before they were handed over by Haughey at a luncheon in the Shelbourne Hotel'.[9]

Following the release of this report, Denis Brosnan, the head of the Kerry Group and chairman of Leisure Holdings UK Ltd, defended the investment by the Saudi Sheik, which, he claimed, had pumped £15 million in investments into the Irish economy. Brosnan, who chaired Leisure Holdings UK Ltd and Kerry Airport PLC, both of which benefited from the PFI money, said that he was introduced to Khalid bin Mahfouz by Haroon Rashid Kahlon, who was on the board of Leisure Holdings. Another beneficiary was Butler Engineering in Portarlington, the major competitor to JMSE in Ireland at the time, which received £4 million but went into examinership in 1996, owing creditors more than £20 million. Brosnan said that the controversy surrounding the issue of the passports 'had damaged the prospects of a further £5 million in a proposed technology park in Tralee' and cost jobs.[10] It is unclear how many jobs were created in Ireland with the Sheik's money given that Leisure Holdings was based in the UK.

When I asked Haughey where the rest of the Sheik's promised £20 million investment had gone, during an exchange in the National Gallery a few months after the *Post* published the story, the former taoiseach replied simply that it was the 'best investment ever' in the country. He then queried why I bore him 'such animus', reminding me that he had known my father, a fellow scholarship student in University College Dublin (UCD) in the 1940s. I did not tell him what my late father thought of him. They had studied and socialised together at college. Both from poor family backgrounds, they were among the UCD students who marched to Trinity College on VE day in 1945. The Trinity students had raised a Union Jack on the roof of the college's entrance to celebrate victory by the Allied forces but had placed a tricolour below 'the butchers' apron' and attempted to burn it. This sparked an angry response from the UCD students, who attempted to get through the Trinity gates on College Green and were baton-charged by the police. My father was injured during the confrontation. Years later, as a public servant and volunteer with our local credit union, he believed that Haughey and many of his associates in Fianna Fáil had long sacrificed whatever integrity they once had for power and money.

Burke was now fighting on two fronts, with a Market Research Bureau of Ireland (MRBI) opinion poll in September showing that 70 per cent of respondents did not believe his assertion that 'there were no strings attached' to the £30,000 'donation'. Holes were starting to appear in the contradictory accounts of the various people involved in the affair and Burke's attempt to draw a 'line in the sand' had patently failed. Bertie Ahern could no longer keep his closest political ally on board his dangerously leaking ship, particularly when the Progressive Democrats gave ominous signals about their unwillingness to remain in government with Burke as minister for foreign affairs.

Two days after the release of the report on the passports scandal, Ray Burke resigned. On Tuesday 7 October, in a statement to the media, he said that he was resigning as a minister and TD while still insisting that 'I have done nothing wrong.' In the Dáil that day, Ahern defended his long-time colleague and complained of 'the persistent hounding of an honourable man' in what he described as 'a sustained campaign of incremental intensity' against the former minister. 'There comes a time when even the strongest shoulder bows, the stoutest heart falters and the very best can resist no longer.'[11]

A day later, blaming the media and the opposition for Burke's unfortunate departure from politics, the Taoiseach expanded on his criticisms: 'I believe he resigned both as the strongest protest that he could make at the shameful treatment to which he has been subjected by certain parties in this House and by certain sections of the media who cynically regard politics as a blood sport.' Referring to his appointment of Burke as minister for foreign affairs six months earlier, Ahern said, 'I appointed him after careful consideration in the firm belief that he had done nothing wrong and that he had earned the Foreign Affairs portfolio. Accepting an unsolicited gift of £30,000, of which less than half was retained for his personal campaign, was certainly imprudent, but a few weeks ago in this House almost no one considered it a hanging offence.'[12] He went on to formally declare the establishment of the 'Planning and Payments Tribunal' to be chaired by former High Court judge, Feargus Flood.

Burke's resignation was a major vindication of Gogarty's claims, of my relentless pursuit of the story and of the work of other journalists who joined in the search for truth. For the *Post*, its editor and owners, it was a significant achievement by a small and relatively new media outlet that had defied many months of legal and other attempts to shut down the investigation.

Notwithstanding the public defence of his 'honourable' friend, Ahern had to know that some of the statements made by Burke in Dáil in his September speech were misleading, to say the least. As the co-treasurer of Fianna Fáil in 1989, he should have been aware, as other party officers were, that Burke's contribution of £10,000 to the party during the election campaign that year did not, as he claimed in his 'line in the sand' speech, come from the JMSE contribution. If he did not know where the money came from, he would soon learn.

Chapter Five

Out of Africa

LESS THAN SIX MONTHS INTO HIS first term, Ahern was under severe political pressure, including from the senior ranks of his own party. He lost a key ally in Burke, one he had hoped would play the role of his enforcer during the imminent peace negotiations by keeping Sinn Féin in its place. Ahern also alienated supporters of Albert Reynolds after he engineered his predecessor's defeat in his quest for the party's endorsement for the presidency. Lawyer and Catholic activist Mary McAleese secured the nomination and went on to win the presidential election in October 1997.

Ahern's relations with his coalition partners in the Progressive Democrats were increasingly fraught as Mary Harney belatedly withdrew her already shaken confidence in Burke following months of confusion and chaos over the payments and passports controversies. As a consequence, his government's stability, dependent on Harney and three of her party members, as well as four independent TDs, was uncertain. Within weeks of Burke's resignation, Harney and her colleagues became embroiled in a financial predicament of their own, when a story landed, in most unlikely circumstances, on my desk.

In early December 1997, I took a call from Ian Lumley, a prominent member of An Taisce and colleague in the heritage organisation of environmentalist Michael Smith. One afternoon, Lumley came across a most distressing sight as he cycled past the offices of the Progressive

Democrats in South Frederick Street in Dublin, just a few hundred yards from Leinster House. Outside the Georgian-era party headquarters, a rubbish skip was filled with boxes of documents. On closer examination, he found hundreds of leaflets promoting environmental protection initiatives, printed by the European Commission and intended as handouts for citizens across the country. Instead of being distributed, they were headed for the landfill in what Lumley perceived as a gross dereliction of the Progressive Democrats' duty as elected representatives. I suggested that he deliver the contents of the skip to the *Sunday Business Post* offices on the Liffey quays opposite the Four Courts, where they duly arrived by taxi.

When we opened the contents, we found the leaflets and much more. The discarded documents also contained a detailed history of the financial donors to the party since its foundation by Des O'Malley, Harney and others in the mid-1980s. It was a scoop in more ways than one, and it provided front-page and inside stories for a number of weeks, as well as a heavy dose of embarrassment for the right-wing party and its benefactors, and great amusement for the readers of the *Post.*[1] It was also sufficient to ensure that Harney and her team, absorbed with an unexpected credibility, and potentially financial, crisis, were quickly dispatched from their self-proclaimed position on the high moral ground. They sought the immediate return of the material under threat of legal proceedings. The newspaper complied, but only after a thorough investigation of the haul, which identified hundreds of donors to the party from 1985 to 1992.

The discovery of the skip and its financial secrets was humiliating for the small but influential party, with many of the donations described as 'confidential', although its contents did not imply any obvious illegality. The 'bankrolling' revelations exposed a network of powerful business interests and individuals who put their considerable political weight and money into the party. Among them were people with a great deal to gain from the party's policies of government deregulation, tax breaks and other incentives intended to benefit the wealthiest at the expense of the majority. Despite their small numbers in the Dáil, the Progressive Democrats were an effective vehicle for ensuring that the interests of the well-endowed were embedded in the fiscal, economic and political decisions of the Fianna Fáil-led government.

It seemed that the party, formed by O'Malley when he could no longer put up with the perceived stench of corruption surrounding Haughey and his circle of friends, was tainted by association with the same members of the business elite. Among the correspondence and records were financial contributions from meat baron Larry Goodman, whose close relations with Haughey were part of O'Malley's motivation for splitting from Fianna Fáil to form the new party. Details of a 'confidential meeting' in 1992 between O'Malley and Michael Smurfit, head of the Smurfit Group, accompanied by a cheque for £30,000, were also among the papers, while Frank Reynolds, former managing director of JMSE, was named as another donor. That company was clearly hedging its bets when it came to political sponsorship.

The Haughey legacy would continue to haunt Ahern and his government colleagues into 1998, and questions about how the former taoiseach accumulated his wealth during his decades in office were revived by another exclusive story in the *Post* in February that year.

Weeks earlier, I had made contact with Patrick Gallagher, the former builder and banker who was convicted of fraud offences and jailed in the North of Ireland. His imprisonment followed charges of fraudulently signing off an addendum to the accounts of Merbro Finance, based in the North, and its associated company Merchant Banking, both founded by his late father, Matt Gallagher, in the 1960s. Matt Gallagher, with his brothers, was founder of the Gallagher Group construction company and a significant benefactor of Haughey until the businessman's untimely death in 1974. His sons, Patrick and Paul, inherited the Gallagher Group, which their father had started in 1956, and which built a successful business in mining, plant hire, pubs and housing across the UK and Ireland. The Gallagher Group made a fortune building low-cost homes for young families in Dublin and also by destroying large swathes of the city's Georgian streetscapes for office and retail developments. It had a reputation for playing fast and loose with planning, labour and banking regulations, and for buying off politicians and the odd property editor. In the late 1970s and 1980s, before his companies crashed and burned, the cigar-smoking Patrick swanned around the city in a Rolls-Royce making property and other deals in bars and hotels.

I flew to Zimbabwe to meet up with Gallagher, who was rebuilding his life after serving two years in prison. A series of taped interviews with the former businessman over five days where he lived in a safari park, near the capital, Harare, provided a unique and fresh insight into the source of Haughey's wealth. Gallagher was a sad character, recovering from cancer yet a heavy drinker. Most of our discussions took place in the mornings, as he was prone to having a glass or few of whiskey in the early afternoon and his recollections grew hazy as the day wore on.

It was not until the day before I was due to return to Dublin that he recounted the story of how he rescued Haughey from bankruptcy just days before the latter became taoiseach for the first time in late 1979. Haughey had been chosen as party leader two days after the resignation of then Taoiseach Jack Lynch in early December 1979. Gallagher described how he, with his brother Paul, was summoned to Abbeville, the politician's home in Kinsealy, where Haughey explained that he needed £750,000 to pay off his debts to Allied Irish Bank (AIB). If he did not repay the money, Haughey said, he would not be allowed to take up the position of taoiseach.

'Can you get someone to raise half of it?' Gallagher asked. When Haughey said that he could, Gallagher said, 'Say no more, I'll sort it out with Des Traynor.' Traynor was a former partner in Haughey Boland, the accountancy firm formed by Haughey and Harry Boland in the 1950s, and was hugely successful in convincing an array of rich people to fund the Taoiseach's lavish lifestyle from the late 1970s until his death, aged sixty-two, in 1994. Traynor served as a director of the Gallagher Group and Merchant Banking in the early 1960s and as a tax advisor to both Matt and Patrick Gallagher.

Gallagher went on to explain to me how the deal was done; he told me that £375,000 was put down as a deposit on lands at the edge of the Kinsealy estate, a sale which would never go through. It was a ruse to cover what was a direct payment to the politician, with no strings attached. Gallagher forfeited any claim to the property, or the deposit, when his company, with assets worth an estimated £70 million, collapsed in 1982. He also described how his father and other leading businessmen financed Haughey in order to allow the politician to concentrate on 'building the nation'. His father encouraged Haughey to buy his first home, Grangemore, near Raheny, in 1959 for £13,000 with a promise to buy it back from him, which he did, ten years later, for £260,000. By this time, with the help of political contacts, it had been rezoned for housing and had planning permission for over 380 homes. The Gallagher Group went on to build a large housing development on the land in north Dublin, while Haughey relocated to Rath Stud, which he purchased with the proceeds of the sale; he then moved to Abbeville in Kinsealy.

As I reported in the *Post* following my trip to Africa, Gallagher explained how Haughey was like a latter-day chieftain or noble, fed and watered to his heart's content. 'Haughey was financed in order to create the environment which the Anglo Irish once enjoyed, and that we as a people could never aspire to,' Gallagher told me. He described how in the 1960s, his father had helped to form Taca, 'a secretive fund-raising arm of the party which brought builders, architects, accountants and other businesspeople together in the great crusade to reconstruct the nation'.[2]

'Fianna Fáil was good for builders and builders were good for Fianna Fáil, and there was nothing wrong with that,' says Gallagher. 'Taca took up about a day a month of my father's time. He saw it as building the nation by fundraising for Fianna Fáil. The "young turks" who met for dinner at the Gresham Hotel and retired for drinks late into the night at Groom's had from early days recognised Haughey as their future political leader.' These included Donogh O'Malley (an uncle of Des O'Malley), Neil Blaney, Brian Lenihan and a number of prominent businessmen and professionals.

According to Gallagher, Traynor looked after Haughey's finances. 'Traynor was asked to look after his personal finances while he looked after the affairs of the nation, and Des Traynor had no problem with that,' he said. Traynor created and managed what became known as the offshore Ansbacher Cayman deposit tax evasion scheme, whereby hundreds of rich people in Ireland, including some politicians, lodged large sums in the Caribbean island during the 1980s and 1990s. The Ansbacher scheme was uncovered during the investigation into Haughey's finances by the McCracken Tribunal, and was operated by Traynor out of the Guinness & Mahon bank in Dame Street in Dublin and later at the headquarters of Cement Roadstone Holdings in Fitzwilliam Square in Dublin 2.

Traynor established the Guinness Mahon Cayman Trust in 1970 in George Town, Grand Cayman, as a tax-avoidance scheme, which also allowed clients to withdraw funds locally from the Dame Street bank. On the day Haughey was elected taoiseach in December 1979, a bank account with a lodgement of £780,662, including the contribution from Patrick Gallagher, was opened and managed by Traynor in Guinness & Mahon bank in Dublin. In 1988, the bank was sold by Traynor to the Henry Ansbacher Group.

At the end of our interview, Gallagher offered to return to Ireland to give evidence on Haughey's behalf, if asked, saying, 'He is isolated because all his old cohorts are gone. He has nobody to turn to. People should be very careful because the big hand comes back to twelve and what goes around comes around. I have told Haughey that I will defend him at the tribunal, sober and word-perfect.' Gallagher was unapologetic about his complicity in the corporate and banking practices that led to his two-year jail term. By this time, he was a shadow of the former man about town of the 1980s, whose financial fortunes had been greatly assisted by his political connections, to Haughey in particular. Former assistant city and county manager for Dublin George Redmond had also been on his company's payroll and enjoyed frequent foreign holidays at Gallagher's expense.[3]

Zimbabwe in 1998 was an oppressive and dangerous place, and during the week I spoke to political and human rights activists, who were subjected to vicious repression and frequent imprisonment under the regime of former revolutionary and then president Robert Mugabe. As I departed, I read that just that week Mugabe had imported a dozen, top-of-the-range Mercedes Benz cars from Germany as a gift for his wife, Grace, and other friends. Corruption knows no boundaries.

The detailed, and unforced, admissions by Gallagher served to remind people of the litany of scandals that forced Haughey from office in 1992. His description of arriving in Kinsealy that evening in late 1979 and passing a row of Cabinet hopefuls awaiting appointment as he entered Haughey's office was cringeworthy. His recollection of how he and other benefactors opened their cheque books so readily to ensure their man took the top job in Irish politics revived memories of the politician's alleged role in not-so-distant controversies.

These included the sale of a lucrative site in Ballsbridge to Telecom Éireann, which led to the resignation of its chairman Michael Smurfit. There was the controversial, and below-market-value, purchase of the former Carysfort College in Blackrock by another party supporter, Robert 'Pino' Harris, which never went to Cabinet for approval. And, of course, there was Haughey's promotion of Larry Goodman, who gave

£50,000 to Fianna Fáil during the 1989 election campaign and another £25,000 in an 'anonymous' contribution to the Taoiseach's party leader's fund during the same period. Haughey's government then underwrote a £135-million contract for the supply of beef by the Goodman group to the Iraqi regime led by Saddam Hussein, which became the subject of the Beef Tribunal.

Bertie Ahern needed all of these reminders like a hole in the head, as he, in his capacity as co-treasurer of the party, had signed the blank cheques from the leader's fund used by Haughey to bankroll his lavish lifestyle, including the £25,000 a month cost of maintaining Abbeville, the Charvet shirts, the yacht, the island retreat in the Blaskets and his well-stocked wine cellars.

Meanwhile, the Planning and Payments Tribunal (commonly called the Flood Tribunal), continued to gather evidence in advance of public hearings. However, it faced an early High Court challenge to an order it served on Bank of Ireland seeking financial records relating to Mick Bailey and Bovale Developments as part of its investigation into the company's alleged 1989 payment to Ray Burke. In early March 1998, Bovale, Michael Bailey and his wife, Teresa, obtained a temporary order restraining the bank from handing over documents relating to them to the tribunal. This mirrored the ongoing High Court case taken by Haughey and his family against the Moriarty Tribunal in its quest for documents relating to the payments made by Ben Dunne to the former taoiseach.

Small in stature but firm in his determination to expose those involved in planning corruption in the city, Judge Feargus Flood had set about his task with urgency, despite the legal and other challenges to his inquiry. Current and former members of the Oireachtas and county councils received letters from Flood asking them to disclose any dealings they had with JMSE or Gogarty, and any knowledge they had of payments to any public representative, local government official or any member or employee of An Bord Pleanála.

Among those who responded to Flood's call for information was former Dublin county councillor Jim Geraghty, who provided an affidavit recounting the incident when he witnessed Burke receiving large amounts of cash from two separate individuals on different occasions in the offices of Dublin County Council in the mid-1980s. Geraghty had already provided a detailed account of what he witnessed when I met him at his home in Rush, in north Dublin, some months before he made a formal statement to the tribunal. He was nervous of the potential reaction from Burke and his former colleagues in Fianna Fáil, and so did not wish to have his name revealed when the *Post* first published details of the bribery he witnessed. Ahern had dismissed Geraghty's allegations, which he knew Burke would deny and which were unlikely to be proven unless another witness could corroborate the claim, but it was not so easy to avoid the collateral damage resulting from the revelations of yet another large payment in 1989 to his former minister for foreign affairs.

It was widely accepted that Ahern's election success in June 1997 was in no small part due to an unprecedented intervention on the day before polling by the *Irish Independent*, which carried an editorial headlined 'Payback Time' calling on voters to support Fianna Fáil. The newspaper promised that a Fianna Fáil/Progressive Democrat government would deliver tax cuts and roll back public spending.[4] It now emerged that its owner, Tony O'Reilly, had done more than simply endorse Ahern and his party. The uncomfortable news came after an order for discovery served on Fianna Fáil by Flood in February 1998 uncovered another previously undisclosed payment to Burke. The £30,000 payment, made during the 1989 election, emerged after Fianna Fáil party officers found a receipt for this amount provided to sign-makers Rennicks in return for a contribution to Burke. A photocopy of a compliments slip from Rennicks confirmed Burke as the recipient of the donation. Rennicks was a subsidiary of the Fitzwilton company owned by O'Reilly. This revelation compromised the ability of the *Independent*'s journalists to cover the payments scandal, as its wealthy owner became part of the corruption story.

It also tore to shreds the narrative promoted by Ahern and his finance officers that Burke gave the party £10,000 from the JMSE 'donation' in 1989. Fianna Fáil told the tribunal that Burke made only one payment to its finance office by way of a bank draft for £10,000 in 1989. Along with the receipt issued to Rennicks, the party officers found evidence that the donation came from the payment to Burke by the Fitzwilton-owned company. Ahern was forced to concede in the Dáil that his previous statement claiming that the £10,000 given to the party by Burke in 1989 was from the JMSE donation was incorrect. Despite his claim to have climbed all the trees in north Dublin to establish the truth about the Burke payments, it turned out that his 'thorough investigation' did not involve even a cursory examination of his own party's financial records.

The last vestiges of Burke's credibility were fast disappearing when further details emerged of the Rennicks payment. The £30,000 from Rennicks was paid in the form of a cheque made out to cash, which was solicited by Burke during the election campaign. So, his claim to the Dáil in September 1997 that he never received another payment as large as that given to him by JMSE was exposed as patently untrue. The Fitzwilton-linked payment also provided some context to the question posed by Donegal TD Tom Gildea after Burke's emotional speech in the Dáil the previous September. Gildea had asked Burke whether the minister received any monies in connection with the granting of MMDS licences in his capacity as minister for communications in 1989. Among the companies awarded permits in 1989 for the MMDS used for the transmission of television signals was Princes Holdings, in which Independent Newspapers took a 50 per cent share in 1992.

The tribunal also uncovered a payment of £35,000 to Burke from Oliver Barry, the promoter of Century Radio, which was established in 1989 during the politician's time as minister for communications.

Haughey's son-in-law, John Mulhern, was an investor in the company, which benefitted from Burke's decision in 1988 to promote a commercial television service to compete with the State broadcaster, RTÉ. The amount involved in this payment contradicted Burke's claim that the largest single amount he ever received in a donation was the £30,000 from JMSE. His insistence that he never had an offshore account was also later holed in the water, when it emerged during the Flood Tribunal that he lodged substantial sums in banks in the Isle of Man and Jersey in the 1980s. These were filled with payments from his benefactors, the most generous of whom were builders Tom Brennan and Joe McGowan, estimated in value to be more than £275,000.[5]

Burke was later jailed on charges arising from his failure to declare for tax purposes the monies he received from the backers of Century Radio. On 24 January 2005, he was sentenced to six months in prison, making him the most senior Irish politician to serve time in prison since the foundation of the State.

If the Taoiseach thought that Burke's departure from politics would provide some relief from the allegations of sleaze and corruption that marred his first year in office, he was sorely mistaken. It was not long before another story surfaced that would rock Ahern and his party to the core and ensure that his first term in office would continue to be overshadowed by corruption inquiries and his alleged complicity in bribery, deceit and the diversion of public funds that they exposed.

Chapter Six

The Gilmartin Story

IN THE SUMMER OF 1998, I was given a lead by the former taoiseach Albert Reynolds that was worth following. He mentioned that a man called Tom Gilmartin, an Irish emigrant who lived in Luton, England, was making allegations about a number of politicians and businessmen, including some household names. When I asked him for contact details for Gilmartin, he directed me to property consultant Colm Scallon, who gave me the number in Luton without hesitation.

One quiet afternoon in the offices of *The Sunday Business Post*, I talked on the phone for the first time to Gilmartin, a soft-spoken man from Sligo who certainly had a story to tell. At first he was hesitant, as he believed that he had been unfavourably treated by the *Post* in previous articles by other reporters. He complained that journalists in other media outlets in Dublin had misrepresented statements he made and failed to honour his request for anonymity. However, following my sincere assurances that he would not be quoted or named in any article without his express permission, he gave me an outline of his experiences at the hands of people he described as corrupt politicians, businessmen and public officials whom he encountered when he tried to do business in Dublin.

Almost two hours later, I put down the phone, having agreed to travel to Luton as soon as possible to meet up. I ran into the office of Damien Kiberd. If true, this was the most incredible story I had come across in my expedition through the morass of sleaze the country had endured since Gogarty raised his head three years earlier. 'Rocket fuel,' Kiberd said, 'but go easy', or words to that effect.

Within days, I was on a flight to London to meet for the first time a man with whom I would spend many hours and days in various locations over several years, both in person and on the phone, as his story and battle for justice and respect unfolded. Many of our conversations were taped with his consent, providing a valuable and verifiable record of his account. Over time, we developed the level of trust essential for any journalist engaged in such a sensitive and politically explosive investigation. He recounted an extraordinary tale of corruption and graft that was almost beyond comprehension, but it was told with such heartfelt honesty that I was convinced. Gilmartin had a suitcase full of documents, records and diaries that backed up a detailed recollection of his experiences in Dublin from the late 1980s to the mid-1990s.

He met many politicians and business people who supported his plans, but some of them, he later discovered, were working against him to feather their own nests. Among those he encountered were Haughey and various Cabinet members, including Pádraig Flynn, Ray MacSharry and Bertie Ahern, as well as elected members of Dublin County Council of different parties and none. Liam Lawlor TD, George Redmond, Frank Dunlop and businessman Owen O'Callaghan were identified as particularly nefarious characters in Gilmartin's remarkable tale of alleged graft in Dublin. Judges, lawyers, solicitors, accountants and other professionals were drawn into what amounted to a conspiracy that almost ruined Gilmartin, personally and financially, devastated the health of his Donegal-born wife, Vera, and damaged the lives of their young family. From a successful career as an engineer, factory owner and property developer in England, he was bankrupted and almost broken, after striving to build two shopping centres and create jobs in economically deprived parts of Dublin in 1987.

Before our first conversation, the *Post* had previously reported on the proposed schemes that Gilmartin envisioned along the north quays in Dublin city centre and at Quarryvale in the west, close to the M50 ring road stretching from Dublin Port to Wicklow. But the coverage in the newspaper and in other media outlets wrongly suggested that he withdrew from the projects and returned to England due to financial difficulties. As he explained, he was, instead, the victim of a corrupt network that dominated politics, business and banking at the highest level and forced him out of the company he had formed to progress the ambitious retail developments.

Gilmartin described to me how his UK financial backers, Arlington Securities Ltd, were prepared to advance the funding for his plans in Ireland, having previously worked with him on the development of a major retail centre at Milton Keynes. Gilmartin had also invested in a shopping centre in Bangor in the North of Ireland, and he had a reputation for identifying viable locations for commercial development. The first Dublin scheme involved a major rejuvenation of the quays at Bachelors Walk and the purchase of properties fronting the River Liffey and along O'Connell Street and Abbey Street. It was an audacious proposal that required support from central and local government authorities if it was to succeed.

In the mid-1980s, Ireland was struggling with high unemployment, mass emigration and poverty. Indeed, it was the plight of emigrants arriving in Luton from Ireland that motivated Gilmartin's decision to try and assist with the recovery of the country he had left in 1957, following hundreds of thousands of others seeking a better life in England and America. Born in 1935 in Lislary, near Grange in County Sligo, Gilmartin left school at thirteen to work on his father's small farm and clear drains for the local council. After a night course in the local technical school, he won a scholarship to the agricultural college at Ballyhaise, County Cavan. Despite coming first in the civil service examination, his application for a position in the Department of Agriculture was unsuccessful, and the post was awarded to another graduate from the college who had poorer results but better connections. It was a case of 'who you know and not what you know,' as he said in our early conversations.

Against the wishes of his father, who had fought against the British in the War of Independence and preferred that his son emigrate to anywhere but England, Gilmartin took the boat to Holyhead in July 1957 and joined many of his friends from north Sligo who had settled in Luton, thirty miles from London, where jobs were plentiful and opportunities ripe. Within two years, he had developed his skills as a welder and completed further training in structural and precision engineering, before setting up his own company in Cross Street, Luton, in 1959. He became an expert in mechanical handling systems and special purpose machinery, and progressed to building and installing conveyor systems for local car manufacturers, including Ford in Dagenham and Vauxhall, owned by General Motors. His company, Gilmartin Engineering, was registered in 1965, the same year he married Vera Kerr from Urris in the Inishowen peninsula, whom he met at a dance in the George Ballroom in Luton.

His thriving business suffered during the industrial disputes of the late 1970s and early Thatcher years, and was forced to close in 1981, resulting in the loss of 400 jobs. Using the £1 million he received from the sale of a factory he was building in Northampton, he began identifying suitable sites for office and retail schemes, which he then helped to design. He raised a further £1 million after he acquired, and then sold on, a proposed scheme in Milton Keynes, north of London. He gradually made his name as a shrewd investor and property developer, winning the trust of finance companies and pension funds, whose executives were prepared to back his projects with investment capital.

Among them was Raymond Mould, chief executive of Arlington Securities, who supported his proposal to investigate the potential of Dublin as an investment opportunity. In early 1987, he was offered a fee of

£250,000 to develop the site around Bachelors Walk for a large shopping centre. He met with established retailers Arnotts and Clerys, with a view to purchasing their stores for the development. He met other property owners in the vicinity, including the chief executive of Independent Newspapers, Joe Hayes, with whom he discussed the acquisition of its premises on Middle Abbey Street. In exchange for the lands, he offered Hayes a site in the docklands owned by semi-state transport company Córas Iompair Éireann (CIÉ), which Gilmartin proposed to buy.

Using the first £10 million of a projected £200 million expenditure by Arlington Securities, Gilmartin began to assemble the properties, including derelict buildings along Bachelors Walk, while opening discussions with politicians who could support his project through legislation. During 1987 he met Minister for Finance Ray MacSharry, Minister for Labour Bertie Ahern, a TD in the north inner city, and Minister for the Environment Pádraig Flynn. He specifically wanted the Urban Renewal Incentive scheme extended to include the entire site, as, at that time, it only covered part of the area of the planned development. Arlington executives wanted to ensure that the required tax reliefs were in place before they spent more money on acquisitions. They dismissed concerns expressed by Gilmartin that property prices would escalate if their owners learned that there was a potential buyer with deep pockets willing to purchase their derelict buildings. His worst fears were realised when people he described as 'Mickey Mouse' or 'Middle' men began to surface with outlandish demands, with the cost of one property on Abbey Street jumping from an asking price of £400,000 to £1.5 million in a matter of weeks.

In early 1988, Pádraig Flynn proposed that the entire area from the quays back to Abbey Street would be included under the incentive scheme. At a meeting with Flynn and Seamus Brennan, the minister of state for trade and marketing, Gilmartin and the Arlington executives were asked to include a bus station in the planned retail complex for which finance would be available from European Economic Community (EEC) structural funds. They agreed that adjoining land already in the ownership of CIÉ could accommodate a bus terminus. When Gilmartin and Arlington were subsequently informed that the EEC would only finance a bus station within the retail complex, and after CIÉ and government officials suggested that it could be located on the roof of the new development, Arlington rejected the proposal. Not long afterwards, the company began to be subjected to media attacks over their 'bus station in the sky proposals' and the threat that they posed to the historic buildings on Bachelors Walk. They also faced increasingly extortionate demands from some owners and their agents for the properties essential for the success of the retail scheme.

Gilmartin, meanwhile, was exploring the potential of the Quarryvale development at the junction of the M50 and the N4 to the west for an 'out of town' retail scheme. The Dublin Development Plan agreed by Dublin County Council in the 1970s had envisaged the development of three shopping centres – at Tallaght, Blanchardstown and Clondalkin – to cater for the growing population in the western suburbs of the city. The first two were already under construction, while the Clondalkin centre had yet to get underway, not least, as Gilmartin believed, because the chosen lands at Neilstown were unsuitable for commercial development. He identified a 180-acre parcel of land at Quarryvale on the other side of the motorway from Clondalkin with far greater commercial potential and set about tracking down the owners of the site and a further 300 acres surrounding it.

One day a friend, Paul Sheeran, manager of the nearby Blanchardstown branch of the Bank of Ireland, introduced him to a local businessman who was in the bank at the time. Garage owner Brendan Fassnidge suggested that Gilmartin talk to a man who, he said, knew every blade of grass in west Dublin, and he arranged a meeting that very evening in the local and aptly named Deadman's Inn. Gilmartin went to the pub in Palmerstown for the 7 p.m. appointment. He recalled:

> I was in the Deadman's Inn for about ten minutes when this big man came tearing in the door, all hail-fellow, well-met. He wasn't the slightest bit interested in what I wanted to know. He only wanted to talk about Bachelors Walk, which he said was on his patch. He told me he knew I was involved in a big scheme in Bachelors Walk and he said the government allocated him to take care of me and get the deal into Dublin. He said that he wanted to meet the people behind the proposed development. I said that I was meeting the people in London on Thursday and I would ask them if they would like to meet him. I told him I was interested in a piece of land in the Palmerstown area. He said that this land was zoned industrial and he told me he would have a map for me the next time I came over from England. That was my first encounter with Liam Lawlor.[1]

Loud and brash, the Fianna Fáil TD for Dublin West and long-serving county councillor had his fingers in many pies. Born in 1944 and raised in Crumlin, he was a former hurler for Dublin and Leinster and had a reputation for throwing his weight around long before he bullied his way into Gilmartin's life. He ran a successful refrigeration business before he won a Dáil seat in 1977. Lawlor enjoyed considerable influence in commercial and political circles and was used to getting his own way. He made money in property deals from Dublin to Prague, falsely promoted himself as a representative of the Irish government in Iraq while doing business for Larry Goodman, and moved around in expensive clothes and a chauffeur-driven Mercedes while living in Somerton, his mansion in Lucan.

A week after he met Gilmartin, Lawlor turned up unannounced at the Arlington offices at Brewer's Green in London while the board meeting Gilmartin had mentioned was underway. Lawlor claimed that he could knock at least two years off the time to develop the scheme if he was on board. By the time the meeting ended, and despite Gilmartin's protestations that the man was nothing but a 'hustler', he had extracted a monthly fee of £3,500 in exchange for helping the company 'through the corridors of power' in Dublin. Arlington directors Raymond Mould and Ted Dadley ignored Gilmartin's warnings, convinced that the uninvited visitor might help clear political hurdles in Dublin.

Lawlor was not finished hustling, and a week later he turned up, unexpectedly, to collect Gilmartin when he landed at Dublin Airport. From there he drove to the headquarters of Dublin County Council in O'Connell Street and ushered his guest into the office of Assistant City and County Manager George Redmond. Almost immediately after their introduction, Redmond produced a 24 x 24-inch colour-coded sheet which identified every owner of the Quarryvale lands. Lawlor told Gilmartin that, in return for the map, he would have to 'look after George' and himself, at nothing less than £100,000 each. Otherwise, he said, the projects were going nowhere. Gilmartin rejected the outrageous demand, stuffed the map into his bag and made two powerful enemies.

After months of delay in acquiring the land around Bachelors Walk, Arlington Securities, with a lost investment of £12 million, including Lawlor's monthly fee, pulled out of the city-centre project. Gilmartin decided to concentrate his efforts on Quarryvale, working out of an office in St Stephen's Green in Dublin funded by Arlington. In late 1988, he formed a new company, Barkhill Ltd, and raised the finance to purchase the main blocks of land fronting the N4 to form the core of the planned multi-million retail development. However, the site previously chosen by the county council for a shopping centre at Neilstown in Clondalkin already had official zoning, and Gilmartin knew that transferring that to the Quarryvale lands posed a significant challenge. Senior council officials invited him to purchase the zoned Neilstown site, but, in his view, it was not viable and would not provide the working-class community of Clondalkin with opportunities for secure, long-term employment or the range of social, sports and other community facilities that could be provided at the more extensive Quarryvale lands.

By not accepting the offer of the Neilstown lands, Gilmartin exposed himself to exploitation by others because of their ransom potential. Lawlor was the first to recognise that Gilmartin would need to get the existing zoning on Neilstown transferred to Quarryvale, which would require a vote by the elected members of Dublin County Council, over whom he and his party wielded considerable influence. He lined up a key party supporter with more than enough financial and political strength and tactical ingenuity to match Gilmartin's.

In November 1988, during a meeting between Gilmartin and his architects, Taggarts of Belfast, who had worked with him on the successful Clandeboye Shopping Centre in Bangor some years earlier, Lawlor again turned up without notice. The politician had learned about the meeting after calling Gilmartin's home in Luton to establish his whereabouts. He arrived at the Trust House Forte hotel with a ready-made plan. He told Gilmartin that another developer, Owen O'Callaghan, had an option to buy the Neilstown site from Welsh retailer Albert Gubay, who had purchased the lands from the council after Gilmartin refused its offer. Cork developer O'Callaghan had already discussed the potential of the Quarryvale site with Lawlor, and he wanted a slice of the action. O'Callaghan had been building houses and commercial developments for more than twenty years, including the Merchants Quay retail centre in Cork and a smaller one at Arthur's Quay in Limerick. He was appointed as a board member of the State-owned energy company, Bord Gáis Energy, by Charles Haughey and was an influential back-room player for Fianna Fáil in Cork.

If O'Callaghan had control of the Neilstown site, it would force Gilmartin to negotiate with him and, as a shrewd operator with influence in the spheres of high finance and Fianna Fáil, the Cork man had a strong hand to play. When Gilmartin insisted that no one in their right mind would build on Neilstown, Lawlor replied that O'Callaghan didn't have to. 'All he has to do is threaten to build it and you'll be [stuck] there forever,' he said.

The Cork developer had first heard about Gilmartin's ambitious plan at Quarryvale from Lawlor and another Lucan-based Fianna Fáil councillor, Finbarr Hanrahan, a few months earlier. He secured the option to buy the Clondalkin land from Gubay in early November 1988, having recognised its ransom value. At his first meeting with Gilmartin, a month later, O'Callaghan said he wanted the Quarryvale site or 50 per cent of the entire retail development, a demand which was immediately rejected. The Cork developer then sought £7 million from Gilmartin in exchange for the Neilstown lands; by the new year they had settled for half that amount, to be paid in stages.

A total of £3.5 million for lands that would never be developed was a high price for Gilmartin, and the punishing contract required him to pay £800,000 upfront to cover the money O'Callaghan had paid Gubay for the site. A further £1.35 million was due a year later, in January 1990, and the balance of the same amount when zoning for Quarryvale was approved or in January 1991, whichever came sooner.

At their first meeting in early December 1988, O'Callaghan made no bones about his extensive political contacts and boasted of how he had discussed the prospects for Quarryvale with Minister for Industry and Commerce Albert Reynolds and senior executives of AIB at an event in Cork only days earlier. He showed Gilmartin a photo from the local newspaper, the *Evening Echo*, featuring himself and Reynolds at the Merchants Quay shopping centre.

In early 1989, Gilmartin found himself in Leinster House at the invitation of Lawlor, who said he had arranged a meeting with 'the boss'. At a pre-arranged meeting at Buswells Hotel, across the road from the parliament complex, Lawlor told Gilmartin that 'the boss', Taoiseach

Charles Haughey, wanted to meet him to discuss his plans for the city. In Leinster House, Lawlor took his guest in a lift, in which a silent Ray Burke was also travelling, to an upper floor. Lawlor remained in a lobby area after ushering Gilmartin into a large room, where the developer encountered a group of Cabinet members, including some familiar faces, standing and sitting around a table. Among them were Pádraig Flynn, with whom he was in regular contact, Bertie Ahern and junior minister Seamus Brennan, all of whom greeted him. Also present were Minister for Justice Gerry Collins, Albert Reynolds and Brian Lenihan. Soon afterwards, Burke entered, followed by their leader.

'I know you, you're Gilmartin from Lislary,' Haughey said to his visitor as they shook hands. Haughey told him that he had a holiday home by the sea in the Sligo townland where Gilmartin was reared. The Fianna Fáil leader knew a lot about the Gilmartins as he had, some years previously, sought to acquire, by dubious means, land belonging to Gilmartin's sister, Chris McGoldrick. She had confronted Haughey in Sligo town in 1986 about an attempt to register 1.5 acres of her land in the name of his company, Larchfield Securities Ltd. A few years earlier, Haughey had obtained a property adjoining the Gilmartin lands from a relation of theirs, John Andrew Currid, a client of the taoiseach's former accountancy firm, Haughey Boland. In 1984, the politician sought to extend this to include land given to Chris by her father, James Gilmartin. After their confrontation in Sligo, Haughey agreed to meet Chris at Strandhill, where he was addressing a Fianna Fáil function that evening. Before she arrived at Strandhill, Haughey departed for Dublin. The Gilmartin family eventually recovered control of their land after some fraught legal exchanges. There is little doubt that the Taoiseach would have recalled this sordid land-grabbing exercise when he met with Tom in the Dáil in February 1989, but he didn't mention it.

After a brief chat, the Taoiseach assured Gilmartin that no obstacles would be put in his way to ensure the success of his business plans at a time when jobs were so desperately needed in the capital city. The Taoiseach mentioned that his brother, Seán, was an assistant city and county manager for Dublin. Haughey then asked whether 'Liam is taking good care of you?' During the conversation, another minister, Mary O'Rourke, entered the room and was introduced to Gilmartin by Flynn.

After the informal meeting, Gilmartin was led back into the lobby area where Lawlor was standing in a corner. At his side was another man, short in stature, with 'salt and pepper hair' and wearing a casual jacket. The man approached Gilmartin and told him that he was likely to make millions out of Dublin with his business projects. '[W]e think you should give us some of the money up front … we would like you to deposit 5 million pound [*sic*] before you start … and we want it deposited into an Isle of Man account.'

'That's not much,' Gilmartin replied sarcastically. The man, who never identified himself, then took out a piece of paper about an inch and a half wide from his jacket pocket and handed it to a now perplexed Gilmartin. The note contained a bank account number. 'I want you to deposit the money into that account,' the man said. Gilmartin took the piece of paper, put it in his pocket, looked at the man and said, 'You make the fucking Mafia look like monks.' The man grabbed his arm, tried unsuccessfully to retrieve the piece of paper and threatened, 'You could wind up in the Liffey for that statement.'

'I told him to fuck off and walked on,' Gilmartin recalled. There were no apparent witnesses to the conversation, Lawlor having disappeared. As Gilmartin walked towards the lift, Seán Walsh, then a Fianna Fáil TD for Dublin South-West, beckoned him into his office. He warned the shaken developer that he was being set up by Lawlor, Hanrahan and other named party councillors, as well as Redmond, adding that these were individuals he 'should watch out for'. 'You are being shafted ... You must watch your back,' said Walsh.

Over the coming days and weeks, Gilmartin told several people about his meeting with the Taoiseach, his ministers and the anonymous man who attempted to extort £5 million from him outside the room in Leinster House. Among those he informed were Paul Sheeran, chief city valuer Michael McLoone, and investment banker Johnny Fortune. As Gilmartin said later, there was only one opinion he could take from all of this:

> I was invited by Mr Lawlor to meet the Taoiseach. I went to meet the Taoiseach. I met the majority of ministers, who were around the table, and on my way out, just at the door, a gentleman asked me – told me, because of the amount of money I was going to make out of all the help they were going to give me ... that I should give them five million pounds. So all in all, I could only come to one conclusion: that the place was totally corrupt.

It would not end there, as he discovered weeks later when he was advised by Lawlor to get some other important councillors 'on board' and was summoned once more to Buswells. There he saw O'Callaghan, along with his solicitor John Deane, also from Cork, and his architect, Ambrose Kelly. Lawlor was at the bar with another man, who then approached Gilmartin. It was Hanrahan, who asked about Quarryvale. Gilmartin showed him the brochure that set out the scale of his ambitious retail scheme for west Dublin. Hanrahan responded with a demand for £100,000 in return for his support. 'I've met people like you who when they get what they wanted didn't pay up, so I want £50,000 up front,' Hanrahan said. Gilmartin walked away in disgust.

'Did he tap you?' O'Callaghan asked, to which Gilmartin replied, 'What do you think?' His business partner seemed unsurprised and even amused by this latest attempt to extort money. Adding salt to the wound, O'Callaghan told Gilmartin that Lawlor was working on his instructions and getting well rewarded.

Chapter Seven

Pub Crawl for Bertie

TOM GILMARTIN'S REFUSAL TO ENTERTAIN ANY of these outlandish demands, amounting by early 1989 to some £6 million, led to a pattern of obstruction by some of those involved, notably George Redmond and Liam Lawlor. Redmond interfered with a deal made by Gilmartin with Michael McLoone for the purchase of council-owned lands at Quarryvale, which caused a delay of several months before it was completed and led the cost to almost double on the price previously agreed.

Redmond also frustrated an important meeting with council engineers, forcing Gilmartin to contact Charles Haughey's brother, Seán, the other assistant city and county manager for Dublin. He was present when Seán Haughey confronted Redmond over the delay in the meeting and asked what his 'fucking game' was, to which Redmond replied, 'Ask your brother.' An angry Haughey responded, 'I'm not my brother's keeper and George, your game is going to stop, I can assure you.'[1]

As his retirement from the council in June 1989 approached, Redmond contacted John Corcoran, the founder and managing director of Green Property, asking for a consultancy job. Green Property was developing the Blanchardstown shopping centre, the closest rival to the Quarryvale retail project. Redmond suggested to Corcoran that he put in a tender for the council lands at Irishtown in Quarryvale that Gilmartin had already agreed to buy. It was another attempt to scupper or delay the Quarryvale project, or at least to make the land purchase more expensive for Gilmartin.

Gilmartin decided to make a formal complaint about Redmond's behaviour to the city and county manager, Frank Feely, who met him with Seán Haughey a few days after the delayed meeting with the county engineers. During a three-hour discussion, Feely agreed that the complaints about Redmond, Lawlor and Hanrahan should be brought to the attention of Environment Minister Pádraig Flynn. On 22 February 1989, Gilmartin met Flynn and informed him of the various demands for money that had been made of him, including by Lawlor and Redmond. Following consultations between Flynn and the Taoiseach, and involving Minister for Justice Gerry Collins and Attorney General John Murray, the gardaí were asked to investigate Gilmartin's complaints as part of another inquiry they were running into allegations of planning irregularities in Dublin.

Yet the investigating officers did not interview Lawlor, Redmond or Hanrahan in relation to Gilmartin's claims, and their final report made no reference to the £5 million demand in Leinster House. They concluded that there was no evidence of criminal conduct by either Redmond or Lawlor. The report stated: 'Gossip and rumour abound in Ireland and many an innocent, defenceless person has had his good name tarnished as a result. Therefore, it was an important part of this enquiry to delve fully into the allegations made by Thomas Gilmartin and others concerning Liam Lawlor TD … [who] emerges from this enquiry with his good reputation unscathed.'

The investigation was headed by Detective Chief Superintendent Hugh Sreenan, who, with Superintendent Brendan Burns, interviewed a range of witnesses, including Owen O'Callaghan, Ted Dadley and Raymond Mould of Arlington Securities, and senior council officials Redmond, Feely and Seán Haughey. While Gilmartin was also interviewed, his decision not to sign a formal statement was justified when he learned that none of the serious incidents of criminal and corrupt behaviour he had raised were actually put to Redmond or Lawlor. Signing a formal statement would, in his view, have been an endorsement by him of what he believed was a sham of an exercise, which not only exonerated Lawlor and Redmond, but also failed to mention the demand for the £5 million in Leinster House in the final report.

The flawed inquiry arguably encouraged those involved in making and receiving illicit payments in relation to planning in the city to believe that they were untouchable by the law. This was evident when a man who identified himself as 'Garda Burns' called Gilmartin to say that he should 'fuck off back to England' and that similar allegations of the type he had made had also resulted in the people accused emerging with their 'reputations unscathed'.

At a subsequent meeting with Flynn in April 1989, when Gilmartin reported that nothing much had changed despite the Garda investigation, the minister suggested that 'a substantial donation' to Fianna Fáil 'could help to curb these activities'. Flynn told Gilmartin that he was one of two national treasurers of the party trying to clear its debt of some £3 million. The other was Bertie Ahern. Coming out of the meeting, Ted Dadley, who had accompanied Gilmartin, commented, 'Everybody's looking for money. Dèja vu.'

With a general election looming, Gilmartin decided, against the advice of McLoone, to make the donation suggested by Flynn, and he arranged an appointment to see the minister at his office in the Custom House along the city quays. 'They'll take your fucking money and they'll still do nothing for you,' McLoone warned before Gilmartin left the chief valuer's office for the Custom House.

Flynn was packing his briefcase when Gilmartin arrived. He told Flynn that he had decided to give a donation of £50,000 to the party. The minister said that there was 'a car waiting for me'. 'He was in a great hurry, and he was standing behind the desk. So, I wrote out the cheque and I asked to whom should I make it payable … and he said, "Oh just leave it on the desk." So I left it on the desk.' The payee section on the cheque was left blank.

'All I wanted was to give some chance to the scheme getting off the ground,' Gilmartin said of the reason for the donation. 'After all, it was creating twenty thousand jobs. I risked everything to put it there, including my name. And it had been suggested to me by a government official that I had to pay to get justice, so I felt I had no option but to do that.' Flynn provided no receipt for the donation and apparently told no one else in the party that he had received the huge payment, equivalent to a year's salary for a government minister, just days before the 1989 election. The politician from Castlebar, County Mayo, and his wife, Dorothy, bought a plot of land for forestry with the proceeds, which were first lodged off-shore.

As McLoone had predicted, the contribution failed to resolve the delay in closing the purchase of the Irishtown lands from the council, which were crucial to the completion of the land bank required for Quarryvale. Gilmartin was forced to put in a fresh, higher bid, after Redmond and Lawlor forced a new tender process following unfounded allegations they made of a 'cosy deal' between Gilmartin and the council. Gilmartin eventually paid £5.1 million, or £70,000 an acre, for the property, compared to the £40,000 per acre he had previously agreed with McLoone, and substantially more than the amounts he paid for other parcels of land in the area. It was also a far greater amount than the bid submitted by John Corcoran of Green Property on Redmond's advice.

In a last-ditch effort to rescue the land deal, Gilmartin reached out to another senior politician who had offered his full support for the Bachelors Walk and Quarryvale projects soon after he landed in Dublin in 1987. Bertie Ahern was the minister for labour and had previously welcomed Gilmartin to his department office in Mespil Road in autumn 1987. At their first meeting, they discussed the plans for Bachelors Walk, part of Ahern's north inner-city constituency. 'Mr Ahern was affable and approachable and he was very supportive of my plans,' Gilmartin recalled.

He met Ahern again in October 1988 in the politician's office above Fagan's public house in Drumcondra, where he recounted the difficulties he was having in relation to the purchase of the Irishtown lands. According to Gilmartin, he called on Ahern in early June 1989, and the politician listened to his complaints about the continuing delay over the land purchase at Quarryvale and said he would see what he could do. A few days later Councillor Joe Burke, a friend and political associate of Ahern, called into Gilmartin's office on St Stephen's Green, where he repeated the promise to assist with his problem over the land purchase. Burke was a member of the Planning and Development Committee of the city council, which had approved Gilmartin's bid for the lands in late May. The land disposal still required the approval of the full council. A few days after their discussion, Burke called Gilmartin to confirm that the council members had approved his tender at a meeting the previous night.

Gilmartin phoned Ahern to thank him for his help, and during their conversation the party co-treasurer mentioned that Fianna Fáil was holding a fundraising event in the Reform Club in London that November. He said that the party finances were 'in a bit of a state' and asked Gilmartin if he would consider a donation. The weary businessman replied that he had recently given Pádraig Flynn £50,000 for the party, but that he would try to attend with his Arlington colleagues.

Some months later, when he arrived with Raymond Mould and Ted Dadley at the function in the Reform Club, where Ahern and Flynn were among the speakers, Gilmartin was asked by the Mayo politician to go to a nearby restaurant where he would join him later. In Gilmartin's absence, Flynn asked the Arlington executives for a donation 'for the boys', which Dadley assumed meant Fianna Fáil, but the pair refused. Later in the evening, Flynn arrived in a flustered state to meet Gilmartin but avoided questions about the fundraiser. Later, Gilmartin realised that he had been diverted from the Reform Club to ensure he did not alert Mould and Dadley to the £50,000 donation he had already made to Flynn for the party.

By late 1989, Gilmartin, having rejected demands for millions in bribes, including from Lawlor, Flynn and the anonymous man in Leinster House, was facing further challenges in his efforts to get the Quarryvale project over the line. He had spent over £4 million of the funds he had raised on the land acquisitions at Quarryvale and on professional fees, and he was nearing the deadline to pay the second tranche owed to O'Callaghan for the Neilstown purchase. He had commitments from Arlington for £10 million in funding and also had a positive response from his contacts with the British financial lenders Norwich Union, as well as the London and Edinburgh Trust, but only on condition that the land at Quarryvale secured the proper zoning for the retail scheme. AIB was also prepared to advance a loan facility of £8.5 million, but this was subject to strict conditions, which included the deferment of the monies due to O'Callaghan and an assurance that tax designation for the development would be approved by the government. Gilmartin was forced to put up the lands he had assembled at Quarryvale and other assets as collateral for the AIB loan, giving the bank significant leverage over his ambitious project.

On his visits to AIB in Ballsbridge for negotiations on his loan during 1990, Gilmartin and his business partner, Richard Forman, noticed that O'Callaghan and his solicitor, John Deane, were often at the bank at the same time. Gilmartin was put under pressure by some AIB executives to engage with O'Callaghan and to provide equity and even cede control of the Quarryvale development to the Cork man. One bank official described O'Callaghan as someone with the 'political clout' to get the scheme done.

At a public event for the Westpark scheme, as the Quarryvale development was being marketed, which took place in the Berkeley Court Hotel in Ballsbridge in July 1990, Gilmartin presented an elaborate thirty-two-page brochure outlining the project. It set out his plans for a 'high quality regional shopping centre, with leisure, sport and entertainment facilities as well as a major business park on the 820 acre site'. He told an audience of business leaders, politicians, local government officials and media representatives that he intended to invest £750 million and provide up to 20,000 jobs in the economically depressed part of west Dublin. So, he was more than surprised to encounter a distinctly hostile response from some of those present and in subsequent media coverage, which, he believed, was orchestrated.

Angered and depressed by the apparently unending obstruction to his efforts and the recurring experience of people putting their hands in his pockets, Gilmartin decided to close his Dublin office and return to Luton and his family. As he packed his bags in the office on St Stephen's Green, he had an unexpected visitor when Councillor Joe Burke walked through the door. He explained to Burke that he was returning to Luton in frustration over the obstacles he faced and the demands placed on him for financial favours from several quarters over the previous two years. Following his litany of complaints, he said to Burke that he 'would pay a fucking half a million to get out of here' if he could recoup the £5 million and more that he had spent on the Quarryvale project.

'Would you?' asked Burke, a Donegal man, who then reminded Gilmartin that Bertie Ahern was 'looking after him'. Gilmartin remarked, 'It wasn't a demand, it was like talking about £500,000. Whether I would pay it. It wasn't a question like Lawlor. "Hand me, you know, £100,000." This wasn't a demand like that. It was what I call typical Donegal fashion, talking in circles. Talking around half a million.'

Burke, a building contractor, then asked Gilmartin whether he wanted a lift to the airport and suggested that they could meet up with Ahern on the way. Gilmartin got into Burke's pick-up truck with his suitcase and off they went, pulling up at two different pubs on the way to the airport. The first stop was Fagan's in Drumcondra. Burke went into the pub and came out 20 minutes later to say that Ahern was not there. They then stopped at the Beaumont House, where Gilmartin waited in the truck for another ten minutes while Burke went inside. He returned to say Ahern would be there shortly. Concerned that he would miss his flight to Luton, Gilmartin insisted that he needed to head for the airport immediately. An extremely upset Burke tried to persuade him to wait, but Gilmartin said he had an important meeting in London the following day and could not afford to miss the plane.

Before he left for Luton, Gilmartin had had a conversation with Colm Scallon during which he told him about his mistreatment by various political figures. Scallon described the demands for cash by Lawlor and others as 'horrendous' and 'disgraceful', and he brought Gilmartin to see Seán Sherwin, the Fianna Fáil national organiser, at the party's headquarters in Lower Mount Street in Dublin, where Gilmartin recounted his experiences during a two-hour discussion. Sherwin professed to be astounded and shocked at the brass neck of Councillor Finbarr Hanrahan, who had asked for £100,000 in Buswells Hotel. Gilmartin also told Sherwin about the donation given to Pádraig Flynn in the Customs House during the 1989 election campaign, and the national organiser promised to investigate whether it was received by the party. Sherwin subsequently asked the Fianna Fáil fundraiser, Paul Kavanagh, who confirmed that there was no evidence in the accounts of any such donation. Remarkably, neither Kavanagh nor Sherwin approached Flynn about the missing donation nor raised it with their party leader, Haughey.

Gilmartin's return to Luton in mid-1990 did not mean an end to his Irish business dealings, as he remained a director of Barkhill and was still involved in bringing the Quarryvale project to fruition. But he left Dublin with his faith in the Irish political system totally shattered after the less than subtle request by Burke for a huge bribe for Ahern, the one politician he thought he could trust. A few months later when he met O'Callaghan in Dublin, he was shocked to learn that Ahern had received a large payment from the Cork developer in relation to the acquisition of the Irishtown lands. O'Callaghan 'laughed out loud' when Gilmartin mentioned that the only politician who had helped him was Ahern when he intervened, through Joe Burke, with Dublin City Council to confirm his successful tender for the Irishtown lands. Gilmartin was absolutely stunned when the Cork developer told him that he had paid Ahern £50,000 to ensure Gilmartin secured the tender and Green Property did not get its hands on the land. O'Callaghan said the money was paid to Ahern at a football match in Dublin in autumn 1989. It was evident that O'Callaghan had not been exaggerating when he boasted about his influence with senior government ministers and AIB executives.

By November 1990, unable to raise the finance to repay the AIB loan, now amounting to more than £9 million including interest, and with other lands yet to be purchased at Quarryvale and O'Callaghan seeking his due payment of £1.35 million, Gilmartin was forced to concede an equity stake to the Cork developer. Reluctantly he agreed, in mid-December, to give O'Callaghan a 25 per cent stake in Barkhill, the company he had formed to develop Quarryvale, in exchange for an additional loan facility from AIB. The arrangement included an unlikely option to terminate the deal if he fully repaid his debts to O'Callaghan and AIB by January 1991. On 14 December 1990, Gilmartin signed the faxed copy of the deal at his home in Luton without taking legal advice.

In order to raise the funds he needed to clear the loan and debt, Gilmartin knew that the Quarryvale lands had to be zoned, and that was a decision that could only be made by a majority of elected members of Dublin County Council. Councillor Colm McGrath, with whom Gilmartin was in occasional contact, agreed to submit a motion to this effect in advance of a meeting of the council to review the Dublin Development Plan, which was due to take place in February 1991.

On 15 February, three days before the deadline for putting down the motion, AIB called in the £9.35 million loan to Barkhill with immediate effect, unless Gilmartin agreed to a re-drafted 'Heads of Agreement', which required him to hand over a 33 per cent stake of his company to O'Callaghan. McGrath, who was being directed in the background by Lawlor, the strategist acting for O'Callaghan, phoned him in Luton to say that he had been advised not to submit the zoning motion until Gilmartin had signed the agreement. Fianna Fáil councillor, Seán Gilbride, likewise said that he could not support the motion unless the deal was in place. O'Callaghan and senior AIB executive Jim Donagh piled pressure on Gilmartin to close the deal, which also required him to find an outside investor to purchase a further 33 per cent of Barkhill by the end of March 1991.

The 'Night of the Long Knives', as Gilmartin described it, ended with him consulting his solicitor, Seamus Maguire, and signing the new agreement, which he faxed to AIB late in the evening. The motion was then submitted by McGrath, which proposed removing the town centre zoning for Neilstown and effectively transferring it to Quarryvale, the value of which would immediately increase by some £20 million. When the motion was carried, Gilmartin believed that he was now in a position to buy out his partners, cover his debts and complete the project, unless, of course, further obstacles were put in his way.

Gilmartin had a poor grasp of the wheels within wheels that kept much of Dublin's political and commercial life in motion, and was encouraged to find someone experienced in public relations to improve his image and provide the lobbying skills required to ensure that councillors would support further votes crucial to the success of the Quarryvale project. Unfortunately, it was evident that those on whom he most depended for financial, political and media support were among those who could be least trusted.

Chapter Eight

An Oppressed Shareholder

FRANK DUNLOP, A FORMER FIANNA FÁIL and government press officer in the 1970s and 1980s, had offered his services to Tom Gilmartin soon after he first arrived from Luton, but Gilmartin was advised not to go near the PR guru, who was described to him as a 'political bagman'. However, he had reason to suspect Dunlop's interference in his affairs when he saw the dapper and smooth-talking lobbyist in the company of Owen O'Callaghan and Bertie Ahern during a visit to Leinster House in 1989.

In April 1991, at the request of the bank, Gilmartin was brought by O'Callaghan to meet Liam Lawlor, ostensibly for another engagement with politicians in the Dáil. Instead, Lawlor brought him through the Leinster House complex and across Merrion Square to a building in Upper Mount Street. Gilmartin recognised Dunlop when he arrived, but he was left sitting in another room while O'Callaghan and Lawlor had what he gathered was a heated conversation with the PR man in his office. As time dragged on, the impatient Gilmartin walked out in disgust, only to be followed by an irate O'Callaghan with Dunlop. Gilmartin agreed to take a lift from them to the guest house on Merrion Road where he was staying and which was owned by Paul Sheeran.

During the trip, Dunlop loudly complained to O'Callaghan about Lawlor, alleging that Lawlor had tried to bully a payment from him, which the politician claimed to be owed. Gilmartin recalled:

> Dunlop was fuming and said that he thought Lawlor was going to hit him. He wanted £100,000 but had received only £40,000 of what he was owed. O'Callaghan laughed and said he would 'try and square it' by giving 'a bit more' to Lawlor ... It was obvious that they wanted me in the offices [of Dunlop] for a reason, but that was never explained. The bank had contacted me to meet Lawlor on the basis that he was going to introduce me to some senior politicians in the Dáil. Clearly it was a set-up.

It soon became clear to Gilmartin that he was being introduced to the PR man as yet another cog in O'Callaghan's machine of political, financial and media handlers.

In 1989, Dunlop had established his own PR business, Dunlop and Associates (subsequently renamed Frank Dunlop and Associates), and had opened a Channel Islands-registered company, Sheafran Ltd, an amalgamation of his name and that of his wife, Sheila. The name was later changed to Shefran Ltd. In 1990, Dunlop opened another offshore Jersey-based company, Xerxes Consult (Jersey) Ltd. At the time of their meeting in 1991, Gilmartin was not aware that Dunlop's role was to assist with the 'advancement of zoning' and 'to advise on media issues' in relation to the Quarryvale site. Substantial fees were being paid to Frank Dunlop and Associates Ltd by O'Callaghan for his efforts, and even greater amounts were given to Shefran Ltd. In May and June 1991, the offshore company was used to filter £100,000 in payments to councillors in return for their votes on the Neilstown/Quarryvale rezoning motion.

Local elections in June 1991 meant that candidates were hungry for funds, an appetite O'Callaghan was ready to feed from the war chest he employed to ensure that the Quarryvale lands were rezoned for a major town centre and for industrial use, and to remove the existing zoning for Neilstown. The successful motion to that effect was submitted by Colm McGrath, but it also capped the scale of the proposed retail centre in deference to the concerns of some political representatives about its size. During the election campaign O'Callaghan expended some £230,000 through his company Riga Ltd for what were termed as 'Westpark expenses' in his company accounts. O'Callaghan expected to recoup the expenses when he took control, as he intended, of Gilmartin's company, Barkhill Ltd.

Following the election and the successful rezoning vote, Gilmartin was asked to cede further control of his company in return for a loan of £3 million from AIB and £1 million from Riga Ltd. This would have left him with a 33.5 per cent stake in Barkhill, with Riga holding just over 44 per cent and AIB just over 22 per cent. Gilmartin refused the offer and said he would not accept less than an equal share of 40 per cent with O'Callaghan. He also refused to replace the Belfast firm, Taggarts, as architects for the development with the one favoured by O'Callaghan: Ambrose Kelly.

Greater pressure was placed on Gilmartin when he inadvertently mentioned to AIB officials that the Inland Revenue (IR) in the UK was pursuing him for a debt of almost £7 million for taxes he did not owe. He had previously settled his tax affairs with a £120,000 sterling payment arising from a property deal he completed in Milton Keynes, but suddenly his dealings with the IR hit the headlines of *The People*, the British tabloid newspaper. He told me:

> I had informed AIB that I had a settlement agreed with the Inland Revenue for £120,000 in relation to a property deal in Milton Keynes. The next thing the newspapers in England had a headline 'Tom's tax problems' with a photo of me and a claim that I owed £7 million plus penalties. When the media called to my home, Vera opened the door and was knocked to the ground. The Revenue came looking for up to £14 million, and I was made bankrupt by the courts in 1992. They seized my car and other assets in front of

> my wife and children. Then they realised their mistake and told me they had been misled with information from Dublin. I didn't owe them anything but the £120,000 we agreed. They offered me compensation for their mistake, which I refused. But that destroyed any chance of keeping control of my business in Ireland. I could not even afford the price of an air fare to attend board meetings of Barkhill. On one occasion, O'Callaghan offered to pay my fare with money he had taken from my company. My family suffered terribly at this time. I learnt later the whole plan was hatched in Dublin.

His bankruptcy left him unable to pay basic household bills. He recalled how he privately wept when his son, Thomas, a schoolboy, gave him his savings, including his Holy Communion money, to help his parents. Family members in Sligo and Donegal, some of whom he had helped out financially over preceding years, sent money and other supports. He was devastated, ruined and ashamed.

The fingerprints of Frank Dunlop were all over the dissemination of information about Gilmartin's alleged difficulties with the IR. The PR man spoke to various politicians in Dublin and tipped off the English tabloid about the developer's tax problems. *The People* was happy to run with an inflated and inaccurate account of Gilmartin's financial challenges. The sordid attack, and the campaign of false information about his tax affairs, which a senior IR official confirmed came from Dublin, almost destroyed him and his family. Vera, who had multiple sclerosis (MS), suffered a rapid deterioration in her health following the stress of confronting a manufactured bankruptcy. It also revealed the extraordinary depths to which his rivals were prepared to descend in order to take over his business.

The immediate effect was to force Gilmartin into signing another shareholders agreement in September 1991, which gave both him and O'Callaghan a 40 per cent stake in Barkhill, with AIB holding the balance of 20 per cent. In return, the company received a £3 million loan facility, which was to be used exclusively 'for the purchase of properties' required to complete the Quarryvale development. Notwithstanding this requirement, O'Callaghan continued to make payments from his company Riga Ltd to various politicians, including Lawlor and McGrath, as well as large sums to Shefran. With the new agreement in place, these 'expenses' were invoiced by Riga to Barkhill Ltd, thus depleting the funds Gilmartin required for property purchases.

In May and June 1992, £70,000 was paid to Shefran and reimbursed by Barkhill, even though Gilmartin had never heard of the company and didn't know that its owners were Frank Dunlop and his wife. Dunlop processed the payments to Shefran through an account he opened at AIB in College Green, while he also lodged funds at the Terenure branch of AIB on Rathfarnham Road. He continued to use the Xerxes Consult (Jersey) account in the Midland Bank in Jersey and another with the Irish Nationwide Building Society (INBS) in Dublin to disperse and disguise the funds he received. Between April 1991 and January 1993, Dunlop received from Riga or Barkhill £150,000 through Shefran and another £100,000 through Frank Dunlop and Associates. These and other funds were used to pay numerous politicians during their election campaigns before the November 1992 general election and in advance of another crucial vote on Quarryvale at Dublin County Council a month later.

The election provided perfect cover for illicit payments, and, as Fianna Fáil's campaign director of publicity, Dunlop was in a prime position to both finance and lobby selected candidates running for the Dáil. Among those favoured by O'Callaghan were Cork Fianna Fáil TD Batt O'Keeffe, who received £5,000, and Dublin Fianna Fáil councillor G.V. Wright, who was given £10,000 during the campaign. Councillor Seán Gilbride took a sabbatical from his teaching job and was paid £3,500 a month for his lobbying efforts to secure a further rezoning of the Quarryvale lands at the December meeting of Dublin County Council.[1]

The Flood Tribunal later established that AIB was informed of the legally dubious campaign to lobby politicians and that the bank released £40,000 in funds, which benefitted candidates of different parties and none. Liam T. Cosgrave of Fine Gael, a son and grandson of former taoisigh, was handed £5,000 by Dunlop in the car park of a church in Blackrock in November 1992. It did not seem to bother Dunlop that, while employed by Fianna Fáil, he was assisting political rivals of his party with money.

But it was Fianna Fáil candidates who were the main beneficiaries of O'Callaghan's generosity, with Lawlor topping the list with a contribution of £25,000 from Dunlop. The PR man drew down £55,000 on 10 November, the day he supervised the launch of the Fianna Fáil election manifesto, which was attended by senior ministers of the outgoing government. O'Callaghan's financial contribution to the party's election effort was confirmed in a letter he wrote to Taoiseach Albert Reynolds during the campaign, in which he stated that he had provided an amount 'in excess of six figures' to the cause. 'It is vital for the country that we have a Fianna Fáil controlled government,' he wrote and enclosed a cheque for £5,000 for good measure.[2]

Nine months earlier, Reynolds had replaced the former party leader, Charles Haughey, following the spate of financial and other scandals that finally brought down 'the boss'. In his farewell speech in February 1992, Haughey quoted Othello: 'I have done the state some service; they know't. No more of that.'[3] He did not refer to the service he provided to his friends over his thirty-five years in politics, or to their generosity to him in return. O'Callaghan boasted to Gilmartin how he, with other powerful backroom party figures, had forced Haughey's resignation and thrown their support behind Reynolds as their favoured successor. It seemed that a Fianna Fáil-led government was vital for him as well as the country.

Though depleted in numbers, Reynolds secured enough votes to form a coalition government with the Labour Party, which had won an unprecedented thirty-two seats following the election on 25 November 1992. Bertie Ahern was reappointed minister for finance, a role that was essential to the delivery of O'Callaghan's wish list of projects, among them Quarryvale, a stadium on the nearby Neilstown lands, and the Golden Island shopping centre in Athlone.

In December 1992, Dublin County Council voted to revise the zoning of Quarryvale to a town or district centre (Category C in the Development Plan) and for industrial use (Category E) subject to a cap on the retail space to 250,000 square feet, a restriction to which Gilmartin was adamantly opposed. This vote altered the decision of the council in May 1991 to zone the lands as categories D (for a major town centre) and E (industrial use), and had been proposed due to growing opposition among local councillors to the scale of the proposed development. Gilmartin believed that the cap would further diminish the value of his interest in Barkhill and the potential viability of the Quarryvale project, but efforts he made to postpone the vote were successfully frustrated by O'Callaghan, who was satisfied that the decision would later be reversed.[4]

For several months, Gilmartin challenged the bank's failure to explain payments from his account to Lawlor, McGrath and Shefran, which were wrongly listed as expenses that he solely had incurred. The amounts, which were paid from monies belonging to Barkhill, were incorrectly reimbursed to O'Callaghan's personal account, he claimed.[5] AIB had reason to be fearful of any legal consequences, as some of its senior executives were only too well aware that its officials had assisted with the transfer of some £250,000 to Dunlop over the previous two years, which was used to 'lobby' elected representatives on the council in relation to the Quarryvale zoning motions.[6] O'Callaghan had not bothered to disguise these activities and, at one point, showed Gilmartin a cheque for £10,000 made out to McGrath, who was also being paid substantial amounts to provide security and plant hire services at Quarryvale. O'Callaghan showed him the cheque while he was driving the now financially embarrassed Gilmartin to the airport following a board meeting in Dublin in early 1993, a flight paid for by the Cork developer, and once again boasted of his control over councillors and other politicians.

In September 1993, Dunlop, according to his own diary records, handed over £25,000 in cash to a senior politician in Power's Hotel near Leinster House although, for the life of him, he could not remember the name of the beneficiary when later asked by the tribunal.[7] This payment came during a period when O'Callaghan was providing large sums to senior Fianna Fáil politicians.

The Quarryvale project was granted its final zoning at a special meeting of councillors on 19 October 1993, and the development plan for Dublin was adopted two months later. In early 1994, Dublin County Council was abolished and replaced with three separate local authorities: Fingal County Council, Dun Laoghaire–Rathdown Council and South Dublin County Council (SDCC). The cap on Quarryvale remained, but O'Callaghan's confidence that it would be removed by the SDCC later transpired.

Along with his concerns about the cap, which diluted the value of his shareholding and of the development, Gilmartin was worried that a lucrative tax designation might be granted by the government to the rival town centre owned by Green Property in Blanchardstown. This, he feared, would allow it to entice away some of the more significant UK and Irish retail investors at the expense of Quarryvale. Gilmartin's concerns were prompted by the news that former Fianna Fáil minister Ray MacSharry had been appointed to the board of Green Property, which was lobbying for the favourable tax incentive under the Urban Renewal Scheme. MacSharry was central to the party's efforts to clear its £3-million debt and, in December 1993, he obtained a commitment from O'Callaghan and other 'high net worth individuals' to pay £100,000 to Fianna Fáil. Although Gilmartin was not aware of MacSharry's key role in the fundraising exercise, he correctly suspected that the politician had influence at the highest levels on government policy.

When Gilmartin raised the designation issue at one of the rare board meetings of Barkhill that he attended, O'Callaghan revealed a further nugget of information about his business dealings with senior Fianna Fáil politicians. Gilmartin described how the Cork developer left the room during the discussion and returned a few minutes later. At the end of the meeting, he told Gilmartin how he got it 'from the horse's mouth' that Blanchardstown would not receive the lucrative tax designation. The horse in question was none other than Minister for Finance Bertie Ahern.

Unknown to Gilmartin, Ahern and Reynolds were providing valuable assistance for a stadium project that O'Callaghan was planning for the Neilstown lands and were in regular contact with the property developer on this and other schemes. Gilmartin knew nothing of the proposal for the Neilstown site, even though it was ultimately owned by Barkhill, in which he had a major shareholding. But O'Callaghan told him of other questionable activities involving Fianna Fáil's unorthodox financial affairs. For instance, he told Gilmartin that Ahern was given £30,000 to ensure that the Blanchardstown centre would not get the favourable tax designation. It was also decided by the Minister for Finance that Quarryvale would not benefit from the incentive either.

On a regular basis, O'Callaghan made it clear to Gilmartin that he nurtured close relations with the highest-placed figures in Fianna Fáil and the government, and that large amounts of money were required to keep the politicians 'on side'. The amounts were staggering, and to add insult to injury, a significant portion of the hand grease was removed as 'Westpark expenses' from Barkhill. The involvement of Ahern in these financial dealings was becoming more apparent but was still shocking for Gilmartin. O'Callaghan disclosed that he paid the politician £25,000 in exchange for ensuring that the Golden Island retail centre in Athlone secured the favourable tax designation under the Urban Renewal Scheme from the Minister for Finance. All of these claims were subsequently and repeatedly denied by Ahern.

As he continued his legal battle to escape from bankruptcy, Gilmartin's family suffered another blow when Vera collapsed in a supermarket in Luton in August 1994, as her medical condition and MS worsened further. The proud Donegal woman, who had endured so much as she tried to keep house and home together, was now paralysed and confined to a wheelchair for the rest of her days. She had been bitterly opposed to Tom getting involved with business in Dublin, and he blamed himself and his decision to ignore her distrust of the political and financial machinations in the country she had left behind. He blamed himself for the stress and pain that she suffered as a result.

Over the following months, as he adapted their home and family life to his wife's new circumstances, Gilmartin was distanced from his business projects in Dublin and was in danger of losing control of Barkhill to his fellow shareholders. He was unable to attend board meetings on a regular basis and believed that he was not being provided with accurate information about the company's affairs, so he authorised Paul Sheeran to represent him.

In May 1995, at one board meeting he did attend, in AIB headquarters, Gilmartin openly accused the other shareholders of fraud and collusion in suppressing his interests in the company and of bribing politicians to achieve their objectives. Sheeran recalled that Gilmartin 'made it very clear as regards bribery and corruption to the other parties [shareholders] concerned' and specifically made reference to the lack of information he had been given about the payments to Frank Dunlop and Shefran Ltd. Sheeran proposed that the board might consider returning to Gilmartin some of the considerable funds he had invested, or at least cover his travel and other expenses so that he could attend board meetings and participate more effectively in the Quarryvale project.[8]

Although this reasonable request was ignored, Gilmartin continued to seek out investors and potential tenants for the scheme, with the result that Grosvenor Holdings, the huge retail and property firm owned by the Duke of Westminster, offered to take shares in Barkhill and ultimately took a 50 per cent stake. This was achieved with the assistance of Gilmartin's colleague, Richard Forman, and they also successfully attracted the interest of UK chains Marks and Spencer, Debenham's, John Lewis and Topshop, along with prominent Irish retailers, to Quarryvale, subsequently named Liffey Valley Shopping Centre.

When it became clear that his work in securing these investors and retail tenants was welcomed but would not be rewarded by his fellow shareholders, Gilmartin told a senior AIB official, Mary Basquille, that he was considering an invitation to co-operate with a British television company investigating planning corruption in Ireland. The programme makers were following up on the reward posted by Newry solicitor Kevin Neary in August 1995, for anyone who provided information that resulted in a criminal conviction for planning corruption. Unsurprisingly, the bank was disturbed at such a prospect, and the promise of a significant investment by Grosvenor allowed a more amicable course to present itself, with the option of a buy-out of Gilmartin's shares put on the table.

After protracted negotiations over the terms of a sale of his interest in Barkhill to Riga Ltd, a board meeting was held in February 1996. Gilmartin retained a new solicitor, Noel Smyth, a high-profile negotiator of commercial property deals and someone well equipped to confront his client's adversaries on the board. At the heated meeting, Gilmartin threatened O'Callaghan, his solicitor John Deane and AIB with legal action over their 'criminal' behaviour. Smyth accused the bank of making Gilmartin 'an oppressed shareholder' and said he was prepared to issue legal proceedings and subpoena witnesses, including elected councillors, to give evidence, if necessary.

'Tom could be described as naïve or stupid or maybe a combination of both, but he was an honest man,' Deane recorded in his notes of the meeting. 'He had been treated very badly: the situation regarding some of the matters were criminal. When challenged on use of this word, he said he would withdraw the word but did not withdraw the implication contained by the word, that there had been very grave and serious misconduct.'

Subject to the condition that Gilmartin would not interfere with the deal under negotiation, in which Grosvenor Holdings would take a 50 per cent share of Barkhill, the board agreed that Riga Ltd would pay him £7.675 million for his shares. Following the deal in March 1996, Gilmartin left Ireland declaring that he 'never wished to see the sky over Dublin again.'

Chapter Nine

A Shithouse Consultant

WITHIN MONTHS OF THE ESTABLISHMENT OF the Flood Tribunal in November 1997, its legal team came across the 1989 Garda report into allegations of corruption made by Tom Gilmartin, which ended up on the desk of Minister for Justice Ray Burke in 1990. They learned that Gilmartin had informed Garda investigators how Liam Lawlor secured his monthly fee from Arlington by promising to overcome planning obstacles to the Bachelors Walk scheme and sought a huge bribe for himself and George Redmond in exchange for information about the ownership of lands at Quarryvale.

The Garda report exonerated Lawlor and Redmond while accusing Gilmartin of failing to co-operate with its inquiries and of besmirching the name of respectable people. It was given to Burke, who promptly buried it. It surfaced again when the tribunal lawyers discovered it in early 1998, which sent them on a quest to find Gilmartin. Weeks later, with the help of a Mayo-born priest, Fr Liam Murtagh, who was known to one of the lawyers, John Gallagher SC, they tracked Gilmartin down in Luton. Murtagh was friendly with Gilmartin, a parishioner who had helped to build and roof Catholic churches in Luton and who was well respected among the higher ranks of the clergy in England.

Despite his initial reluctance to have anything to do with political inquiries in Ireland, Gilmartin agreed to meet the tribunal chairman, Feargus Flood, along with Gallagher, Pat Hanratty SC and solicitor

Máire Ann Howard, at the Trust House Forte Hotel at Heathrow Airport. In our early conversations some months later, Gilmartin recounted to me how he laughed when he read the letter Flood handed him setting out the terms of reference for the tribunal and explained his role as its chairman. The judge said that he was appointed by the Oireachtas as sole member of the inquiry with a mandate to uncover the truth about allegations of corruption in the planning process in Dublin. When Flood asked him what was so funny, Gilmartin replied:

> I told the lawyers that I'd heard a lot of Irish jokes over the past forty years in England. Some of them were corny, some offensive, and some of them funny, but this was the funniest of all. This takes the biscuit. You were probably appointed a judge by Charles Haughey. Now you hand me a letter saying you were hired by the same people who caused me these problems, and that you are to report back to them. That is the funniest thing ever.

Flood, however, did enough to impress on Gilmartin that he intended to carry out his work thoroughly and impartially, and then he left the room, as he was precluded from participating in interviews with potential witnesses. The lawyers asked Gilmartin why he failed to co-operate with the 1989 Garda inquiry and were shocked to hear how he had been told to 'fuck off back to England' by a caller who described himself as a senior garda during the so-called investigation.

When he informed them how the same caller said that others like Gilmartin had made 'spurious allegations in the past about respected public figures who subsequently emerged with their reputations unscathed', the two barristers were stunned. The lawyers immediately realised that the exact same words were used in the 1990 Garda report given to Burke, which Gilmartin did not know about and had never seen. He then showed the legal team a document showing a list of payments to

Frank Dunlop and Shefran Ltd from Barkhill Ltd, which was compiled by accountancy firm Deloitte & Touche. In a letter accompanying the list, the accountants had sought an explanation for the large round-figure payments from his company. Gilmartin asked the tribunal team to investigate why payments were made from his accounts to a company with which he had no business dealings.

At further meetings in the Strathmore Hotel in Luton, Gilmartin outlined the nightmare he had endured in his dealings with some of Ireland's highest-ranking politicians, councillors and council officials, bankers and businessmen, when he tried to bring retail schemes and jobs to Dublin in the late 1980s. While he was uncertain about the details of transactions, dates and locations of some events and encounters, his narrative was convincing enough to persuade the tribunal team of his integrity and honesty, and, crucially, for them to offer him immunity from prosecution in return for his full co-operation.

Separately, after I made several trips to Luton and had numerous telephone interviews with Gilmartin, we agreed on a strategy for publishing the details of his extraordinary experience without naming him as the source of the information. The first opportunity to publish arose after the *Sunday Independent* reported on 20 September 1998 on Gilmartin's donation to Fianna Fáil at his meeting with Pádraig Flynn during the general election of June 1989. The newspaper, whose journalists had also been speaking to Gilmartin, reported that Flynn denied receiving a cheque for £50,000 from him.[1] A few days later, Gilmartin called me to say that he had received a phone call from an irate Flynn, who was then based in Brussels.

Flynn told Gilmartin that it was being suggested by some people that the money he received was not passed on to the party and that he wanted to meet with him urgently in Luton. He said he suspected he was being 'hung out to dry' by elements within Fianna Fáil, including some close to party leader Bertie Ahern, and that the tribunal was investigating the payment. Gilmartin expressed his anger to me at another false rumour that he had paid a bribe to Flynn. Now, he said, Flynn wanted him to lie and say the donation was returned, or that it was a personal donation to cover the politician's 1989 election expenses. In response, Gilmartin insisted that the donation was for the party and he would not commit perjury for anyone. He told Flynn it would be unwise for the politician to travel to Luton, as the tribunal lawyers were frequent visitors to the area.

Our discussion opened the way for my first exposition of Gilmartin's story and a journey that would lead to many more exclusive reports and unprecedented political convulsions over several years. In the lead story, on 27 September 1998, the *Post* published Gilmartin's insistence that the cheque he gave the former minister and serving European Union (EU) Commissioner for Social Affairs was intended for the Fianna Fáil party. It confirmed that Gilmartin had agreed to co-operate fully with the Flood Tribunal's inquiry and 'would provide details of his alleged contacts with politicians in Dublin during the 1980s and 1990s', including the £50,000 political donation to Fianna Fáil through Flynn.[2] It was also reported that 'informed sources' agreed that the contribution 'was made in good faith and was not tied to any demand for assistance with his business plans', and that senior Fianna Fáil sources had 'no recollection of the minister passing on such a sum to party headquarters'. The payment by Arlington Securities of £3,500 a month in the 1980s to Liam Lawlor in his consultancy role for the multi-million-pound retail complex on Bachelors Walk in Dublin was noted. Lawlor confirmed to the newspaper that he had been paid the amount in 'consultancy fees' in the mid-1980s.

'Gilmartin was involved in the initial attempt to develop the Quarryvale project in west Dublin as a massive shopping complex. But the project was taken over by developer Owen O'Callaghan with financial support from AIB,' the lead story recounted. The article went on to explain how Gilmartin had implicated 'a now retired local government official' in accepting large amounts in relation to property transactions in Dublin. It noted that the former senior council figure came under the scrutiny of the Flood Tribunal after James Gogarty, former chairman of JMSE, 'accused the same official of accepting a sum of £25,000 from his company'.

For legal reasons it was not possible to identify George Redmond as the official in question. Neither could Gilmartin be quoted directly, as he had been advised by his solicitor, Noel Smyth, not to speak to the media while engaged in discussions with the tribunal, and I had agreed to co-operate with his request not to attribute any comments to him. On this basis, we had agreed to pursue a relationship based on mutual trust and the understanding that he was telling me the truth and providing documentation to back up his claims, and that I was not going to distort the information he provided nor breach his confidence. However, this arrangement did not survive longer than a week after the first article was published, thanks to Lawlor.

The naming of Lawlor in the first story provoked an immediate response from the politician, who contacted me to say that he mistakenly described the monthly payments from Arlington Securities as 'consultancy fees' when they were in fact 'political donations'. On Sunday, 4 October 1998, I reported how 'Lawlor reclassified the payments as political donations after he was told by *The Sunday Business Post* that the payments from Arlington Securities of £3,500 per month were never listed on the register of interests of Dublin County Council, on which he served at the time.'[3] Lawlor's claim that the payments he received were political contributions meant that he was not obliged to register them as 'consultancy fees' as required under the terms of the Local Government (Planning and Development) Act 1976 if related to 'dealing in or developing land'. As the article explained:

> Political donations are not normally taxable, whereas consultancy fees would be treated as income for tax purposes. A week ago

> Lawlor told this newspaper that he was employed on a consultancy basis by Arlington[,] with whom Gilmartin worked on developing a site at Bachelors Walk in Dublin[,] and had helped prepare demographic and economic data for the company as well as identifying and approaching property owners along the quays when the site was being assembled.
>
> On Friday last, he said the payments he received from Gilmartin, amounting to £3,500 per month, were normal political donations.

Lawlor told *The Sunday Business Post*:

> I got about two or three contributions or subscriptions from Tom Gilmartin, when there was a series of elections in the first half of the 1980s. I did up a report for them and went to England at my own expense. We were talking about the possibility of me taking space in the development for a bowling leisure idea. I advised him [Gilmartin] but there was no formal consultancy arrangement. There was no requirement on me to register my interest.

Gilmartin was incensed by Lawlor's dishonest replies, telling me that 'he had never personally retained Lawlor as a consultant. "I would not have that man consulting on a shithouse," he told the *Post* in one of his rare public outbursts.' The bowling proposal was also an invention by Lawlor, he said.

The article also reported on the massive payments received by Frank Dunlop from Owen O'Callaghan, outlining the £500,000 he was paid 'in fees for his assistance in acquiring the rezoning and planning permission on the Quarryvale site … over the past seven years. Dunlop has confirmed that a part of this sum was used to make political donations, which are fully documented.' Dunlop was very annoyed at the way his generous fees were reported on and called me just after publication to register his anger. Unused to personal criticism in a newspaper which, like most others, normally deferred to PR practitioners, he let loose with both barrels telling me that, if he had a shotgun and I was beside him, he would shoot me.

For years, 'Pirelli', as Dunlop was nicknamed by friends and Fianna Fáil associates, obtained frequent and positive coverage for his clients and for his company, and he considered himself immune from media criticism. However, he had volunteered the information on his financial success, and the *Post* was satisfied that revealing the damning material on payments to Frank Dunlop and Associates and Shefran Ltd was in the public interest. Two days after the story was published, the PR man was served with an order from the Flood Tribunal to provide extensive documentation on his financial affairs and to attend in person at its offices in Dublin Castle.

In that same October edition of the newspaper, we ran a profile of Tom Gilmartin, which elaborated more fully on his experience in trying to develop the ambitious business projects in Dublin. It captured a flavour of the complexities involved in circumventing the political, planning and rezoning obstacles to the Quarryvale development, as well as the number of palms that needed greasing. In the profile, Dunlop was quoted as accepting that he may have said certain things 'out of turn', which led to the unfair persecution of Gilmartin by the IR authorities in Britain some years earlier, and offered to apologise to Gilmartin. The article explained how:

> Either way, the AIB forced his exit from Barkhill, the vehicle developing Quarryvale, leaving Gilmartin a deeply aggrieved and angry man and also a man with financial problems. A confidentiality clause in his exit contract precludes him from responding to the rumours and allegations he claims have been

> unfairly directed at him. Despite some suggestions that he will not come back to Dublin to give evidence to Flood or Moriarty, or both, Tom Gilmartin will have his day.[4]

A week later, Gilmartin raised the stakes when he contradicted Liam Lawlor's claims and made a sworn statement that the TD had received a total of £85,000 in the late 1980s and 1990s in connection with Bachelors Walk and Quarryvale. In another front-page story, the *Post* reported:

> In a submission to the Flood tribunal last week, Gilmartin has claimed that Lawlor was paid £35,000 in the mid-1980s by Arlington Securities over a ten-month period. The monies – paid at a rate of £3,500 monthly – were ostensibly consultancy fees.
>
> Seven of the payments were made through offshore accounts, according to Gilmartin, and details of the relevant cheques have been made available to tribunal lawyers. Lawlor has stated on the record that he received between two and four payments of £3,500 each.
>
> Gilmartin claims that a further £50,000 was paid to Lawlor when the Quarryvale project was being progressed. Gilmartin claims that this payment was handled by public relations consultant and former Fianna Fáil press officer, Frank Dunlop. Dunlop has forcefully denied making any such payment to Lawlor. He said that he met Lawlor for briefings on the Quarryvale project but made only one contribution of some £500 towards a golf classic organised by Lawlor.
>
> When contacted on Friday night, Lawlor refused to comment on the claims.
>
> 'He can claim what he wants. We will deal with it all at the tribunal,' he said, before terminating the telephone call abruptly.[5]

The story went on to describe how Lawlor had demanded a 20 per cent stake in the Quarryvale development and later a lump sum of £100,000, the latter amount a reference to the discussion that took place in Redmond's office in the late 1980s.

The mention of payments to Lawlor through offshore accounts, and of a £50,000 sum given to the politician by Dunlop in relation to Quarryvale, opened a fresh can of worms. Coupled with the revelation that Gilmartin had 'named various former officials and politicians in a detailed statement signed for the tribunal in London 12 days ago', the report rocked the Dublin political establishment. It also unleashed a barrage of legal missives both to the *Post* and to the tribunal. At the same time, Flood signed a raft of discovery orders that were served on the politicians, businessmen, professional advisors and companies named in Gilmartin's lengthy statement of September 1998. Along with Lawlor, Dunlop and Flynn, those asked to provide information and financial records included Owen O'Callaghan, Riga Ltd, solicitor John Deane and AIB.

Following the publication in the *Post* of details of the large payments provided by O'Callaghan to Frank Dunlop and Associates and to Shefran, the PR man, concerned at the tax implications of his newly exposed finances, sought an immediate injection of funds. I learned that Dunlop met O'Callaghan near the PR man's home in Dunshaughlin, County Meath, and negotiated what later emerged was a payment of £300,000, plus VAT of £63,000, to cover his tax liabilities.

At the Fianna Fáil Ard-Fheis in late November 1998, delegates were consumed by the developing tribunal story, and Gilmartin's claims in particular. Word circulated that party leader and Taoiseach Bertie Ahern would not attend at the official opening of the Liffey Valley Shopping Centre, as he had previously agreed, which was due to take place within weeks.

In response to the correspondence from the tribunal seeking the financial records of their clients, a group of senior barristers attended a long and heated meeting at Dublin Castle with Feargus Flood, during which Michael McDowell SC, acting for O'Callaghan, assailed the chairman and his legal team for committing a 'serious criminal offence' by allowing the contents of their correspondence to get into the hands of the *Sunday Independent*. The private meeting, held over two sessions on 9 and 10 December 1998, was demanded after the newspaper published details of a letter from the lawyers to the tribunal chairman setting out their concerns about its wide-ranging discovery order. McDowell, along with Colm Allen SC, representing Dunlop, demanded that action be taken against the journalist and editor of the newspaper for the damage caused by the publication of correspondence sent to his client. 'If necessary, lock them up,' Allen told Judge Flood, in what would be just the first of many fractious exchanges between the two men.[6]

In fact, the offending letter quoted in the newspaper was not 'leaked' by the tribunal, as confirmed by the journalist Jody Corcoran, who wrote the article. This was an overblown controversy, as large numbers of orders, letters and other documents were issued by the tribunal, which meant that any one of the recipients could have provided a copy to the media, or it could have been obtained from one of the PR handlers employed by the wealthy subjects of Flood's inquiry. The protests by McDowell were noteworthy as he was a frequent contributor to the newspaper, something Allen himself inferred in the meeting when he described his law library colleague as 'intimately connected' to the *Sunday Independent*. However, the narrative that the tribunal was leaking like a sieve, even before its public hearings began, was repeated so often following this, that it became almost an accepted truth. It was a claim that I first heard from Liam Lawlor, who clearly, along with other powerful individuals, had a vested interest in discrediting the investigation before it came to his door.

At the meeting with Flood, McDowell also questioned the extent of the discovery order made against not only his client, O'Callaghan, but against 'his accountants, his bankers and his PR consultants, arguing they were not justified by the allegations that some elected councillors in Dublin had taken payments'. Adrian Hardiman SC, acting for Lawlor, complained in the same meeting about the order directing the politician to attend a public hearing of the tribunal, as well as the order for discovery seeking all his bank accounts and financial transactions because of the allegations made by Gilmartin. He singled out what he called the 'bizarre' claim that Lawlor had told the Arlington Securities executives at a meeting in London that he was 'a representative of the Irish government', while at the same time demanding a share of the company's development on Bachelors Walk.

The content of the private sessions between the tribunal and the lawyers for O'Callaghan, Dunlop and Lawlor, which were recorded, was the first significant indication of how those facing corruption allegations would use their ample resources to fund any and all legal means to frustrate the inquiry, eventually resorting to the highest courts in the land to protect their interests.

Chapter Ten

Beware of Greeks Bearing Gifts

JUST WEEKS BEFORE THE TRIBUNAL'S PUBLIC hearings commenced, the *Sunday Independent* found itself in hot water when the newspaper published Jim Gogarty's confidential affidavit for the inquiry. In late December 1998, Judge Flood said that the publication of the legal document, the property of the tribunal, was a breach of the law and an obstruction of his investigation. Flood welcomed the general co-operation of the media, with the exception of Independent Newspapers, which, he said, gave the impression that 'they consider themselves in some fashion to be above the law'.[1]

While much of the substance of Gogarty's claims had previously been reported by the *Post*, mainly as the result of my interviews with him, the affidavit published by the *Sunday Independent* report named several individuals and companies not previously identified, and in a manner which Flood said was in breach of their constitutional rights. The row took place in advance of Gogarty's keenly anticipated appearance at the tribunal in early 1999, when public hearings were scheduled to begin. An eleventh-hour application by George Redmond to have Gogarty's evidence heard in private was rejected by the Supreme Court, but not before it heard evidence that the powerful council official was handed an envelope containing £15,000 by JMSE executives in Clontarf Castle in June 1989.

The legal attempt to restrict public access to the hearings only whetted the appetite of those who had followed the planning scandal for over three years. Meanwhile, another former senior politician, Ray MacSharry, was doing his best to keep his name out of the tribunal proceedings. In October 1998, he contacted Peter Kearns, a friend of Gilmartin who lived in Cork, looking for the developer's fax number in Luton. MacSharry wanted Gilmartin to sign a document, which the former minister for finance and EU commissioner drafted and faxed, stating that they had never met. Gilmartin refused on the simple grounds that he had met with MacSharry to discuss his business projects in 1987, first in Dublin at the finance department and later in his constituency office in Sligo.

MacSharry was more informed than he let on about the corruption allegations circling his former Fianna Fáil colleagues. He was the man who had provided Pádraig Flynn with Gilmartin's phone number in August 1998, when the EU commissioner called the developer to seek an urgent meeting after the details of the £50,000 donation to Fianna Fáil emerged. MacSharry, who served as EU commissioner for agriculture and food before he left politics in January 1993, could not escape the political controversies that he might have thought were behind him. His assumption that he could force Gilmartin to bend to his instructions to lie for him was badly misplaced.

Gilmartin told MacSharry in no uncertain terms that he would not comply with his request, but also that he did not intend to be dragged into the tribunal and the media circus surrounding it. He was already having reservations about giving public evidence at the tribunal in light of attacks he was hearing and reading about on his credibility. He was particularly incensed at the suggestion being put about that his payment to Flynn in June 1989 was a bribe intended to secure a favourable tax designation for the Bachelors Walk project from the minister for the environment.

Adding to his reluctance about coming to Dublin to give evidence was Gilmartin's outrage at a decision made by Revenue Appeals Commissioner Ronan Kelly in relation to Haughey's tax liabilities. Kelly had assessed that the former taoiseach owed nothing to the Revenue on the £1.3 million he had received in payments from Ben Dunne. The fact that the commissioner was a brother of Bertie Ahern's wife, Miriam Kelly, from whom Ahern was then separated, only served to deepen Gilmartin's reservations.

If it had not been for Flynn's unbridled ego and self-importance, Gilmartin may well have followed through on his determination to stay away from the Flood Tribunal. But an appearance by the politician on the country's most popular chat show on 15 January 1999 changed his mind dramatically. Flynn's appearance on *The Late Late Show* would rouse the well of deep anger and resentment smouldering inside Gilmartin since his departure from Dublin. As he sat with Vera in the living room of their Luton home, he watched as the Mayo man deflected questions from the programme's host, Gay Byrne, about the £50,000 donation he had received during the general election campaign almost a decade earlier.

'What are you going to do about the Flood Tribunal and the £50,000 [and] Gilmartin,' Byrne asked.

Flynn replied nonchalantly, 'I've said my piece about that. In fact, I've said too much, because you can get yourself into the High Court for undermining the tribunal, so I ain't saying no more about this … except to say just one thing, and this is all I'll say: I never asked nor took money from anybody to do favours in my life.'

'But you know Gilmartin?' Byrne asked.

'Oh yeah, yeah,' Flynn replied. 'I haven't seen him now for some years. I met him. He's a Sligo man who went to England and made a lot of money. Came back. Wanted to do a lot of business in Ireland. Didn't work out for him. Didn't work out for him. He's not well. His wife isn't well. And he's … out of sorts.'

'But you're saying that you never took money from anybody at any time, for whatever reason?' asked Byrne.

'I never took money from anybody to do a political favour as far as planning is concerned,' Flynn replied.

The interview moved on to the challenges facing Flynn's daughter and Fianna Fáil TD Beverly Cooper Flynn, whom, he said, was the innocent victim of false allegations of involvement in irregular practices when she worked with National Irish Bank. Then, before the largest audience he could have mustered, he shot himself in the foot when he spoke of how difficult it was to keep no less than three homes – in Mayo, Dublin and Brussels – on his EU commissioner's annual salary of £140,000.

'Three homes, three housekeepers … [a] very expensive business. Try it sometime,' he said, as hundreds of thousands of viewers erupted with laughter, while at the same time angered by his arrogance.

It was no laughing matter for Tom and Vera Gilmartin, as their phone started hopping with calls from distressed relatives and friends in Ireland, who had watched Flynn's bombastic and self-serving live performance. It had been a hard Christmas for his family, as Vera's condition rendered her virtually immobile, while the attacks on his reputation in Dublin had added to their stress. Gilmartin was furious at Flynn's reference to Vera's medical condition and his supposedly poor mental state.

His sister, Una, called RTÉ from her home in Grange, County Sligo, and complained to the researchers, who then spoke to Flynn. As the two-hour show ended, Byrne attempted to mitigate the potential damage, especially for RTÉ, and announced that 'Pee' Flynn wished to correct the earlier comments he made.

'In the interview, it was suggested by Pee Flynn that Tom Gilmartin was sick. As far as Pee is concerned, Tom Gilmartin is not sick and has never been seriously sick, and we would just like to say sorry and apologise for that,' Byrne said.

No apology would deter Gilmartin, who was still angry when I spoke to him over the following days, by which time his Luton home had been besieged by television and newspaper reporters seeking more information about his allegations of corruption against Flynn and others. Casting caution, and our unwritten agreement with him not to engage with other media, to the wind, Gilmartin threw a few grenades into an already charged political battlefield. He told the *Irish Independent*:

> I didn't want to get involved. I kept my mouth shut for ten years. I will be giving evidence now. Flynn has seen to that. On the *Late Late Show* he made me out to be a mental patient. I am not a bitter man, and I was never money oriented ... But as far as I am concerned I am the victim of the most scurrilous carry-on perpetrated right from the top – including the current top.[2]

Asked what he meant, he replied, 'I think I will leave that to the tribunal. But I can tell you this: they all have a lot to worry about, right from the top. Everything I say will be proven: it will all be proved ... What I have to tell the tribunal will explode at the heart of the current Government.'

If Bertie Ahern and his most senior aides did not get the message earlier, they certainly could not ignore it now. After the media presence had calmed down, a still furious Gilmartin remarked to me:

> When I saw that clown on the TV I was incensed. The only thing missing was the red nose. I never wanted to be the centre of attention and I never wanted my wife to be involved in any of this. And then that comedian went on TV. The irony is that Flynn was not the worst of them, and I'm not saying that because he is from the west of Ireland.

The 'clown', meanwhile, was keeping a low profile in Mayo. Instead of making his usual appearance at Sunday Mass in Castlebar, where he often sat on the front pew and did a reading to the faithful, he decamped to the five-star Ashford Castle for consultations with his friend MacSharry. It was a brief respite for the embattled politician, who was now faced with multiple unanswered questions, including why the donation to Fianna Fáil from Gilmartin was not handed over to the party, and why he had obstructed the tribunal when he tried to get Gilmartin to lie about the motivation for the 1989 cheque.

With O'Callaghan, Lawlor, Flynn, Ahern and others now in Gilmartin's sights, there was no end to speculation about the intentions of the disgruntled developer and, more importantly, about the ammunition he intended to provide to the tribunal in its efforts to expose the scale of corruption in Dublin's planning system. Elements of the media came under pressure from powerful political and business interests to undermine the credibility of the main tribunal whistleblowers. Gogarty was already the subject of various rumours and false allegations surrounding his past role in JMSE. Among the reports published before he arrived to give evidence was an unfounded claim in *The Sunday Times* that he sent a bullet in the post to militant workers during a dispute involving the company at Moneypoint, County Clare, in 1981.[3] When the tribunal resumed two days later, Gogarty's lawyer, Frank Callanan strenuously objected to the content of the article, which was based on an affidavit made to the tribunal by a former employee of JMSE. Chairman Feargus Flood adjourned hearings for a week due to the upset caused to Gogarty and his family and to allow the gardaí to investigate how the shocking and unsubstantiated allegations made their way to *The Sunday Times* and the *Sunday Independent*, which also published information damaging to Gogarty.

Under its legally binding procedures, the tribunal was required to circulate all relevant documents, including confidential affidavits, to all those affected by their contents, and it was inevitable that some of the more contentious material would find its way into the media. Some of those served with legal orders by the tribunal echoed Lawlor's condemnation of 'leaks' from the tribunal, including Ray Burke, and threatened to withdraw their co-operation because of them. It was patently obvious to most of us reporting on the tribunal that Flood and his team were the least likely suspects responsible for attempts to derail their own investigation. A Garda investigation subsequently established that there had been extensive contact between Bovale Development's Michael Bailey and the *Sunday Independent* in the days prior to the publication of the sensitive material about Gogarty by the newspaper in late 1998.

Meanwhile, others were hatching a more sophisticated plot to undermine Gilmartin's credibility, and, by doing so, simultaneously damage the tribunal, by targeting me and the *Post* with the offer of another sensational, but false, set of allegations. In early 1999, soon after Flynn's humiliation on *The Late Late Show*, I received a phone call from a man with a thick Cork accent that triggered a wild goose chase ultimately aimed at impeding the Flood Tribunal's work. The man said he was close to the *Post* office across the river from the Four Courts in Dublin and wanted to meet immediately. We met in the coffee shop next door, where Denis 'Starry' O'Brien[4] said he wanted to share a particularly explosive account of how he personally paid £50,000 to two prominent Fianna Fáil politicians on behalf of property developer Owen O'Callaghan in autumn 1989. He said he had proof of the payments, including copies of the cheques made out to the politicians, bank statements and a lodgement book issued by a branch of the INBS in Patrick Street, Cork, ostensibly used in the transfer of the monies.

The self-described property developer said that he had been mis-treated in the same way as Tom Gilmartin. He claimed that O'Callaghan had forced him out of a planned housing scheme in Carrigaline in their home county. He said that, at O'Callaghan's behest, he gave one of the two cheques for £50,000 to Bertie Ahern in Dublin in September 1989. He freely admitted that he was a willing participant in the two corrupt payments and that he had previously been accused of perjury and forgery by a judge of the High Court. He was just the sort of character a wealthy person might use to carry out their dirty work.

Over the following weeks, Starry O'Brien travelled to Dublin on several occasions, in order, he claimed, to meet lawyers in connection with his legal battle over large outstanding debts he owed to Anglo Irish Bank. He had paperwork to back up the story of his litigation with the bank, the Revenue Commissioners and various professional firms. He had a letter, written in the mid-1980s, from Charles Haughey, offering him assistance. He wanted to meet Gilmartin to discuss their shared misfortunes, a request I made clear would not be possible. He signed an affidavit for the *Post* detailing his claims, which was passed on to the tribunal's legal team.

'Beware of Greeks bearing gifts,' Gilmartin said when I told him of Starry O'Brien's approach. The detail of the payment made in 1989 was suspiciously close to one that O'Callaghan had once described to Gilmartin in relation to an alleged payment the Cork developer said he personally made to Ahern. That was enough to raise concerns about O'Brien's unexpected contribution to the already fraught cauldron of tribunal claims and counterclaims. My editor and I had deep reservations about this latest witness and shared Gilmartin's suspicions about the circumstances of this alleged payment to Ahern, so we let the story sit. I did continue to follow the trail of evidence laid by O'Brien, but we had plenty of stories to fill pages in the meantime.

Chapter Eleven

Warts and All

BETWEEN LEGAL AND MEDIA REPRESENTATIVES AND an eager public audience of more than a hundred people filling the Printworks in Dublin Castle, James Gogarty attracted a full house when he finally arrived at the tribunal on 12 January 1999. The crowds that flocked to hear the octogenarian with his walking stick and sharp wit, many of them older citizens, were not disappointed. It would soon become the best show in town.

Accompanied by his solicitor, Gerard Sheedy, the elderly and ailing witness was first brought through his many years in the employment of Joseph Murphy senior and the row that ensued between the pair when pension commitments to Gogarty were not fulfilled. Describing how Murphy senior reneged on a promise made in the 1980s that he would receive £500,000 on retirement, Gogarty broke down a number of times in the witness box as he explained how his family circumstances dictated his decision to take on his former boss. Gogarty explained, as his eyes watered and his voice weakened, how his main concern was for his wife:

> First of all I was 65, I was married to a girl, a fine girl, but she was nearly 20 years my junior and we had six or seven in the family at that time, we had a big responsibility and our finances were not good because I was depending on my salary which, looking back, wasn't big at the time for the work I was doing. I was anxious too,

> if anything happened to me, because I was suffering from diabetes too. If anything happened to me, she would be reasonably secure in the family and that was my prime aim at that time and for years after, and it broke my heart.

He told the tribunal lawyer, John Gallagher SC, how he first resigned as managing director of JMSE in 1982, after twenty years' service, but that the Guernsey-based Murphy senior and his wife, Una, then persuaded him to return for a few years more. This arrangement continued until the late 1980s, during which time he helped to save the company from a planned hostile takeover by its then chief executive, Liam Conroy. Over a number of days, Gogarty explained how his relations with Murphy senior were fractured after he had faced down this attempt by Conroy and other executives to take over the trust that controlled the multi-billion-pound enterprise but was then left high and dry with nothing to show for his efforts.

Fortuitously, Gogarty had kept extensive documentation and financial records, which could prove widescale tax evasion, currency offences and other illegal transactions by his former employer, and, of course, details of the payment of £40,000 by JMSE to Ray Burke at his home in June 1989. When it came to this part of his evidence, the visiting crowds grew larger and more excited as Gogarty graphically recounted his trip from Santry to Burke's home in Swords with Joseph Murphy junior in a car driven by Mick Bailey. A few days earlier, they had agreed with Bailey that both parties would each give £40,000 to the politician in exchange for his assistance with rezoning over 700 acres of land owned by JMSE in north Dublin, thus multiplying their value. When he mentioned Bailey's 'Will we, fuck!' response to the question of whether they would get a receipt, there were huge roars of laughter in the Printworks.

Gogarty described how Bailey took a large envelope from the dashboard when they arrived at the house, where they were offered tea and biscuits before a conversation that lasted over half an hour. He recalled the fact that he offered Burke a document containing the schedule of lands that JMSE was seeking to rezone and develop with Bovale, as well as the minister's response that he had already been given a copy by Bailey. He continued:

> So I put that back in my pocket … and Bailey put over his envelope, and Burke never opened them or touched them as far as I was concerned at that time, but I then said it was a substantial payment, you know, against an open-ended commitment, and my anxiety was that I would go back to [Joe Murphy] Senior and allay his anxieties about paying out this money, and Burke says that Murphy and Bailey were well aware of how he had honoured his commitments in the past, and immediately Bailey intervened and said: 'That's alright Jim, leave it with me and Ray,' and then Joe Murphy Junior said: 'That's alright too as well, Jim. I'll have a word with my father,' so I took that as being I shouldn't be saying much more, so I left it at that, and Mr Burke was looking at his watch several times.

It was the middle of the general election campaign, Gogarty recalled, and Burke mentioned that he had to go back on the campaign trail and was due to do an interview on television later that day.

Over the following months, relations with Murphy senior went downhill, until Gogarty threatened litigation against his former employer, a development which was of concern to Bailey and Burke. Gogarty described to the tribunal the occasion when Bailey stuffed a cheque for £50,000 into his breast pocket after tea and biscuits at the Skylon Hotel in late August or September 1990, over a year after the visit to Burke's house. According to Gogarty, the cheque was intended as an inducement 'not to drag Burke or Bailey into his bitter battle with

Murphy Senior over the alleged failure of his employer to honour his pension entitlement'.[1]

Gogarty brought George Redmond into his narrative when he explained how the senior planning official was given a £12,000 payment from JMSE in 1988 in return for obtaining a two-year extension to planning permission on lands owned by the company at Forest Road, Swords. Gogarty told the tribunal that he met Redmond at the council offices on O'Connell Street in Dublin on two occasions in May or June 1988, just weeks before the expiry of the permission. During their first meeting, Redmond reminded Gogarty that he had been promised a consultancy position with JMSE when he retired from the council in return for the favours he had done for the company. The promise of the post-retirement perk had been made by the company's former chief executive, Liam Conroy. Gogarty also recalled that Redmond asked him whether he could supply any painters to do a job on his house.

Gogarty said that he met Redmond again at the council offices, this time accompanied by Joseph Murphy junior, when the assistant city and county manager handed them a draft letter, which he said should be sent by JMSE to the planning department of the council. The letter set out the request for an extension of the Forest Road planning permission and an offer to pay £122,460 in outstanding service levies. As the *Post* reported, 'Redmond, according to Gogarty, was to receive 10 percent of the amount [about £12,000] saved by JMSE in levy charges for water, sewerage and road services. If the permission expired and a new application was made, Redmond had said the charges would double.'

Gogarty's detailed recollection of his encounters with Redmond revealed the calculating methods of the retired senior council official, who twice interrupted the witness during his evidence, much to the amusement of the rapt audience. In one outburst, Redmond claimed that he was wrongly described as the county manager for Dublin and insisted that he had no reserved functions in relation to planning, so he could not have done the favours, as alleged, for JMSE. He also claimed never to have met Murphy junior, despite Gogarty's precise recollection of their encounter at the council offices.

Murphy junior was again dragged into proceedings when Gogarty, in his final week of direct evidence, recalled how he received a threatening and abusive phone call from the son of the company owner one night at 2.30 a.m. during June 1994, at a time when legal proceedings were underway between the parties. Murphy junior allegedly said, 'I am going out to your house and I will break every fucking bone in your body and then I will kick the fucking shite out of you, and when I am finished with you, you won't have a roof over your head and I will put a stop to all your legal hassles.' Gogarty reported the calls to the gardaí, to little effect. On another, later occasion, a conversation that also contained abuse was overheard not only by Gogarty's wife, but also by a garda, who was at their Sutton home at the time.[2]

The failure of the gardaí to properly investigate the threatening phone calls to Gogarty contributed to his decision to respond to the offer of a reward posted by the Newry solicitors in 1995 for information leading to a conviction for corruption. Not unlike Tom Gilmartin, he was frustrated at the refusal of the gardaí to carry out a thorough inquiry into his concerns and indeed to attempt to justify events by partially blaming the complainant. As Gogarty told the tribunal in the final days of his questioning by its lawyers, there would have been no need for a tribunal if the gardaí had prosecuted Murphy junior for his abusive behaviour. In response, Garret Cooney SC, acting for JMSE and the Murphys, called for the full disclosure of Gogarty's allegations of corruption against some members of the gardaí. Gogarty replied that he had not made any such claims in his affidavit to the tribunal, even though he was dissatisfied with the Garda response to his complaints.

Expanding on the reason why his statement to the tribunal did not include such details, Gogarty reminded Cooney and his gripped audience how he had served as a member of the force in his younger days. He described an event in the 1940s, when he was present during a house search and a Garda colleague was shot dead. Bringing cheers from the assembled crowd, he said:

> I was within six feet of being shot dead and a comrade of mine was shot dead. George Mordaunt. We were trying to arrest an escaped IRA convict, up in Donnycarney. Even if I try to erase it from my memory, every time I read the paper and see where there is a Guard killed or injured it brings me back to what I went through, and thank God I wasn't in the same boat. So to say I disparaged the Guards is completely wrong.

When Gogarty was asked whether he had ever discussed the payment to Burke with Joseph Murphy senior, he replied that he had spoken about it to him when they met at the funeral of his former employer's wife in 1991. It was the final day of his direct examination by John Gallagher for the tribunal, and he recalled:

> I was at the funeral of his wife, Una, Lord have mercy on her. I went up and shook his hand and sympathised with him and I said we'd be in touch, you know, he said, whether he was serious or not, he says any chance of getting the £40,000 back … I think he meant that I'd get the money back from Bailey.

While the payment had been made in return for Burke's assistance with rezoning the 720 acres of land, because JMSE sold the land bank to Bailey for £2.3 million in 1990, the company did not actually benefit from any actions taken by the politician. The motivation for Murphy senior to dispose of the lands so rapidly was rooted in his fear that the contents of an affidavit made by Liam Conroy would emerge during threatened legal proceedings by his former chief executive. Gogarty explained that Conroy's affidavit, made in a High Court action against JMSE, contained very damaging revelations about the business dealings and financial transactions of its owners and subsidiaries. Before the case was settled, the Murphys decided to dispose of their land assets in north Dublin in case their dirty linen was aired in public.

Gogarty also recounted how Bailey reminded Murphy junior during their car journey to Burke's house about the promise of a consultancy made to Redmond by Conroy. Bailey said that Redmond wanted £25,000 in lieu of the promised consultancy on his retirement from the council. Gogarty described how Murphy junior baulked at the amount and said he would 'have to talk to his father about it'.[3]

The consultancy was due to commence when Redmond retired in 1989, but instead he was given £15,000, ostensibly for a different reason. Bailey was with Redmond when this amount was paid by Murphy junior in cash at the Clontarf Castle Hotel, Dublin, in 1989. Gogarty, who was also present, said the money was in exchange for Redmond's help in protecting the company from a possible court action and hefty fine after it carried out the unauthorised demolition of Turvey House, a listed building owned by JMSE in north Dublin.

Redmond's insistence that he did not know Murphy junior was undermined by the details of their encounters in the offices of the council and in the hotel in Clontarf, as described by Gogarty. The parsimonious planner was not pleased when the tribunal learned that he also enjoyed free tickets to shows at the Gaiety Theatre in Dublin, which was owned by the Murphys during the 1980s. Further evidence revealed that Bailey personally gave Redmond at least £20,000 in cash payments during the 1980s.

The car journey to and from Swords in 1989 was the subject of further discussion in the final days of Gogarty's evidence, when he corrected a version of the trip he had given to Labour Party TD Tommy Broughan and me in our discussions in 1996. I reported in the *Post* that three unnamed JMSE executives visited Burke's home, but Gogarty now recalled that he had wrongly stated that Frank Reynolds, the company's construction manager, was present on the day. Gogarty said that Reynolds was aware of the cash payment of £30,000 and co-signed the cheque for £10,000 with him but did not travel to the politician's home.

This inconsistency between his evidence and his earlier statements was seized on by Cooney as evidence of Gogarty's unreliability and allowed the lawyer to raise an objection to a statement I provided to the tribunal concerning my reporting on this and other matters. I had recounted Gogarty's mistaken claim that Reynolds was in the car, and Cooney's objection was based on his claim that I had 'a vested interest in the outcome of these proceedings'. Judge Flood overruled the objection. As I pointed out in my article on this, '*The Sunday Business Post* and this reporter have a vested interest in the outcome of these proceedings, one we share with the majority of citizens. Our interest is that the truth about the relationship between politicians and business people, past and present, emerges "warts and all"'.[4] Gogarty had been the first to employ these final three words in the first days of his evidence, when he declared, 'I came here to the tribunal to get to the truth, warts and all, and if I did wrong I am ready to take my place in the queue to pay for it.'

It would not be the last time I was subjected to criticism by lawyers acting for some of the politicians and businessmen under scrutiny during tribunal proceedings. Cooney also objected to comments I made during a discussion on *The Last Word*, hosted by Eamon Dunphy on Today FM on Thursday, 18 February 1999. I reported on the tribunal on a regular basis for Dunphy, and this particular broadcast saw a remarkably contentious exchange between me and Sam Smyth, after it emerged that a story he had published earlier, suggesting that Bailey had withdrawn £50,000 from Anglo Irish Bank as an 'under the table' payment for Gogarty, was totally false.

This narrative was an attempt to undermine Gogarty's explanation for the cheque for £50,000 that Bailey stuffed in his pocket in order to ensure that he did not bring the Burke payment into his litigation with the Murphys. Gogarty shrewdly retained but did not cash the cheque, which was made out to his name and dated 30 September 1990. When I interviewed Bailey in the summer of 1997, after the payments to Burke were first confirmed, the builder claimed that the Skylon cheque was intended to buy Gogarty's assistance with the purchase of a property owned by JMSE at 23 Baggot Street in Dublin, in 1989. This was almost a year earlier than the date on the cheque, and the explanation was not only denied by Gogarty but provably untrue.

During his cross-examination of Gogarty, Colm Allen, who was representing Bailey as well as Dunlop, referred to a recent report I had written on this discrepancy. Addressing the tribunal chairman, he asserted, 'I don't know about you sir, but I do not believe everything I read in the newspapers. Therefore, the fact that it appears in something as *The Sunday Business Post* [*sic*] doesn't exactly mean it is true.'[5]

In a front-page 'exclusive' in the *Irish Independent* in early February 1999, Smyth explained how Bailey had informed an official of Anglo Irish Bank in 1989 that he needed to withdraw a sum of £50,000 in order to pay Gogarty for a property transaction. The newspaper reproduced what purported to be handwritten notes by the Anglo Irish Bank official recording a figure of £50,000 with Gogarty's name beside it.[6] In my view, this *Independent* story about an alleged payment to Gogarty was invented and fed to Smyth in order to verify Bailey's earlier and false story about the Skylon hotel cheque.

Following its investigation into Smyth's report, the tribunal established that the Anglo Irish Bank files made no reference to Gogarty in relation to the £50,000 withdrawal by Bailey in November 1989, contrary to what was stated in the article. It found that there was no basis for the claim that contemporaneous notes made by an

Anglo official recorded that Bailey wanted the money for Gogarty, as published in the newspaper.[7]

Garrett Cooney also took exception to some of my remarks concerning Bailey and his clients, JMSE, during *The Last Word,* and he made a formal complaint to Judge Flood about an alleged conflict between my role as a journalist and as a likely witness at the inquiry. Specifically, he complained that I had made observations that went beyond the evidence and had introduced material that could possibly be the subject of my own future evidence.

However, Flood ruled that it would be inappropriate for him to direct that I should desist from commenting on the proceedings of the tribunal merely because I was a witness in respect of certain factual events. He said, 'The proceedings of the tribunal are not subject to the sub judice rule. Furthermore, this is not a situation where a jury might be inappropriately influenced by any statement concerning its proceedings.' He declined to make any form of order against me and, in his comments, referred to the comments of legal philosopher Jeremy Bentham, who once wrote: 'Publicity is the very soul of justice. It is the keenest motivator for effort and the most reliable safeguard against dishonesty. It keeps the judge himself, while trying, under trial.'

The ruling was a relief to me and to a number of other journalists who were listed to give evidence before the tribunal, but a disappointment to Cooney, who promised that he would give me a roasting when it came to my turn. As it transpired, he delegated my cross-examination to his junior counsel, Michael Cush BL, who adopted a non-adversarial approach.

When Cooney, a brother of former Fine Gael Minister for Justice Paddy Cooney, vented his rage at the tribunal chairman on one occasion too many, he was somewhat astounded when Judge Flood got to his feet and dramatically walked out. It followed an exchange during which Cooney claimed that his clients, JMSE, were not being given a fair hearing by tribunal lawyers. After an unsuccessful attempt to introduce a document that a tribunal lawyer claimed was put to Gogarty in an incorrect context, Cooney asked, 'Mr Chairman, what is going on here? Are you going to give us a chance to defend ourselves in this tribunal?' When Flood described his remark as 'both insulting and insolent', Cooney replied that it was 'well justified', prompting the diminutive and angry chairman to leave his bench to raucous applause from the packed public gallery. To add insult to injury, Cooney appeared to join in the applause before sitting down and lighting up a cigarette.

When he failed to provide an apology the following day, there was speculation, including in the media and the Dáil, that we were witnessing an attempt by some parties to 'collapse the scrum' in Dublin Castle. The stand-off lasted for two days before Cooney made a grudging apology to the chairman, while managing to avoid using the word 'sorry'.[8]

Chapter Twelve

Finnegan's Wake

GEORGE REDMOND'S BLUSTERING WAS EXPOSED WHEN he was dramatically arrested on arrival at Dublin Airport from the Isle of Man on Friday, 19 February 1999. Officers from the Criminal Assets Bureau (CAB) seized £300,000 in cash (punts and sterling), bank drafts and cheques, which Redmond had withdrawn from banks on the offshore island earlier that day.

While he was held overnight and questioned in Harcourt Terrace Garda Station in the city, his home in Castleknock, in west Dublin, was searched by detectives. Redmond had authorised the tribunal to obtain details of his Isle of Man bank accounts prior to his arrest, and there was much conjecture over the motivation behind the actions of the CAB and its implications for the ongoing public inquiry. Many people were also scratching their heads as to why Redmond made the day trip on Manx airlines and ended up in custody.

What concerned the tribunal lawyers was the potentially significant documentation seized at the airport and from Redmond's home by gardaí, to which they required access. Before he was caught red-handed at Dublin Airport with the bag of offshore monies, the tribunal had sought details from no less than fourteen financial institutions in Dublin where Redmond also had accounts. The CAB followed him to the island and watched as he visited the bank, which he had telephoned before his departure from Dublin that morning. He was now facing further interrogation by the tribunal, as well as the Revenue Commissioners, and a very uncertain future in retirement, concluded one of his associates. As an article in the *Post* put it: 'George is a sitting duck at this point. The financial institutions will report within days to the CAB. The tribunal has notified him that they are seeking the same information. I expect he is going to get a tax bill in the not too distant future, said the source close to Redmond.'[1]

Redmond's arrest was significant, as it undermined his attempt to portray himself as a humble public servant whose only mistake was to provide advice to various builders and businessmen. It also generated further leads that could potentially unmask other, hitherto unknown, participants in his web of corruption. The CAB found bundles of cash in his bathroom, bedroom and other parts of his home. A person close to his family confirmed to me later that Redmond kept envelopes full of cash in his house for years. This proved to be an expensive habit when the garage at his Castleknock home caught fire one morning, wiping out bundles of his hidden stash before it was extinguished.

Redmond's love of money was well known. People who worked in the council spoke of an incident when a senior official arrived at the office to find a crew with a digger lifting the pavement outside. 'George lost tuppence on his way in this morning,' was the explanation. While that may have been apocryphal, one colleague recalled going to the chip shop on Parnell Square on occasion for his lunch, invariably followed by Redmond. He liked the fish but not the batter, which George would scoff instead of buying his own food. At the tribunal he famously refused to pay for his lunch at a nearby restaurant, as he considered his celebrity status entitled him to a free cup of tea and a sandwich.

In early March 1999, in a statement to the tribunal just weeks after his arrest, Redmond accepted that he had received payments from builders and developers. He said that he had been given large cash payments by Bailey and JMSE, as well as by Tom Roche of National Toll Roads (NTR) and co-founder of Roadstone Ltd and Cement Roadstone

Holdings, and had received improvements to his home worth £20,000 from construction firm Dwyer Nolan. However, he denied that any of these payments were bribes, despite the undoubted influence he wielded at the highest level of local government.

After obtaining access to his offshore holdings, the tribunal found that he had twenty accounts in more than a dozen banks and building societies, through which he moved some £1.2 million between 1979 and 1989. Although he continued to deny receiving bribes, he agreed that he was 'looked after' by builders Brennan and McGowan, Mick Bailey and JMSE, among others. Redmond disputed the claim by Gogarty that he took at least two large payments from the Murphys in the late 1980s, but, contrary to his earlier denials of any meetings with JMSE executives in a hotel in Clontarf, he now confirmed that they had met there on two occasions.

Redmond was further undone when I reported in late March 1999 that a west Dublin car dealer, Brendan Fassnidge, told me that he had paid £10,000 in cash to Redmond in return for assistance with road access from his garage to a new road. He described how he obtained permission to get a leeway from his Esso filling station to the Palmerstown bypass in 1988:

> Former VW dealer, Brendan Fassnidge, has told the *Sunday Business Post* that he gave Redmond £10,000 in £50 and £100 notes in 1988 in return for the documentation which allowed building contractors to make a leeway from his Esso filling station to the public road. Such access to a major new dual carriageway is regarded as exceptional in planning terms.
>
> According to Fassnidge, he was at his then home at Laurel Lodge, Castleknock when Redmond collected the cash and provided the garage owner with the necessary documentation to proceed with the access road.

> 'I remember collecting the cash at the National Irish Bank in Blanchardstown because on the day I called they did not have sufficient large denomination notes. So I came back the next morning.'

Fassnidge was the man who had arranged Tom Gilmartin's first meeting with Liam Lawlor at the Deadman's Inn to discuss the acquisition of lands at Quarryvale in the late 1980s.[2]

Jim Gogarty's forty days 'in the dock', as he once described it, concluded after his cross-examination by lawyers for the Baileys, Redmond and Burke, with a somewhat calmer approach adopted than by the JMSE team. In his lengthy and abrasive cross-examination of Gogarty, JMSE's barrister Garrett Cooney raised Redmond's claim that he had been given £25,000 by the witness in connection with the extension of planning permission at Forest Road, Swords, in the late 1980s. Gogarty dismissed this allegation and stood by his claim that Redmond took money on two different occasions from JMSE – when £12,000 was handed over by Joseph Murphy junior to the public official in his council office in 1988 and £15,000 at Clontarf Castle Hotel in June 1989.[3]

Mick Bailey insisted that he gave £150,000 to Gogarty in cash and cheques in November 1989 but could not provide any evidence to back this up other than a petty cash book, which contained no proof of when or how the payments were made. Gogarty contradicted further claims by Bailey's lawyer, Colm Allen, including that he asked the builder for money to buy a home for his daughter, a teacher in Athlone. 'That's a damn lie. Because I haven't got a daughter in Athlone, a teacher. More of the damn lies,' Gogarty asserted.[4] He also refuted Bailey's description of the meeting in Burke's home, and the builder's insistence that Murphy junior was not present.

On occasion, Allen called Gogarty a liar, but he could make little headway with the uncompromising witness. When the lawyer said that his client would deny that he introduced Redmond to Gogarty and mentioned the alleged payment of £25,000 by JMSE to the now disgraced planning official, the witness responded, '[T]hat poor man is in enough trouble of his own, so he is.' The Baileys insisted that they had made secret payments to Gogarty, but none of these were recorded in the annual accounts of their company, Bovale Ltd, and could not be independently verified.[5]

Redmond's solicitor, Anthony Harris, had no luck either in his attempts to back up his client's latest effort to damage Gogarty's reputation, and the tribunal chairman accused the lawyer of 'wandering around the desert' in his cross-examination. When Harris suggested that the £25,000 was a finder's fee from Gogarty for getting Bailey to buy the Forest Road lands, the witness replied, 'I refute that completely but what can you say to a man like that? He is operating as city manager, auctioneer, casino runner, the whole bloody lot.'

His reference to the casino runner was in response to media reports of Redmond's habit of dropping into the amusement arcade owned by one of his business friends, Jim Kennedy. The connection between the pair went back to the time when Kennedy's house in Strawberry Beds was acquired by NTR during its construction of the M50 in Dublin. The official file on the property controversially went missing from the offices of Dublin County Council but turned up in the search of Redmond's home by the CAB following his dramatic arrest at Dublin Airport. Kennedy permitted Redmond to take bags of coins from the amusement arcade in Westmoreland Street and to use his account at a wholesale store in the city where the public official did his shopping. Redmond must have felt he was in heaven with all the free cash and the stock of cheap food at his fingertips.

During his cross-examination of Gogarty, Joe Finnegan, Ray Burke's SC, finally confirmed that the former minister had received £20,000 in cash, withdrawn at the AIB in Talbot Street, Dublin, as well as a cheque from Gogarty, which differed from the politician's assertion in June 1997 that he got £30,000 in cash from JMSE at his home. This belated admission followed an earlier confirmation from JMSE that a cheque for £10,000 was involved in the transaction, as Gogarty had always insisted. Finnegan claimed that the meeting in Burke's home took place in the morning, not the evening, that no tea was served and that it lasted just ten minutes.

When Finnegan's light interrogation ended, Gogarty turned to the barrister and said, 'I am coming here for the last three months and I didn't realise we would be having Finnegan's Wake so soon. It's only a matter now of getting the plot, the burial plot, and there should be no problem there. Mr Finnegan, a good man. Finnegan's wake.'[6] With that comment, and the aid of a stick, the eighty-one-year-old walked off the stage and into tribunal history.

If anyone expected the tribunal temperature to fall in the wake of Gogarty's departure, they were sadly disappointed, as further evidence emerged that placed the focus back on the man who had set it up in the first place. Bertie Ahern may have been among those hoping that his decision to establish the tribunal would have pushed any embarrassing questions for him down a long and winding road of fruitless enquiries, but nothing could have been further from the truth. Deep contradictions in his earlier statements about the Burke payments were exposed when a statement to the tribunal made by one of his Cabinet colleagues, Minister for Social, Community and Family Affairs Dermot Ahern, found its way into my hands, and from there to the front page of the *Post*.[7]

In his affidavit for the tribunal, Dermot Ahern revealed details of his two conversations with Joe Murphy junior in late June 1997, after he was sent by his party leader to talk to the JMSE executive about the alleged payments to Burke as part of Bertie Ahern's less-than-thorough investigation before Burke's appointment to Cabinet. When the minister, a solicitor experienced in taking detailed notes, returned from his first visit to the JMSE executive, which took place in London, he reported Murphy junior's account of events involving Burke, Bailey and Gogarty in the summer of 1989 to the Fianna Fáil leader.

During the two meetings, Joseph Murphy junior made 'explosive allegations' to Dermot Ahern, which he outlined in his statement to the tribunal and I reported on. According to Ahern, he first asked Murphy junior whether he, his father or their company paid a substantial sum to Burke at his home in June 1989. The reply was a clear and absolute denial: 'He [Ahern] said that at the first meeting at a hotel near Heathrow Airport, the JMSE executive denied any knowledge of a company payment to Burke …' Ahern's statement outlined the counter-allegations made by Murphy junior in their second meeting, including 'that Bailey had told Murphy junior of payments to two other Fianna Fáil politicians in return for planning favours' and had 'proposed paying Gogarty £100,000. Bailey suggested that he and Murphy would pay £50,000 each to Gogarty to buy his silence, but Murphy refused.' It was at this second meeting that Murphy told Dermot that Bertie Ahern himself 'had a three-hour meeting with Ray Burke and builder Michael Bailey in June 1997 over allegations that the former minister for foreign affairs had received a corrupt payment of £80,000 from JMSE and Bovale Developments'. When Ahern asked the Taoiseach about this alleged meeting, 'the Fianna Fáil leader denied that any such encounter had taken place'.

The account by Dermot Ahern reflected the blatant lies told by the various people he interviewed in 1989 and contradicted the evidence given to the tribunal just a few weeks earlier, when Murphy junior's lawyer admitted that JMSE had drawn down cash of £20,000 from company accounts and organised a cheque for £10,000 in preparation for the payment to Burke in June 1989. It also revived uncomfortable questions for the Taoiseach, who had staunchly defended his appointment of Burke as minister for foreign affairs in his first Cabinet two years previously on the basis that he 'had established no wrongdoing on the part of the north

Dublin TD', even though Dermot Ahern's inquiries had uncovered some disturbing information about the affair. As I noted in my *Post* article: '*The Sunday Business Post* has also learned that Bailey and Bovale were substantial contributors to Fianna Fáil in 1989 and 1990.'[8] Bertie Ahern, who was the joint treasurer of the party in those years, would have been familiar with its benefactors, and the Bailey brothers were well known for their financial largesse.

It seemed that the Taoiseach's investigation had been designed less to establish the truth of the matter and more as a rather dubious exercise in damage limitation, which would allow him to protect his party and its donors, and to appoint his close political ally to government. When the Fianna Fáil leader denied to Dermot Ahern that he met Bailey and Murphy junior prior to appointing Burke to his Cabinet, it was hard to know who was telling the truth. Either way, the Taoiseach was facing increasingly stormy waters as the slow-moving tribunal continued its exploration of the murky links between politics and business in the capital.

The publication of the contents of Dermot Ahern's statement resulted in an order by the tribunal on the *Post* and on me to surrender any documents we possessed relevant to the minister's account of his meetings with Murphy junior and his report to the Taoiseach or face 'penal sanction'. Detective Superintendent Pat Brehony of the National Bureau of Fraud Investigation arrived at the newspaper offices to interview me. He was told that neither I nor the newspaper had any such documents in our possession.

Ahern told the tribunal that, during their meeting in London, Joseph Murphy junior described me as 'a dangerous bastard', an allegation that led to a statement by Seamus Dooley of the National Union of Journalists in my defence:

> Frank Connolly is no bastard but he is dangerous. As a journalist with the *Sunday Business Post* he has played a key role in exposing

> corruption in the planning process. His work led directly to the establishment of the Flood Tribunal. We do not yet know the full extent of this achievement but already we have gained a glimpse of the darker side of Irish politics, local government and big business. No wonder politicians and businessmen may consider him dangerous.[9]

Such personalised attacks on me were not new, starting with the 'line in the sand speech' by Ray Burke in September 1997, just two weeks before he resigned, where he referred to 'unethical journalism' and the 'type of journalism which, thankfully, is followed only by a minute number of that profession.'[10]

Chapter Thirteen

The £5 Million Man

FOLLOWING PÁDRAIG FLYNN'S DISASTROUS TELEVISION INTERVIEW in January 1999 and the angry public response by Gilmartin, I agreed to publish more details of the latter's encounters with the various politicians who were claiming never to have met him, including Ray MacSharry, Albert Reynolds and Bertie Ahern. Gilmartin was first determined to nail Flynn to the cross for his arrogant and hurtful remarks to the nation, and to refute the claim that he paid a bribe to the 'clown' from County Mayo.

In late January, I published an interview with him in *The Sunday Business Post* in which he recounted the exact circumstances of the donation to Flynn, some details of which he had shared with me previously: 'I wrote the cheque to give a donation to the party. I asked him who I would make it payable to. He said, "Don't, just leave it on the desk." I gave him a cheque because it was traceable.' The cheque was later made out to 'cash' and presented at the Bank of Ireland in College Green, Dublin. Gilmartin also recalled the approach after his meeting with Charles Haughey in February 1989 asking him to lodge money in an Isle of Man account. 'After the meeting, I was approached outside the door by a bloke who demanded £5 million to be deposited in an account in the Isle of Man. He gave me an account number,' Gilmartin recalled.[1]

Among those he claimed were in attendance at the meeting were Albert Reynolds and Ahern. When I called Reynolds to ask him whether he remembered the encounter, he said that he could not recall the occasion: 'If he says he met me, then perhaps he did, but genuinely I do not recall any meeting. He might be mistaken, as Haughey wasn't accustomed to bringing me anywhere near him.'

A week later, the document sent by Ray MacSharry in October 1998 stating that there was no relationship between them, which he demanded Gilmartin sign, was published in the *Post*: 'Reports in the Irish Press [*sic*] suggesting a relationship between Ray MacSharry and myself are completely untrue and misleading. In fact, I would like to state categorically that I do not know Ray MacSharry personally. Ray MacSharry did not introduce me to Padraic [*sic*] Flynn or indeed to any other minister or politician.' Gilmartin had refused to sign the letter, which he took 'as an absolute insult. I met him on three occasions and had one meeting with MacSharry in the ministry of finance, near Merrion Square. He had a delightful disinterest in my proposals. Last September he ran around the country looking for my number to give to Pádraig Flynn. He knows my family. He knows my mother.'[2] When approached for comment about the letter, MacSharry, a board member of Smurfit and Ryanair, among other prominent companies, told the *Post* that he did not wish to be 'dragged' into the controversy surrounding the claims by Gilmartin.

Bertie Ahern arguably suffered the most political damage from the latest revelations made by Gilmartin to me, as they undermined claims made by the Taoiseach to the Dáil on 27 January 1999. In his lengthy statement, Ahern denied that he was present, along with other Cabinet members, at the meeting with Haughey in Leinster House. In his remarks, which were made under Dáil privilege, Ahern disputed the description by Gilmartin of the meeting in the Fianna Fáil offices on the fifth floor of the Leinster House complex when the developer was introduced to Haughey in February 1989. Ahern, who mentioned the date of the meeting as 10 March, said that in 1989 any meetings held by Haughey would have taken place in Government Buildings, rather than in the Fianna Fáil offices. He also said that his diaries and those of Seamus Brennan and Haughey showed that no such meeting ever took place. In fact Gilmartin never mentioned this date in connection with his meeting with Haughey. It was a reporter on RTÉ who referenced it, incorrectly, a few days before Ahern addressed the Dáil.

Ahern also misrepresented the role played by his close political ally and friend, Councillor Joe Burke, in attempts to extract money from Gilmartin in return for their promised assistance with the Quarryvale project. He claimed that the only dealings Burke had with Gilmartin were in relation to the planned Bachelors Walk project. He failed to mention the more sensitive matter of his intervention with Burke on the purchase of the council lands at Quarryvale. Ahern went on to dig a deeper hole for himself by disputing Gilmartin's recollections of their several encounters.[3]

The following Sunday the *Post* published a detailed rebuttal of the Taoiseach's recollections, in which Gilmartin contradicted Ahern's dating of the Leinster House meeting, which he said took place in February 1989, a date previously mentioned in our reporting, as well as his assertions about his dealings with Joe Burke. Gilmartin provided details of how he approached Ahern for assistance later in 1989, after his attempts to purchase the Dublin County Council site at Quarryvale ran into political obstacles and demands for money. He described in precise detail meetings with Ahern that the Taoiseach did not disclose to the Dáil in his January statement. He told the *Post*:

> I trusted Bertie and I thought he could help. I wouldn't pay up the money that was being demanded by various people. After meeting him in Drumcondra twice and in the Ministry of Labour [*sic*], I formed the view that he could be trusted when I was being screwed. I rang Bertie to tell him about how I was being blackmailed and

> I explained how people were giving me difficulty about acquiring the site even though I had placed a £500,000 deposit on it. He didn't make a great deal of comment. He did ask if I had given a donation to the party, and I told him about the money I gave to Flynn the previous June.[4]

Gilmartin said Ahern sent Burke to meet him and that, soon afterwards, a Dublin County Council committee, on which the Taoiseach's friend sat, agreed the sale of 70 acres of land at Quarryvale to the developer. His account of his trip to the airport, when Burke stopped his pick-up truck at two pubs frequented by Ahern in a fruitless search for the politician, added more spice to the story.

Notwithstanding forceful denials by Joe Burke and Ahern of Gilmartin's colourful account, the revelations generated more unease and discomfort among Fianna Fáil's government partners, the Progressive Democrats. They were uncomfortably reminded of the plethora of contradictions and obfuscations surrounding Ahern's and Fianna Fáil's responses to the allegations about payments to Ray Burke just two years previously. As relations with Mary Harney became strained, Ahern complained, 'it was bit unfair on me that when you correct the record you are accused of a loss of memory, senility or something worse'.[5]

The inconsistencies in Ahern's Dáil statement and recollections were further exposed when Gilmartin provided more evidence about the infamous meeting with Haughey, Ahern and other Cabinet members. The details, published in a story in the *Post* in early February 1999, undermined Ahern's poorly researched Dáil speech. To remove confusion over the date of the Leinster House meeting, Gilmartin produced his diary, in which was recorded the exact date and time of his encounter with Haughey and the '£5 million man'. It took place at 5.30 p.m. on 1 February 1989, dispelling any further doubt or dissembling on the matter. Gilmartin's entry for that date had a time of 4.30 p.m. for 'Meet with L. Lawlor at Buswell's Hotel' and 5.30 p.m. for 'Meeting with Ministers in Dáil Éireann (Leinster House)'.[6]

Ahern was dragged deeper into the controversy when the *Post* reported on how a friend of his had received large sums of money from Gilmartin's company, Barkhill Ltd, in the 1990s. Tim Collins was paid sums of £30,000 and £50,000, ostensibly for work he did for Owen O'Callaghan and his architect, Ambrose Kelly. In his Dáil statement in January 1999, the Taoiseach mentioned Collins as a friend who attended his first meeting with Gilmartin in the Department of Labour in 1989. Gilmartin confirmed that Collins was 'with Ambrose Kelly and was paid by Barkhill and O'Callaghan' without his consent as a director of the company. Collins also worked for Kelly in identifying suitable sites for development in Dublin, and with former Fianna Fáil fundraiser and close ally of Ahern, Des Richardson at Pilgrim, another company owned by the architect. Collins resigned as a member of the board of Enterprise Ireland, a State company to which he had been nominated by Ahern, just weeks before the Taoiseach named him during his Dáil statement.

Bertie Ahern could now be linked through his friends to the allegedly dubious financial activities of Dunlop, Lawlor, O'Callaghan and Kelly, among other villains in Gilmartin's story, and it was becoming clearer that his involvement with this particular 'gang of four' was closer than previously understood. This was illustrated by the supportive role he played as minister for finance in the attempt by O'Callaghan to induce US investors into his scheme to develop an all-purpose stadium on the lands at Neilstown, a project in which the four men were stakeholders. Gilmartin's company, Barkhill, had reluctantly acquired the site from O'Callaghan as part of his option buy out, but the former was unaware of the stadium plan for the site being pushed by O'Callaghan after he acquired a stake in Barkhill.[7] Ahern's ministerial diary for 1 February

1989 showed that he met Dunlop at 3 p.m. that day, just hours before Gilmartin's engagement with Haughey.

As the *Post* continued to extract and publish Gilmartin's claims, at the same time exposing the weak denials of those he implicated, the Flood Tribunal continued to join the dots between the senior politicians involved, their business associates and the corruption allegations. This essential work was in preparation for Gilmartin's appearance to give his evidence in public, along with the tribunal's private and public interviews with the senior political and other figures he had named in his accusatory statements.

The Moriarty Tribunal, meanwhile, had uncovered how Haughey had accumulated over £2 million from Ben Dunne alone during his term as Fianna Fáil leader, while he pocketed £750,000 from the dig-out by Patrick Gallagher and his other friends to clear his bank debt in late 1979 to allow him become taoiseach for the first time. AIB wrote off £350,000, or 30 per cent of Haughey's debt, even though it held the deeds to his mansion and lands at Kinsealy worth an estimated £1 million, as well as those of his Blasket island, Inishvickillane, and his holiday home at Lislary, Sligo. The favourable treatment meted out to the former taoiseach by the bank was in stark contrast to its ruthless pursuit of ordinary borrowers in difficulty and of Tom Gilmartin. During a visit to AIB in the early 1990s, Gilmartin saw Haughey rip up and throw a document out the window of his ministerial Mercedes as it left the bank. It was a clear display of the disdain the politician had for his lenders.[8]

Unsurprisingly, Bertie Ahern did not appreciate the unwelcome reminders of the long trail of financial impropriety that overshadowed the legacy of his illustrious predecessor. He faced discomfiting questions about his direct financial dealings with Haughey and why, between 1984 and 1992, he had signed most of the 1,615 cheques from the Leader's Allowance account used by the former taoiseach. Over £1 million was paid by the State to Haughey during that period, including some of the money raised in 1989 to defray the medical expenses of former Tánaiste Brian Lenihan, when he required a liver transplant operation in the US.

Ahern told Moriarty that he had no recollection of co-signing a cheque for £25,000 from the Leader's Allowance lodged in 1989 to Haughey's personal account. Neither could he recall the reason for other cheques he co-signed in 1990 and 1991 amounting to £33,400. He did concede that the pre-signing of cheques 'may transpire to be an inappropriate practice' and that he learned in 1989 that Haughey may have made 'collateral use' of the Leader's Allowance during his term as 'Una Duce' of the party. In total, the Moriarty and McCracken Tribunals had by then established payments of more than £5 million to Haughey and those connected to him from his bountiful patrons.

It was now evident that the roots of corruption in Ireland during the 1980s and 1990s ran far deeper into political and business culture than any outsider could ever have envisaged. It would soon become clear that they were not the only parts of Irish society marred by the illicit dealings and practices of powerful institutions and those vested with authority over the lives of the common people.

Minister for the Environment Pádraig Flynn, who kept a £50,000 donation from Tom Gilmartin intended for Fianna Fáil. © Derek Speirs

Public relations consultant and former Fianna Fáil press officer Frank Dunlop admitted to bribing a host of senior and other politicians. © Derek Speirs

Taoiseach Charles Haughey and Minister for Justice Ray Burke, who were tarred by corruption allegations over many years. © Derek Speirs

Liam Lawlor canvassing during the 1989 general election in west Dublin.
© Derek Speirs

Minister for Communications Michael Lowry leaving Leinster House following his resignation from the government in November 1996, after it emerged that he had accepted large payments and other benefits from Ben Dunne. © Derek Speirs

Bertie Ahern with (left) Mary O'Rourke and Ray Burke, at the Fianna Fáil Ard-Fheis two months before he first became taoiseach in June 1997. © Derek Speirs

Judge Feargus Flood, sole member of the Planning and Payments Tribunal, whose damning reports were hugely popular with the public. © Derek Speirs

Property developer and banker Patrick Gallagher, who helped to clear Haughey's huge bank debt in 1979. © Derek Speirs

Former JMSE chairman James Gogarty, whose story led to the resignation of Ray Burke in 1997, leaving the Planning and Payments tribunal in Dublin Castle. © RollingNews.ie

Denis 'Starry' O'Brien at the Four Courts in Dublin after he lost a defamation action taken against him by Bertie Ahern. © RollingNews.ie

Joseph Murphy junior, managing director of JMSE, who admitted to making threatening phone calls to James Gogarty, arriving at the Planning Tribunal in Dublin Castle with his lawyer, Patrick Cooney SC. © RollingNews.ie

Tom Gilmartin, whose shocking tale of corruption in Dublin brought down Bertie Ahern and other senior politicians.© Derek Speirs

The grave of Baby John in Caherciveen, County Kerry. The inscription reads: 'I am the Kerry baby baptised on 14–4–1984 named John. Rest in Peace.' © Derek Speirs

Sergeant Patrick Reidy, the scene of crime officer following the murder of Baby John in Caherciveen, arriving at the Kerry Babies Tribunal. © Derek Speirs

Joanne Hayes being greeted by supporters at the Kerry Babies Tribunal in Tralee, County Kerry. © Derek Speirs

Detective Garda P.J. Browne, Detective Sergeant Joe Shelly and Detective Sergeant Gerry O'Carroll, whose flawed investigation into the death of Baby John led to false confessions of murder by members of the Hayes family, at the Kerry Babies Tribunal. © Derek Speirs

Frank McBrearty Senior and Frank McBrearty Junior, whose campaign to prove their family had nothing to do with the death of Richie Barron exposed corruption to the highest levels of the Garda Síochána in Donegal.

John O'Dowd was dismissed from the force after the Morris Tribunal found that he had told 'many lies about his behaviour' on the night Richie Barron was killed. © Gerard Cunningham/Guth Publication

Padraig Mulligan, the garda on duty in Raphoe on the night Barron was killed, was dismissed from the force in 2004. © Gerard Cunningham/Guth Publication

Kevin Lennon was dismissed from the force after the Tribunal found he had orchestrated hoax explosives finds in the north-west to further his career. © Gerard Cunningham/Guth Publication

Detective Garda Noel McMahon resigned in 2004 after the Morris Tribunal found he had planted hoax explosives and ammunition. He also threatened his wife and another garda with a loaded gun. © RollingNews.ie

Sheenagh O'Doherty, ex-wife of Noel McMahon, who exposed corruption in the force and the threats and violence she suffered at the hands of her former husband. Courtesy of Sheenagh O'Doherty

PART II

Chapter Fourteen

Who Killed Richie Barron?

IN LATE SPRING 1999, WHILE THE Flood Tribunal was meandering its way through the illicit payments made to Burke, Redmond, Flynn and countless other politicians, I was following another unfolding scandal involving extraordinary allegations of corruption against members of the Garda Síochána in Donegal. Following a tip-off from a solicitor in Dublin, I travelled to Raphoe, in east Donegal to meet publican Frank McBrearty, owner of the Parting Glass in the town. The pub was well known for its adjoining Frankie's Nite Club, which attracted revellers from across the county and the North to listen to well-known performers such as Joe Dolan, Big Tom and other showbands.

At our first meeting in the Parting Glass, McBrearty recounted a three-year nightmare endured by his family at the hands of members of the gardaí in Donegal, which started when his son, Frank junior, and his nephew, Mark McConnell, were wrongly accused of killing a local cattle dealer. A big man and former boxer, McBrearty had worked in Scotland for many years before he returned to Ireland with his wife, Rosalind, also from Donegal, some twenty years earlier, at which time he opened the pub in Raphoe. They raised a family and developed a successful business and solid reputation in the town until their life was torn apart following the death of a man near their public house in late 1996.

Just after 12.45 a.m. on Monday, 14 October 1996, Richie Barron of Townparks, Raphoe, was found unconscious in a pool of blood on a road behind the car park of the Parting Glass. He was found by a local man, Lee Parker, who was driving home from the town. The emergency services were contacted, and an ambulance from Letterkenny arrived at the scene between 1.20 a.m. and 1.25 a.m. Barron was alive but in critical condition, and the ambulance crew transported him immediately to Letterkenny Hospital. They left Raphoe at about 1.30 a.m., but, despite their best efforts, Barron was pronounced dead on arrival in the emergency unit at 1.50 a.m.

The gardaí were contacted at 1.05 a.m., but it was 1.34 a.m. before a squad car from Lifford arrived at Townparks. As the ambulance had already gone, it was too late for gardaí to record the exact location of the incident, the position of the body or the condition of the victim. Garda Padraig Mulligan was responsible for controlling and preserving the accident scene. He arrived there with Garda John O'Dowd just behind the Garda car from Lifford. Mulligan claimed that he witnessed an altercation between 'some men from Northern Ireland' outside the Parting Glass, which broke up when he told them to stop. He said that he and O'Dowd were then told that Barron had been knocked down in Townparks. Just then the Lifford Garda car pulled up beside them, so O'Dowd followed it, with Mulligan, to the accident scene.

Despite being the designated officer on duty that night in Raphoe, Mulligan had instead spent much of the night drinking in Lifford with O'Dowd before returning to Raphoe. They claimed to have left Daly's pub in Lifford at around 1 a.m., arriving in Raphoe some ten minutes later. However, witnesses claimed to have seen Mulligan outside the chipper close to the McBrearty premises earlier than this. Mulligan first told Garda investigators looking into the events surrounding the death that one of the reasons left the town where he should have been on duty was to test out a new car that O'Dowd had purchased. He later admitted that he was drinking with O'Dowd after another garda who saw them in the pub confirmed their presence to investigators. Mulligan claimed he was afraid to admit that he was drinking while on duty. Another peculiar aspect of the case was that Mulligan failed to seal off the crime scene, and blood and other evidence was swept from the road later in the morning, meaning no forensic investigation could be carried out.[1]

O'Dowd's movements and behaviour on that night would later become the focus of inquiries, after he and others falsely attributed Barron's death to a severe beating by McBrearty junior and his cousin. The first examination by a pathologist indicated that Barron's injuries were consistent with being struck by a blunt instrument, although it didn't rule out a traffic accident. The case was transformed into a murder investigation and the two suspects were arrested on 4 December 1996. McBrearty junior was arrested by a force of some twenty-five gardaí close to his home in Raphoe as he was driving his two small children to school, and he said he was taken away in front of them. He was then assaulted, threatened and intimidated by a number of officers, purportedly for the purpose of obtaining a confession of involvement in Barron's death. Claims by the gardaí that he signed such a confession were disputed by him, and both he and his cousin were released without charge.

During our first conversation, McBrearty senior became upset as he described how his son fell into a deep depression following his arrest and the harassment that followed, and how badly Rosalind and their family were affected by the treatment they endured at the hands of members of the force. He named Sergeant John White from Letterkenny Garda Station as a leading figure in a long-term campaign of abuse directed at his extended family and staff, which included their cars being stopped and searched frequently, the imposition of unwarranted car parking and other motoring fines, as well as other disruptions to his successful nightclub business. McBrearty senior told me that, in a further attempt to blacken the McBreartys' reputations, senior officers in the division deployed White to Raphoe to run this campaign of harassment just weeks after Barron's death, while Letterkenny-based Garda Superintendent

Kevin Lennon was particularly active in prosecuting summonses against McBrearty, his family and employees.

There was local speculation that Frankie's Nite Club was seen as a commercial threat to other venues in Donegal, particularly in nearby Letterkenny, some of whose owners were not displeased to see McBrearty's business in trouble. White regularly set up checkpoints on the roads leading into Raphoe on weekend nights, causing delays for the crowds entering the town. Hoax bomb threats and other forms of harassment were also employed against the McBreartys in the effort to disrupt their trade.

Over the three years following Barron's death, McBrearty senior, his family members and staff contested more than 130 separate summonses for various road traffic, licensing and other minor offences brought against them in Letterkenny District Court. Garda witnesses told the court on one occasion that a circular had been distributed to stations in the county advising members that charges should be brought against McBrearty and his workers at every opportunity. McBrearty, who held the honorary title of Mayor of Raphoe at the time of our first meetings, complained that he had also been subjected to wrongful arrest on 5 December 1996. He initiated High Court proceedings against the State and its various agencies over the mistreatment, including the use of excessive force, causing distress to him, his wife and family members.

For legal reasons, it was not possible to name the gardaí involved at that time, but, in early May 1999, with the assistance of McBrearty senior's lawyers, *The Sunday Business Post* published the contents of his statement of claim, along with details of the treatment received by his son and nephew.[2] His statement of claim alleged that he 'was assaulted, threatened and intimidated in Garda custody and he was hospitalised, while in detention, with a life-threatening illness'. He was held in four different hospitals during his detention and was seeking damages for 'false imprisonment, assault, breach of constitutional rights, intimidation and oppressive behaviour'.

Frank McBrearty junior also sought damages relating to his arrest. In January 1997, he was arrested again, this time in connection with an alleged assault, and when incarcerated, he was questioned once more about Barron's death. In his High Court claim, he asserted that, as a result of his mistreatment in custody, he suffered bruising to his upper body and back, psychological trauma and upset. He suffered 'character change, and has become withdrawn, introverted and insecure'.

His cousin, Mark McConnell, suffered two serious assaults, in which his leg and jaw were broken, by people who mistakenly believed he was involved in Barron's death, and he also claimed damages. He said he was 'beaten and battered' when, on 4 December 1996, he was taken into custody, unlawfully detained and had his constitutional rights breached following his arrest. On the same day, his wife, Roisín, was arrested and suffered severe psychological trauma having been 'subjected to mental abuse'. While in custody, she was shown photos of the dead Richie Barron and said she was told that her young son would be taken from her. Roisín was later diagnosed with acute paranoid psychosis, despite never having suffered previously from any form of psychiatric or depressive illness. She presented with post-traumatic stress disorder, was treated with electroconvulsive therapy and a variety of heavy medications, and was still undergoing treatment when I met her at her home in spring 1999.

During my investigation, I made several visits to Donegal to meet with the McBreartys and others whose dealings with some of the same gardaí implicated by the Raphoe victims had raised alarm bells in Dublin. Their allegations led to an investigation into the disturbing revelations of corruption within the force, headed by two senior gardaí, Assistant Commissioner Kevin Carty and Chief Superintendent Austin McNally, which began in April 1999.

A key question for those investigating the death of Barron concerned the vehicle O'Dowd was driving that night. A Toyota Carina was seen by a witness, Joseph Sweeney, behind the squad car as it drove through

Raphoe to the scene of Barron's accident. In a statement given on 18 October 1996, just days after Barron's death, Sweeney said, 'I got into Raphoe at about 1 a.m. I drove to the Vocational School and parked, and Damien Callan and Jackie (Craid) pulled in beside me. We were chatting up at the Tech for five or ten minutes. I remember seeing a patrol car and a Carina behind it. They were driving up toward Mongorry.'[3] Mongorry is the area in Townparks where the badly injured Barron was found.

Garda John O'Dowd and Garda Padraig Mulligan told investigators that they were driving behind the squad car when it sped to the scene. However, O'Dowd's actions between the time he drove Mulligan back to Raphoe from Lifford after midnight and his pursuit of the squad car to the scene of the accident raise serious questions that remain unresolved.

Another witness, Eamon Strain, recalled being stopped by O'Dowd after he left the home of his girlfriend, Anne Toye, that night, a few miles outside Raphoe on the back road to Letterkenny. He and Anne had been to the cinema in Letterkenny, and at her house they spoke for about thirty minutes in the car before he headed home. Sometime between 12.35 a.m. and 12.45 a.m., Strain said, a car came up behind him:

> As I had just turned right, the lights of a car came on behind me. I assumed it was the guards and I stopped. The car behind me then reversed a short distance for about three or four yards. The headlights were still on … This man then got out of his car and came up to the passenger door of my own. 'Don't be afraid. We're investigating a hit and run. There was a poor auld cunt knocked down,' he said.[4]

Strain described how the man opened the passenger door of his van, put his head and shoulders into the vehicle, and rested his knee on the passenger seat, before saying, 'We are investigating a hit and run' in Townparks, Raphoe. He then asked Strain whether he had seen any cars speeding along the road. The man was not in uniform, but he acted like a garda and Strain's description of him – about forty-five, clean shaven with short sandy hair – matched O'Dowd. The man used crude language and did not ask Strain for his name or any identification.

The next morning, Strain heard on Highland Radio about the death the previous night of Richie Barron and was concerned about the circumstances of his encounter with the unidentified garda. He informed his girlfriend, who corroborated Strain's timeline and told her mother, Madge. Madge Toye mentioned it to a garda she met at a Bovine spongiform encephalopathy (commonly known as mad cow disease) checkpoint five days after the incident. The garda reported what Toye had told him to the incident room in Letterkenny station, and it was raised at a case conference a week after Barron's death.

O'Dowd, who was present at the conference, said that he had stopped 'Eamon Strain and the Toye girl' on the night at 1.45 a.m.[5] This statement directly conflicted with the evidence of Strain, who said he was on his own when he was questioned at around 12.45 a.m. O'Dowd claimed that he was on the road to check on an 'uninsured farmer' in Manorcunningham as a potential suspect in Barron's death when he saw the car and decided to talk to them in case they had seen anything suspicious. His claim that Anne Toye was in the car was discredited by Strain's description of O'Dowd placing his knee on the passenger seat, while his timing of the encounter was disputed by the recollections of both Strain and his girlfriend. Anne Toye later confirmed to gardaí that she was certain that she was home before 1 a.m. as she had to travel to Dublin with her mother early the next day.

The unlikely explanation that O'Dowd was travelling from the scene of the accident in Raphoe, 13km away, to visit a farmer who drove a car without insurance, was not credible. No evidence was provided by O'Dowd to prove that he visited any such uninsured driver in the early hours of that morning. The Carty investigation also asked O'Dowd about a phone call to his house from Raphoe Garda Station at 3.50 a.m. on the morning of 14 October. Mulligan was the only one on duty in the station at that time, but O'Dowd said he had no recollection of receiving the call.

O'Dowd told Garda investigators that he was driving his new beige Vauxhall on the night of Barron's death. Motor tax registration records show that O'Dowd registered ownership of a beige Vauxhall in September 1996, but it was not observed by any civilian witness in Raphoe or by Eamon Strain on the night in question. Garda investigators have since failed to track down the driver of the Toyota Carina that Joseph Sweeney said he saw immediately behind the squad car from Lifford as it made its way to the scene of Barron's mysterious death. In June 2026, Frank McBrearty junior said that he was informed by a senior garda in Donegal in 2025 that O'Dowd owned a Toyota Carina in 1996, which he claimed to have sold weeks before Barron's death. The Garda Press Office and O'Dowd did not respond to written queries on this assertion.

It was a year before Strain was contacted by gardaí and two before the Carty team took statements from Anne and Madge Toye. Strain made his first statement to the Donegal gardaí in November 1997 and, almost two years later, spoke to the Carty team in October 1999. His evidence placed O'Dowd on the road from Raphoe to Letterkenny at 12.45 a.m., some nine minutes before Barron's body was discovered. Yet the garda was able to confirm to Strain that a hit and run had taken place, even before it was reported to the emergency services. This would imply that O'Dowd travelled on the road from Raphoe to Letterkenny at the approximate time and passed the location where Barron was hit by a car. If this was the case, he then returned to Raphoe after his conversation with Strain, where he joined up with Mulligan and followed the squad car to the accident scene.

Witnesses also contradicted what O'Dowd claimed he did at the scene. He said he searched a shed in a nearby house to see if the engine was warm on any vehicles that could have been involved in the hit and run. He said he saw three tractors in the shed, yet the owner said he only owned one. His actions were further brought into question by William Doherty, a notoriously unreliable Garda informant, who confirmed to me during my investigations of the McBrearty case in 1999 that he wrongly claimed to gardaí and others that McBrearty junior and McConnell were connected to Barron's death, but then retracted his claim. He admitted to making phone calls to members of the extended McBrearty family, accusing them of involvement in the cattle dealer's death, including from O'Dowd's house a few days after Barron's death. O'Dowd was arrested in June 1999 in relation to alleged extortionate phone calls to Michael and Charlotte Peoples in November 1996.

The search for whomever was actually responsible was hindered by the decision of the most senior garda in the district, Chief Superintendent Denis Fitzpatrick, to cover up the fact that a paid Garda informant had made distressing and accusatory phone calls from a garda's house.[6] Details of the anonymous calls were revealed when Billy Flynn, a private detective employed by McBrearty senior in 1998, obtained records from the telephone company showing that some of them came from O'Dowd's home.

The horrific details of what had taken place in the small town of Raphoe, how the lives of so many people were damaged and how the gardaí were implicated in wrongdoing were only beginning to surface. Meanwhile, the prosecutions against members of the McBrearty family, their staff and even customers of their public house were still the subject of regular hearings of the District Court in Letterkenny. The case of a seventeen-year-old woman who was given the benefit of the Probation Act after she was 'found on' in the Parting Glass after hours, was among the first to be determined. The case was heard in September 1999, a year after she was charged. After it was established that there was no evidence the young woman had consumed any alcohol and had left the pub as soon as gardaí arrived, Judge Tom Fitzpatrick, before giving her probation, said, 'I have never come across anybody being prosecuted for this during my twelve years on the bench.'[7] The judge's comment reflected the growing unease in legal circles in the north-west about the number and quality of prosecutions being taken against people working in or frequenting the Raphoe premises.

A week earlier, Martin Giblin, senior counsel for the McBreartys, told Donegal District Court that a witness who claimed to have told gardaí that he was present in McBrearty's bar when alcohol was served after hours was among those found drinking a pint in the pub in the early hours of the morning when the raid occurred. Sligo man Bernard Conlon, aged in his forties, had a string of convictions for criminal behaviour, many of which had not been made known to Giblin by Garda prosecutors, despite an order for full disclosure granted to the lawyer a year earlier. Conlon, it turned out, was another Garda informant, who was asked by members of the force to remain in the pub after hours until they could arrive.

Judge John O'Donnell ordered the DPP to explain discrepancies between two lists of Conlon's previous convictions prepared by gardaí and given to the lawyers acting for the McBreartys. During the court hearing in September 1999, the court heard that McBrearty junior denied any involvement in the death of Barron, even though a confession with his signature was apparently in the possession of the investigating gardaí. Giblin sought the details of a statement by a named garda, which purported to describe the manner in which McBrearty junior confessed to the murder of Barron after his arrest in early 1997. By the time of the court hearing, the DPP had already confirmed in writing to McBrearty junior and Mark McConnell that no charges would be made against them in connection with the death, a tacit acknowledgement that the confession was either forged, that McBrearty junior had signed a different statement, or that he was forced to admit to a murder that never happened or at least was not committed by him.[8]

In June 2000, more than 160 charges under road traffic and liquor licensing acts against Frank McBrearty senior, members of his family and staff were dropped at the District Court in Donegal.[9] In previous court hearings, Giblin had completely undermined the credibility of gardaí and other witnesses. In particular, he exposed the criminal background and falsehoods told in court by the paid informant Bernard Conlon, who had been 'found on' in the Parting Glass in the prearranged raid by Sergeant John White and other gardaí to catch out McBrearty senior and his staff. Conlon would later be charged in relation to making a false report, when he told gardaí that Mark McConnell and another local man, Michael Peoples, threatened him with a silver bullet. Conlon, the first person prosecuted as a result of the Carty inquiry, falsely claimed that he was told he would be shot if he gave evidence against Frank McBrearty senior in a forthcoming liquor licensing case. Alibi evidence discredited this claim, as Giblin was able to establish that McConnell and Peoples were in the company of two barristers at a hotel in Letterkenny at a time when they were supposedly threatening Conlon at his home in Sligo seventy miles away. Peoples was also one of those whom William Doherty phoned from John O'Dowd's house on the night of the hit and run accident in an attempt to implicate him in Barron's death.

Sergeant White had been arrested by the Carty team in March 2000 and questioned in relation to Conlon's admission that the sergeant had asked him to make the false claim. White was arrested again in June 2001, after another detective, Thomas Kilcoyne, alleged that White had planted a shotgun at a traveller encampment in north Donegal some years previously. He was also responsible for planting an 'explosive device' at the MMDS mast near Ardara in south-west Donegal in 1996 (see Chapter 15).

Following confirmation in July 2000 that the DPP had directed that no charges be made against McBrearty junior or McConnell in connection with the death of Richie Barron, the Garda announced that others would be prosecuted instead. It was reported in the *Post* that the informant, William Doherty, as well as a senior officer (Lennon) and a garda sergeant (White), who could not yet be named, were among those facing criminal charges arising from the now sixteen-month Carty investigation.[10] As reported in the *Post* a week later, the sergeant, who had been arrested and suspended a few months earlier, but was then reinstated and transferred, was potentially facing 'serious criminal charges arising from allegations made against him by a number of sources, including a paid garda informant'. In an attempt to protect himself, the sergeant 'threatened to make public serious allegations against senior ranking gardaí if he is prosecuted, including a claim that they knew he was involved in planting evidence on suspects to secure convictions for serious crimes'.[11] White claimed that senior detectives in Dublin knew about his nefarious activities. The report went on to state that another serving garda claimed she had witnessed a detective practising McBrearty junior's signature in Letterkenny Garda Station, a significant development in the case given the confession to murder he supposedly signed.

A week earlier, Garda Commissioner Pat Byrne had transferred the head of the Donegal Division, Chief Superintendent Denis Fitzpatrick, as well as Superintendent Kevin Lennon, Superintendent John McGinley, Garda John O'Dowd and Garda Padraig Mulligan to other duties and locations; all were involved in the prosecution of the McBreartys and their staff members. Byrne 'insisted that the corruption in Donegal was isolated to the region but lawyers for McBrearty have claimed that a number of officers from outside Donegal were knowingly involved in pressing false charges against him and family members'.[12]

In September 2000, the *Post* reported sensationally that the two gardaí, O'Dowd and Mulligan, had initially lied to the Carty inquiry and did not admit they were in a pub in Lifford on the night of Barron's death. This added to suspicions that members of the force were not just involved in concocting false allegations against the McBreartys, but, worse, were implicated in Barron's death or, at least, obstructing the investigation into an unlawful killing.

Chapter Fifteen

Lawyers, Drugs and Money

A WEEK BEFORE THE FIRST McBREARTY story was published in May 1999, I reported on another remarkable claim that members of the Garda Síochána were involved in planting 'hoax bombs' in other parts of Donegal to enhance their chances of promotion within the force. This information was provided by Sheenagh McMahon, the wife of Detective Garda Noel McMahon, who lived in Buncrana in north Donegal. Sheenagh, who was not identified in the first *Sunday Business Post* article on this allegation, claimed that her husband was using their home for 'the storage of detonators, fertiliser and other equipment'.[1] She said that two 'bomb attacks' were concocted in the North in the early 1990s as part of a plan by a named garda to gain promotion based on their supposed discovery and prevention of supposed IRA actions. At that time, the Royal Ulster Constabulary in Derry received a Garda tip-off about one of the devices, which was later identified as a hoax bomb.

As part of their investigations in Donegal, Assistant Commissioner Carty and Chief Superintendent McNally met with Sheenagh, by then estranged from her husband, and her lawyers. She told them that she had removed some of the incriminating material from her home as proof of her claims and that it had been 'stored in a safe location and may be made available to the investigators'. According to Sheenagh, she also had a letter written by a senior officer, which, she claimed, 'represents an attempt by him to distance himself from the affair', as well as 'other documents potentially incriminating to the garda concerned'.

Lawyers acting for Sheenagh successfully sought immunity for her in return for her co-operation, and also examined the possibility of suing the State for damage to her, her family and marriage. She said she had been subjected to 'telephone threats from "an identified caller" who told her she should be worried about her family and her children', which was what prompted her decision to go public with her claims. She identified her husband, Noel, and Superintendent Kevin Lennon as the gardaí involved, along with Adrienne McGlinchey. The daughter of prominent Letterkenny publican, nightclub owner, former Fianna Fáil senator and serving county councillor Bernard McGlinchey, she helped transport the hoax bombs, allegedly prepared 'in the garage of a Donegal garda'. It was a clever scheme, with Garda sources confirming 'that the fake bombs were made from material which had been withheld from previously genuine finds of IRA arms and explosives'.

Sheenagh claimed that Adrienne had admitted to her that she had helped transport bomb-making material across the border to Strabane on one occasion. Adrienne would later make a detailed statement to the Carty investigation, in which she described being involved in the manufacture and transport of 'hoax bombs' containing ground-up fertiliser to various locations in the north-west. These were subsequently 'discovered' by Lennon and McMahon and claimed as IRA finds.

When I met her at her home in Buncrana, Sheenagh was distressed and anxious about her position and fearful of the consequences, for herself and her young children, of coming forward. Yet over the following weeks and months, a series of revelations would confirm her original claims, notwithstanding a statement by the Garda Press Office that the named gardaí had denied her allegations.

Further claims of Garda corruption in the north-west emerged when a Donegal farmer complained about a three-day raid on his home at Ardagh, near St Johnston, in August 1997. Alfie Gallagher said that William Doherty, one of the paid Garda informants involved in the Barron case, had supposedly tipped off Superintendent Lennon in Letterkenny about an alleged arms dump at his farm. 'About 30 armed detectives raided the farm. They arrived at about 4 pm and said they had a search warrant,' said Gallagher. 'There were up to 80 soldiers hidden in the fields around the farm. There was a helicopter hovering about for most of the time.'[2] No weapons or illegal materiel were found.

Gallagher, his wife and family members were held in the farm from 3 to 6 March 1997, during the raid, at which time his sheds, livestock and plants were damaged, while sheep aborted their lambs. His son's plant hire company was also affected when some customers withdrew their business. I established that Doherty had visited the Gallagher farm days before the raid and planted a stake on the site of an alleged bunker full of arms. Gallagher later sought an apology from the Garda Commissioner.

As the Donegal Garda controversy escalated, with new allegations emerging in different parts of the county, another shocking story revived one of the allegations that had prompted Ray Burke's resignation and the establishment of the Flood Tribunal. While discussing the activities of Sergeant White in the attempted destruction of his business, Frank McBrearty senior had told me about the garda's alleged role in the framing of a man who was wrongly accused of planting an explosive device at a mast for the MMDS used to transmit television signals in the south-west of Donegal in 1996.

The hour-long journey from Letterkenny to Ardara runs through the beautifully scenic and rugged Donegal landscape. Hugh Diver and his family lived a few miles from Ardara, on the side of a mountain with spectacular views of the Atlantic Ocean. What was a life of peace and tranquillity was shattered in another episode of mistreatment and abuse by members of the gardaí, which traumatised the small rural community. The harassment followed public protests by the Divers and their neighbours against the imposition of the MMDS broadcasting system and the removal of the existing service, which allowed them to access the UK channels. The controversy resulted in Tom Gildea's election in June 1997 as an independent TD representing the citizens of Ardara and the surrounding area; he supported the campaign against the MMDS infrastructure. It was Gildea who had asked Burke after his 'line in the sand' speech in September 1997 whether he had received any monies in relation to his role in the MMDS saga. A subsidiary of Fitzwilton was among the companies involved in the erection of MMDS masts across the country, while Rennicks, another Fitzwilton subsidiary, made a payment of £30,000 to Burke in June 1989.

Gildea was one of the four independent TDs who supported the Fianna Fáil coalition after the June 1997 election, until he withdrew his support because of the mistreatment his supporters in the community endured during their protest campaign and the revelations of Garda involvement in 'setting up' Hugh Diver for arrest and wrongful prosecution. Diver, a friendly, humorous and committed member of the campaign, and a well-liked and respected member of the community, complained that he was singled out by Sergeant White and other gardaí because of his role in the protest.

When a picket on the remote and isolated mountain mast was removed, unidentified people entered the site and burned the container owned by MMDS promoters Cable Management Ireland (CMI), causing an estimated £80,000 in damage. What appeared to be an explosive device, containing fuse wire, metal tubing, wood and black powder of the type found in fireworks was planted at the scene. Garda sources confirmed that, while the device could not have exploded, a detonator was placed with wire, tubing and black powder to make it appear like an authentic device.

Hugh Diver told me how he was wrongly arrested in November 1996, along with his brother Anthony (who was terminally ill with cancer) and brother-in-law Barney Shovlin, under Section 30 of the Offences against the State Act in connection with the arson attack and the planting of explosives. The family controlled the right of way to the mast site, and the Shovlins, who lived closest held the keys to one of the gates to the mountain. Diver recalled how, after their homes were searched, they were taken to Glenties Garda Station for interrogation.

The three men were released without charge after twenty-four hours in detention and heard nothing more about the incident. A charge against Hugh Diver for the illegal possession of poteen, found during the raid on his home, was also dropped after evidence was given by a local doctor that it had been prescribed for the treatment of his arthritis. According to Diver, the box containing the twelve bottles of poteen was left at the door of his home by an unknown caller some days earlier. He maintained that he had not been on the mountain at the anti-mast protests for some ten months before his arrest but had openly accused gardaí of illegally entering the Telecom-owned site in December 1995 using bolt cutters, in order to install the CMI Portakabin. According to Diver, a senior garda defended this entry on the grounds of public safety.

Diver pointed out how ill his brother was, saying he rarely attended the picket, while his brother-in-law 'never joined the protest'. The men believed the family was singled out because 'they were the landowners who facilitated access for the anti-MMDS protestors'. Tragically, Anthony Diver's wife, Mary, who was forty-eight, was diagnosed with cancer shortly after her husband's arrest in November 1999 and died very soon afterwards. The family believed that her husband's arrest 'contributed directly to the sudden and unexpected deterioration in Mary's health'. Hugh recalled how she was buried in a suit she had bought to wear to her terminally ill husband's funeral. Anthony himself died in early 2000, aged fifty-one.[3]

Hugh described how Sergeant White had tried to get him to admit that he was a member of the IRA. He believed that White was taping their conversation when the garda drove him home following his arrest, in the hope of obtaining an incriminating confession. It later emerged that it was White who had planted the explosive device, which, another garda confirmed, had been assembled in the local barracks. These extraordinary revelations contributed to calls by Gildea and another TD, Jim Higgins, for an independent inquiry into the activities of some gardaí in Donegal.

The disclosures about the planted evidence at the MMDS mast in Ardara coincided with the conclusion of the year-long investigation led by Assistant Commissioner Carty into other 'explosive finds' across Donegal. In April 2000, I was able to report the sensational claim that members of the gardaí were suspected of having placed bags of ground-down fertiliser of the type used by the IRA at three locations. In late November 1993, a find that included two bags of fertiliser mix was made in sheds near the 19th Hole pub at Bridgend, on the main road from Letterkenny to Derry. Similar bags with ground-up fertiliser were found near Donegal town in early 1994, while in June 1994, at Rossnowlagh, a similar discovery contained material normally associated with IRA bombs. While the gardaí initially believed they were IRA materials, a senior garda source told me that they were 'now being examined again in the context of the current investigation'. The find at Rossnowlagh was particularly sinister as its discovery coincided with the annual Orange Order parade through the south Donegal town.

During the same week, the case involving over 160 summonses against the McBrearty family and associates was adjourned at the request of the DPP, who said that the matter should await the findings of the Carty investigation into Garda misbehaviour in Donegal. Meanwhile, Frank McBrearty senior and junior, and Mark and Roisín McConnell lodged High Court proceedings against the State for the hurt and damage caused by the false allegations made against them.

The claims made by Roisín about her treatment while in Garda custody in December 1996 were particularly harrowing, and, once again, involved Sergeant White, who threatened her that her young child would be put into care if she did not implicate her husband in Barron's death. She recalled him saying, 'I was going to jail for seven years and I probably would never see my son again' and telling her to 'swear on my wain's life that Mark McConnell had nothing to do with the death of Richie Barron'. Following this, Roisín 'swore on my wain's life' that her husband had nothing to do with the death. But 'then he started to roar and shout, I was nothing but a dirty lying murdering bastard, that I would use my child in that way … that was the worst thing that he said to me.'[4]

In January 2001, a development in the High Court in a case involving another Donegal publican, Frank Shortt, exposed more details of the corrupt activities of Lennon, McMahon and McGlinchey.[5] Shortt had been convicted in 1995 for allowing his premises at Quigley's Point, near Redcastle on the Inishowen peninsula, to be used for the sale of illicit drugs, and he served twenty-nine months in jail. Shortt held music events in his pub, and his customers from across Inishowen and Derry commonly used cannabis and ecstasy. His complaints to senior gardaí about the problem of illegal drug dealing were largely ignored. Instead, he came to the attention of McMahon and Lennon, who hatched a plan to get McGlinchey to plant hash and E-tabs at the club.

Statements made by Sheenagh McMahon and McGlinchey to the Carty team cast new light on Shortt's case when they confirmed that the detective and superintendent had arranged for the planting of drugs seized in a raid at the bar in Quigley's Point. McGlinchey admitted to the Carty inquiry that she had purchased the illicit drugs and planted them at Shortt's nightclub. In February 2001 the *Post* was able to report in detail on how she was paid £400 by one of the gardaí to do so: 'She has claimed that she returned with the drugs to a garda squad car and gave them to one of the officers who was accompanied by two other members of the force. She has claimed that the gardai then divided up the drugs into smaller packs or "deals" which she was told to plant in the target building.'[6] Sheenagh McMahon described how she discovered writing in her husband's notebook referring to the 'set-up' of Frank Shortt.

The two women's evidence resulted in a decision by the Court of Criminal Appeal (CCA) to overturn Shortt's conviction. It determined that the conviction was unsafe and that Shortt was entitled to a miscarriage of justice certificate and compensation. The court also found that Lennon and McMahon committed perjury at Shortt's original trial. The evidence provided by Sheenagh, including the notebook where her estranged husband referred to the 'set-up', led to further calls by Jim Higgins TD for a public inquiry into allegations of Garda corruption in the north-west.

In April 2001 Lennon and McMahon were subjected to internal Garda disciplinary proceedings following the admissions by McGlinchey to the Carty inquiry in relation to the hoax bombs and the planting of drugs in Shortt's night club. McMahon was also questioned about the reference to a 'set-up' at the Quigley's Point bar in his notebook.[7] Another entry in it related to the murder of Donegal Sinn Féin councillor Eddie Fullerton, who was killed at his home in Buncrana in May 1991. The note referred to a 'backhander' of £1,000 allegedly given to a man who lived in the town and was an associate of Fullerton. No one was ever charged in connection with the killing of Fullerton, for which the Ulster Defence Association/Ulster Freedom Fighters claimed responsibility. However, a number of gardaí in Buncrana, including McMahon, were involved in what has since been described as a flawed investigation into the murder of the popular politician.

Other national media did not follow the extraordinary events in the north-west Garda division with anywhere near the same energy as the *Post*. The security correspondents of the main newspapers either ignored the emerging story or quoted their Garda sources as denying that any such criminal behaviour, including framing innocent people for murder, planting explosive-like devices and making false bomb finds, had taken place.

On completion of their investigation into Garda malpractice in the north-west, Carty and McNally concluded that serious criminal charges could be laid against seven members of the force. The evidence they collected included the statements by Sheenagh McMahon, Bernard Conlon and William Doherty, who implicated members of the force in various criminal offences. It would take some time to confirm that Superintendent Kevin Lennon, Sergeant John White and Garda John O'Dowd were on the top of the list of those potentially facing criminal charges. White was suspended from the force in 2000 and later charged in relation to his handling of Bernard Conlon and the fabrication of evidence against Frank McBrearty junior and Mark McConnell. He was also prosecuted for planting a sawn-off shotgun at a halting site in Burnfoot, in the Inishowen peninsula, but was acquitted on this charge.[8] Following the CCA hearings in May 2002, Lennon was suspended from duty and was later fired by the government.

Meanwhile, the Department of Justice, the Garda Síochána and the government struggled to respond to the ongoing revelations about corruption in the force.

Chapter Sixteen

Courts and Tribunals

BY NOVEMBER 2001, THREE INTERNAL GARDA inquiries had led to charges against six people, including Sergeant White, who was accused of the illegal possession of a gun. At the same time disciplinary proceedings were being brought against a number of gardaí. As the government continued to resist calls by opposition TDs for a public inquiry and narrowly defeated a motion calling for such an investigation, the political pressure intensified when a new post-mortem on the exhumed remains of Richie Barron carried out for the inquest in 2002 found that the cattle dealer was most likely the victim of a hit and run. Pathologist Marie Cassidy determined that the cause of death was the result of a car mirror or bumper hitting Barron. Wounds on his hands were consistent with a traffic collision rather than defending himself from an assault, she concluded. Due to the massive trauma he suffered, Barron would have lost consciousness almost immediately. Her conclusions raised fresh concerns about how the gardaí obtained the alleged confession signed by Frank McBrearty junior. In response, Minister for Justice John O'Donoghue appointed Senior Counsel Shane Murphy to examine all Garda files relating to the investigation into Barron's death.[1]

As the new year approached Taoiseach Bertie Ahern said that he would not rule out a public inquiry into the McBrearty case and expressed his concern about anything that brought the integrity of members of the force into question. He added that it would be in the interest of both individuals and the Garda Síochána that all the issues arising in the context of Donegal were addressed. As expected, and in the wake of the report by Murphy, John O'Donoghue announced the establishment of a judicial tribunal in February 2002.

Initially, there were concerns that the tribunal might be held in private, as suggested by Attorney General Michael McDowell, who cited the ongoing civil actions by the extended McBrearty family in Donegal, which, he argued, could be prejudiced by a public inquiry. The first of these legal actions, taken by lawyers acting for Roisín McConnell, was due to open in the High Court in mid-April and was likely to expose details of her horrific mistreatment in Garda custody. The *Post* revealed how she was verbally and physically assaulted by members of the force in Letterkenny Garda Station, forced to pray for the forgiveness of her dead father for the killing of Barron and accused by a detective of being a member of the IRA. She claimed that she was shown photos of Barron's body and that lights were 'switched on and off repeatedly in order to disorient her'. She was told her child would be taken from her. The statement alleged that following her arrest, Roisín suffered mental health issues, 'lost her job and has been unable to bear more children because of the medication she required as part of her treatment'.[2] (Fortunately, she recovered, and some years later gave birth to her second child.)

Frank McBrearty senior, who claimed that his profitable pub and nightclub business in Raphoe had been destroyed by the false allegations made against him and his family, agreed to suspend his civil action against the Garda Commissioner, minister for justice and attorney general, pending the outcome of the proposed judicial inquiry. The government announced that the public tribunal would be chaired by Judge Frederick Morris, the retired president of the High Court and a former legal advisor to Fianna Fáil, who participated in the party's fundraising committee in the 1980s. Its terms of reference included an examination of the Garda handling of informers, the circumstances surrounding the arrest and detention of McBrearty junior and Mark McConnell following Barron's death, and other incidents, such as the preparation and planting of 'hoax bombs' around the county and of the device left at the MMDS mast at Ardara.

McBrearty senior criticised the failure to include an investigation into the inadequate response of Minister O'Donoghue and his predecessor, Nora Owen, Garda Commissioner Pat Byrne, the attorney general and the chief state solicitor in Donegal to the revelations of Garda corruption and criminality in the north-west. He said that the inquiry should also examine the conviction of Frank Shortt in 1995, the raid on the farm of Alfie Gallagher in St Johnston in 1999 and the flawed Garda investigation into the assassination of Eddie Fullerton in 1990.[3] Through their solicitor, David Walley, the McBreartys made a complaint to the European Court of Human Rights over the shortcomings of the terms of reference and the failure to include the State's response to their complaints about the Garda Síochána since 1996. They and other victims of Garda abuse in Donegal decided not to seek legal representation at the tribunal due to these shortcomings and because it failed to guarantee their legal and other costs arising from the inquiry.[4] The tribunal commenced its inquiries without enjoying the full confidence of the victims of Garda wrong-doing and corruption.

In the meantime, Martin Giblin SC was still seeking information from the Garda Commissioner and the minister surrounding the alleged statement of confession by McBrearty junior taken in Letterkenny by Dublin-based detectives sent there to investigate, including John Melody and John Fitzpatrick. The detectives insisted that McBrearty made a voluntary confession to murder, but McBrearty claimed that if he signed anything, it was in relation to his father's innocence and that he was not aware of any incriminating information that may have been on the other pages of any document he signed. The legal team also sought the personnel file of Sergeant John White and details of payments made to

Garda informants Doherty, Conlon and Robert McBride. Conlon and McBride had been used by Doherty to make false allegations to the gardaí against the McBreartys.

Garda John O'Dowd was central to another request by Giblin and his legal team, when they sought documents disclosing the minister's level of knowledge in relation to the refusal of some gardaí to disclose their whereabouts and actions on the night of Barron's death.[5] Judge Morris would later describe O'Dowd's account of his conversation with Eamon Strain as 'a complete invention'. 'It is difficult to understand why, if Garda O'Dowd had nothing to hide, he told so many lies about his behaviour that evening,' the tribunal chairman said.[6] O'Dowd denied to the tribunal that he had 'hit' the cattle dealer; he was not charged in connection with Richie Barron's death and was exonerated by Judge Morris in his final report.

During investigations I carried out in 2001, I met with a source in the Nuremore Hotel in Castleblayney, County Monaghan. They had obtained copies of the statements made by dozens of witnesses to the Carty team during their investigation into Richie Barron's death. In the course of several hours together, I took copious notes. When the meeting finished it was after dark, and we left the hotel, with me helping to carry the boxes of documents to my contact's car. As it turned out, he was parked alongside my Nissan Primera, and we said our goodbyes after loading up the boot of his car. After finishing the two-hour journey to Dublin, I parked close to my street and went for a drink. Some time later, I came out of the public house to discover that my car was missing, presumed stolen. It was a calm autumn evening in a quiet neighbourhood where car theft was uncommon. I reported it to the local Garda station and heard nothing for two weeks.

I then got a call to inform me that the car had been found some 400 yards from my home in another estate. It turned out that it was left outside the house of a man who was away for a fortnight and found the car, with its doors unlocked, when he returned home. Nothing was missing, including books containing indecipherable notes in my unique shorthand which were still lying on the back seat.

When, a few days after I retrieved the car, I spoke to Chief Superintendent Austin McNally, who was leading the Carty investigation, he concluded that it had been stolen by rogue members of the force, some of whom must have observed me at the hotel in Monaghan and presumed that I took the boxes of documents with me to Dublin. They included witness statements taken by the Carty team, a number of which raised serious questions about members of the gardaí in relation to Richie Barron's death and the elaborate cover-up that ensued. Among them were statements by John Sweeney, Eamon Strain and Anne and Madge Toye, which exposed major inconsistencies in the accounts provided by O'Dowd, Mulligan and a host of other Garda witnesses to the Carty team and later to the tribunal. They would have been invaluable to members of the gardaí who felt threatened by the internal inquiry and what it might uncover.

Just weeks before the 2002 general election, the dramatic revelations of perjury, corruption and planted evidence that emerged from the appeal by Frank Shortt of his conviction and three-year jail sentence served to intensify the pressure on the government to widen the terms of reference of the Morris Tribunal. Supreme Court judge Adrian Hardiman was scathing of the lawyers for the State when he learned that the Garda Síochána had failed to provide evidence in its possession regarding the perjury committed by Detective Garda McMahon during Shortt's original trial.

Documents presented to the CCA during the hearing in May 2002 showed that Sheenagh McMahon had told the Carty investigation over two years previously that her husband admitted to committing perjury during the trial. She had a copy of her husband's Garda notebook which referred to 'Point Inn – perjury -set up. advice on proofs [*sic*]'.

She witnessed her husband, Lennon and two other gardaí preparing their evidence before Shortt's trial and said that her husband admitted to her that he lied under oath during the trial in 1995. 'He told me he had perjured himself in court and that he did it for Kevin Lennon, to help him get promoted,' she told the appeal court.[7] Her husband was upset, however, when Lennon got the 'Policeman of the Year' award for securing the Shortt conviction.

McMahon also told the court that bags of fertiliser, detonators and tubing were stored in her former home, and how the illicit drugs which she believed were connected to the Shortt case were kept in her house. During her account, she revealed to the court the domestic abuse she had suffered at the hands of her husband, who kicked and punched her and put a gun to her head. Once, after she let another garda into his bedroom to wake him up when he was hungover, he told her, 'I'll blow your fucking brains out.' She said she knew the gun was loaded, as it went off after the incident. In a separate incident, McMahon held a gun to the head of a fellow garda, Séamus Gordon, in Buncrana Garda Station, in 1992.

Adrienne McGlinchey also appeared before the court and confirmed that she had been given money by McMahon to buy the drugs and plant them in Shortt's pub before the raid in 1992. She claimed that then Inspector and now Superintendent Lennon was aware that the drugs were planted and that his promotion was, at least partly, the result of the successful conviction of Shortt. McGlinchey confirmed that she had helped transport hoax bombs across Donegal with McMahon and Lennon. She told the court that she was driven in a Garda surveillance van loaded with 'explosives material' to the disused shed in Rossnowlagh, and that they stopped on the way to purchase a bottle of vodka before leaving the 'hoax bomb'. It was discovered the next day and the media was told that it was 'an IRA arms cache'.

In 1999, Sheenagh McMahon was wrongfully arrested after her

husband produced a court Safety Order, which he obtained from a judge under false pretences. He then arranged for her arrest for breaching the barring order. As a result, her three children were placed in care. It took three years for her to regain custody and many more before she obtained an apology and damages from the State over her wrongful arrest. In the 2018 apology, lawyers for the State, the Garda Síochána, the minister for justice and Noel McMahon said in open court that: 'The Defendants concede liability on the basis that they accept that the Plaintiff was wrongfully arrested and detained on 30th June 1999, by reason of the arresting Garda executing a Safety Order produced by the Plaintiff's husband which in fact had never been issued by the District Court.' Sheenagh was awarded €20,000 in damages. She refused an offer of an additional €5,000 if she would agree to the apology not being read out in court.

Three years later, and much to the horror of his former wife and other victims of his violence and corruption, Noel McMahon was awarded a Scott medal for bravery for the role he played in the rescue of Don Tidey, who was kidnapped by the IRA in 1983. Sheenagh has questioned the veracity of her estranged husband's account of his part in the rescue, which was cited in the award ceremony in 2021.

Following the May 2002 general election, the government agreed to widen the terms of reference of the Morris Tribunal to include the experience of Frank Shortt, the Divers of Ardara, Alfie Gallagher and other incidents. The murder of Eddie Fullerton was not included, even though McMahon was among the gardaí who handled material seized by gardaí from the Fullertons' home. Aspects of the cross-border investigation continue to be questioned by Fullerton's family after it failed to identify any of those involved or lead to any arrests or convictions.

A number of gardaí were dismissed and others disciplined and transferred as a result of the inquiries into corruption in the Donegal division. John O'Dowd and Padraig Mulligan were both dismissed in

January 2003, while Kevin Lennon was sacked in October 2004. However, no one has ever been charged in connection with the mistreatment and abuse of members of the McBrearty family, their staff and other innocent victims of Garda abuse in the case. Hugh Diver died in 2010 while he was helping to cut down trees for a neighbour. His funeral was among the largest ever witnessed in Ardara.

The establishment of the Morris Tribunal was predicated on the myopic proposition that the egregious behaviour of gardaí in the north-west was unique to that division. It was a fundamental but strategic choice that would come back to bite governments and the police in the following years and has led to numerous miscarriages of justice, some of which have since been revisited.

In 1985, Joseph Grogan and Joseph Meleady, teenagers from Tallaght were wrongly convicted of malicious damage to a car in Templeogue in Dublin. Known as the Tallaght Two, the two men spent almost five years in juvenile prison before they were released. I wrote about the case in the *Sunday Tribune*, in *Magill* in 1988 and later in *The Sunday Business Post*, after establishing that three different youths were involved in the theft. Subsequent investigations, including by RTÉ and one which I published in the *Post* in 1993, and which led to me receiving the Justice in Media award, proved that members of the gardaí had misled the court by failing to disclose fingerprint evidence they discovered in the stolen car. The convictions were quashed in 1995 when the CCA ruled that the evidence was unsafe.[8]

Many other examples of such mistreatment of suspects by gardaí and false confessions have since come to light. For example, grievous Garda misbehaviour was evident in the attempt to frame Joanne Hayes for the murder of a newborn baby in Caherciveen, known as Baby John, in south Kerry in April 1984. Hayes had given birth to a child who died soon afterwards and whose body she disposed of on land close to her home in Abbeydorney some 80km north of Caherciveen. In the course of the investigation, the murder squad attempted to frame Hayes, whom they outrageously accused of having twins with two different fathers. Hayes, her sister and two brothers admitted to killing or disposing of Baby John during their interrogations by gardaí in Tralee Garda Station. The now discredited Kerry Babies Tribunal castigated the Hayes family and defended the gardaí involved in extracting the confessions.

It has recently emerged that the baby found dead in Caherciveen may have been killed by a now deceased family member of the young woman who gave birth to the child. It is also suspected that another since deceased family member disposed of Baby John on the beach where he was found. The father of the family was a garda who died several years before the woman gave birth to Baby John. Her brother was a serving garda in County Kerry when the infant was brutally killed soon after his birth. This brother, who lived a troubled life, died some years before a DNA search was commenced. He lived with his mother until she died a few years before his own death. He was previously suspected of vandalising the headstone of the baby's grave on two occasions after it was erected by the local undertaker, Tom Cournane. According to the gardaí, the identity of Baby John's parents was established following a general search for DNA matches among people living in the area, which led to their arrest and questioning in 2023. In April 2026, the Garda Síochána confirmed that a file had been sent to the DPP in relation to the death of the baby.

The solicitor for the child's parents, Padraig O'Connell, said to me in response to this development that his clients denied any involvement in the murder of the child and all other allegations put to them. He said they would not make any further comment until they learn whether the DPP intends to prosecute them in relation to the crime. Gardaí took DNA samples from the couple while under arrest in March 2023, which are believed to have confirmed they were the parents of Baby John.

In June 2026, I spoke to Jack Griffin, a farmer and builder who discovered the body of Baby John when he was running along White

Strand on the evening of 14 April 1984. He described how he found the body of the infant face down between the rocks with stab marks on his back. He ran to his brother-in-law's house and they went back to the scene before contacting the local Garda station. A day after the gruesome discovery, a post-mortem was carried out by the state pathologist, Dr John Harbison, who concluded that the neck of the baby was broken before his death and there were twenty-eight stab wounds to the neck, chest and back. There were two large wounds to the chest where the heart had been stabbed during what Harbison described as a panic frenzy. The umbilical cord had been cut flush with the skin, which was in contravention of best nursing practice, as a clamp could not be applied in the event of unexpected bleeding. This, he suggested, meant that the birth did not occur under medical supervision. The wounds, he believed, were inflicted by a 'sharp pointed knife' or stiletto-type instrument. He estimated that the baby was born three or four days prior to his examination and had died within a day or so of its birth. Others familiar with the case suggested that the wounds could have been caused by a knitting needle.

Griffin said that the body was naked, washed and dry when he found it. He said he was shocked when he learned of the extent of the baby's wounds and was distressed for many years after his shocking and horrific experience. A Goulding's 0-7-30 fertiliser bag, tied at the top but with a hole in the bottom, was found near the body. The first garda who came on the scene found a brown plastic shopping bag with another clear plastic bag inside it. It was assumed by gardaí that the body had been placed in the plastic bags, which were put into the fertiliser bag but then fell through the hole in the bottom. The bags were sent by the exhibits officer, Sergeant Patrick Reidy, to the Forensic Science Laboratory in Dublin, but no fingerprint or detailed forensic testing was carried out on them. They were last handled by Sergeant Reidy but disappeared after he claimed to have left them at Tralee Garda Station during the subsequent investigation. Sergeant Reidy lived on the same street and was friendly with the family of the woman who gave birth to the child. He had also served in the force with her late father. Some years before he died, Reidy informed a source to whom I spoke that he knew who killed Baby John but would 'leave it to others find out'.[9]

Detective Sergeant Joe Shelly with Detective Garda John Harrington were the first members of the Garda Technical Bureau known as the 'murder squad' sent to Caherciveen to investigate the death of Baby John after the discovery of the child's body in April 1984. They were followed by Detective Sergeant Gerry O'Carroll and Detective Garda P.J. Browne, both from Listowel in County Kerry. The investigation into the death of Baby John moved from Caherciveen to Tralee when they learned that Joanne Hayes had recently given birth to a child whose whereabouts were unknown to the local doctor and medical staff at the hospital where she presented with a reported miscarriage. The head of the murder squad, Superintendent John Courtney, from Annascaul in Kerry, later joined the team and participated in the interrogation of Joanne and her family. The confessions were made before the body of Joanne Hayes' deceased infant was recovered. Following the discovery of her baby on the family farm, where she said she had left the body of her own dead child, Joanne Hayes was charged with murder, and other members of her family were charged with concealing the birth and disposing of the infant found on the rocks in Caherciveen. She confessed to killing Baby John in a statement taken by Detective Sergeant O'Carroll.

For many years O'Carroll insisted that Joanne Hayes may have given birth to two children by different fathers in 1984, based on the theory of superfecundation, which explained why her dead infant and Baby John had two different blood groups. There had never been such a case in Ireland or Britain, and the possibility that Joanne Hayes had experienced such a freak biological event was discounted by the State pathologist during the hearings of the Kerry Babies Tribunal. The fact that three senior officers involved in securing confessions from members of the

Hayes family for a murder they could not have committed were all from Kerry did not go unnoticed. Joanne Hayes claimed that Garda Browne slapped her in the face and sat her on his lap in Tralee Garda Station. She claimed that Superintendent Courtney had shoved his finger into her shoulder. She said that O'Carroll told her that her baby would haunt her for the rest of her life. Her brother, Mike Hayes, accused Sergeant Shelly of 'punching him in the stomach' and 'grabbing him by the collar and pulling him towards him' in the Garda station.

The tribunal chairman, Justice Kevin Lynch, dismissed the allegations of assault as untrue and the threats as 'doubtful'. He also concluded that Joanne Hayes was not the mother of Baby John.[10] If superfecundation was a freak event in medical and biological science, the extraction of identical and simultaneous confessions to participation in, and covering up, a murder by four different people in separate rooms must be equally rare in the history of policing.

It was also nothing short of remarkable that Joanne Hayes and family members admitted to placing Baby John in a fertiliser or turf bag, which, they said, was then thrown into the sea at Slea Head on the Dingle Peninsula. Sergeant Reidy told the tribunal that it was common for items from the sea below Slea Head to wash up on the shore at Caherciveen. In fact, it is well known among fishers and maritime experts that the tides in south-west Kerry have carried bodies of drowned people and other material north as far as Clare, rather than down the coastline in a southerly direction. The untrue, contradictory and bizarre confessions to dumping the body of Baby John off Slea Head were made before the baby to which Joanne Hayes gave birth was found. It was discovered in a plastic bag in a pond on land near her home – information she had given to Liam Maloney, the local garda in Abbeydorney, in her first admissions about the child's death weeks earlier.

It has long been accepted that Joanne Hayes had nothing to do with the death of Baby John, and she and her family received an apology from the State in 2020, followed by a payment of damages. The question now is whether the finger was pointed at innocent people for a crime committed fifty miles away in order to disguise the possible role of a member of the force from a Garda family in the murder and to protect its reputation.

In later years, members of the murder squad were implicated in other controversies where Garda corruption or wrongdoing was uncovered. Detective Superintendent Joe Shelly, as he later became, was one of four senior officers whose role in the flawed investigation into the death of Richie Barron in Donegal was described as 'prejudiced, tendentious and utterly negligent in the highest degree' in the report of the Morris Tribunal in June 2005. In 2006, Shelly was named as one of three officers ultimately responsible for the shooting of John Carthy in Abbeylara, County Longford, in 2000. Carthy, who had a history of mental illness, was shot in the back by members of the Emergency Response Unit following a siege at his home. Shelly, the scene commander during the stand-off, refused Carthy's request to see a solicitor and for cigarettes. In 2006, I reported on how, during the siege, Shelly had concealed information from police negotiators about Carthy's poor relations with local gardaí. An inquiry chaired by Judge Robert Barr into Carthy's death, found that this failure was 'the most serious finding made against Superintendent Joe Shelly by the tribunal'.[11]

Superintendent Courtney went on to play a significant role in the wrongful conviction of three men – Osgur Breathnach, Nicky Kelly and Brian McNally – who were accused of the Sallins Train robbery in 1976. They claimed that statements they made while in custody were obtained after they were subjected to severe physical and mental abuse by members of the Garda 'heavy gang'. The men received financial compensation from the State for their mistreatment. In June 2026, the CCA heard that the State was not going to contest the application to the High Court for a miscarriage of justice by Osgur Breathnach after a decades-long campaign to prove their innocence. Brian McNally died the following day.

PART III

Chapter Seventeen

The Pussy Book

IN MAY 1999, PATRICK GALLAGHER FULFILLED his promise to attend the Moriarty Tribunal at Dublin Castle and defend the reputation of his political mentor and guide, Charlie Haughey, who may not have been entirely grateful for the assistance. Gallagher told Judge Moriarty about the payment made to Haughey following the meeting at the politician's home in late 1979, stating that he agreed to pay £300,000 to clear Haughey's debt to AIB,[1] thereby allowing his friend to avoid bankruptcy and take up the office of taoiseach.

In return for the money, Gallagher told the tribunal, Haughey agreed to sell him 35 acres of land at Kinsealy at £35,000 an acre. Zoned for agricultural use only, the land was worth just £4,000 an acre, so it would have been an exceptionally generous deal for the politician. Gallagher said he was surprised to learn, just two days before he gave his evidence at Dublin Castle, that the so-called land sale was not legally enforceable. At any rate, it never went ahead, as Gallagher's company collapsed in 1982.

At the Flood Tribunal, hearings focused on the central character in its corruption investigation, Ray Burke, and those associated with the payments he received in June 1989, including Mick Bailey, Joseph Murphy senior and junior, as well as the politicians who tried to manage the fallout from the controversy. Burke had disappeared from public view following his resignation in October 1997, but, on arrival at the tribunal, he appeared to have lost none of his abrasive and confrontational approach. He seemed most concerned with limiting the damage to his financial position, as well as correcting the misinformation he had provided to the Dáil during his tearful 'line in the sand' speech just weeks before he was forced to step down as minister and from politics.

With his familiar bullish confidence, Burke began his evidence on the 'donations' he received by expressing his amazement at the generosity of the business community towards the Fianna Fáil-led minority government during the 1989 election campaign.[2] He admitted that he misled the Dáil on three separate occasions over the payment he accepted at his home and other monies he got before the election. In contrast with Gogarty's assertion that the cash amount from JMSE was £30,000, he confirmed that he received £20,000 in cash and a cheque for £10,000. In September 1997, he had told the Dáil he got £30,000 in cash. He said Bailey unexpectedly brought Gogarty, whom he had never met before and 'wished he never had at all', who had told him that JMSE wanted to give him an election contribution. He said he hardly knew Bailey but then agreed that the builder was a member of the St Margaret's Cumann of Fianna Fáil in his constituency. He also denied Gogarty's claims that Joe Murphy junior attended the meeting in his home and that Bailey gave him an envelope stuffed with cash on the occasion.

Burke confirmed that he received £129,000 in donations during the 1989 election campaign but could account for less than £20,000 of the total. He accepted that the £10,000 he passed on to the party came from the £30,000 he received from Fitzwilton/Rennicks and not from the JMSE payment. He admitted that he was wrong to claim that £30,000 was the largest donation he received, as he also took £35,000 from another donor whom he declined to identify. This was the payment from Oliver Barry of Century Radio, whose commercial interests were promoted by Burke. He said that mistakes in his 1997 Dáil statement were due to the 'considerable emotional stress' he was under at the time. Burke agreed that he opened an overseas account in Jersey in 1984, into which he placed £94,000. The account was closed in 1994, and he transferred the contents to an Irish account, he said. It was unclear 'whether Burke gave an accurate reply to Fine Gael TD, Jim O'Keeffe [in the Dáil] when he said he had no offshore accounts'.[3]

If Burke was evasive and muddled in his recollections, Bailey was even more confusing as he blundered his way through his evidence, at one point claiming that his 'head was spinning' after five days of grilling by tribunal counsel Des O'Neill SC. As I noted at the time, Bailey's 'inability or refusal to answer simple questions, including non-contentious ones with which he had previously dealt, became more pronounced as the week went on. His hesitancy and the admission that he lied to this reporter on several occasions did not help.'

While giving evidence, Bailey made a dramatic new claim that he paid Gogarty a 'finder's fee' of £162,000, given in payments over six years, in return for the former JMSE chairman's help in acquiring the 720 acres of land in north Dublin from the company. He was rigorously interrogated by O'Neill, who established that there was not a shred of evidence to back up the story. The audience in the Printworks of Dublin Castle was highly amused when Bailey showed a small notebook with a picture of a kitten on the front cover as his proof of three alleged payments to Gogarty in amounts of £15,000, £10,000 and £50,000, purportedly made between June and September 1990. The hand-scrawled entries in different inks were not convincing. Bailey's accountant told the tribunal that he had no records of cheques for £50,000 made out to Gogarty, as Bailey had described in his evidence.

Relying on misleading bank documents and the Bailey brothers' handwritten and confusing ledger, the Baileys' attempt to undermine Gogarty's credibility fell flat on its face. The 'pussy book', as it was referred to, contained details of alleged income and the under-the-counter cash payments to Gogarty in different coloured inks and handwriting, and fell well short of what would be acceptable to any self-respecting auditor or book-keeper.[4]

The builder also contradicted Burke's claim that he was not expecting Gogarty to arrive at the minister's home for their meeting. He admitted to telling a series of lies to me during interviews he gave to the *Post* in 1997, including that he didn't attend the meeting in Burke's home or hand over any money. He had also told me that he saw Gogarty giving Burke an envelope 'stuffed with cash' in the house, but when giving evidence at the tribunal said that he saw two envelopes the size of two '9 x 2'-inch bricks changing hands.

Bailey's credibility was further challenged when O'Neill put to him the contents of a detailed statement I had made to the tribunal about a letter he sent to Gogarty in June 1989, in which he offered to procure zoning in north Dublin in exchange for a 50 per cent share of the company that owned the land and which he had read to me over the phone. The letter was dated 8 June, just days before the meeting in Burke's house, creating the not unreasonable suspicion that they were directly connected to each other. Bailey claimed he did not have the letter, so could not have read extracts to me. Asked why he told a journalist something that was untrue, Bailey replied that he 'did not know'.

'Is that the best you can do, Mr Bailey? Were you trying to mislead Mr Connolly or were you trying to send him on a wild goose chase of some sort?' asked O'Neill.

'I said I don't know,' replied Bailey.

'You don't know why it is that you have given an untrue account of events to a journalist who is asking you for your account of events. Is that right?' O'Neill persisted.

'That's correct.'

He agreed that he had told me that the cheque for £50,000 he stuffed in Gogarty's pocket was in return for his assistance with the purchase of a JMSE property in Baggot Street but conceded that this was untrue.

'Why did you tell Mr Connolly an untruth?' the tribunal lawyer asked.

'Because he was persistently asking questions and that was one question. That was one answer I gave him that was an untruth,' Bailey admitted. Asked why it suited him to lie at the time, he said, 'Because I didn't want to tell him that Gogarty got a finder's fee from me.'

This claim unravelled when he claimed to have 'paid off' Gogarty before the land deal with JMSE was closed. Yet he conceded that Gogarty never cashed any of the supposed cheques or received any of the promised cash that was noted in the company's 'pussy book'. Either way, it would have been illegal to pay a 'finder's fee' to the director of a company from which he was purchasing land, as Gogarty's counsel, Brian O'Moore SC, later pointed out to Bailey.

Bailey admitted that he made an offer to the Murphys to sell them back 50 per cent of the land bank for an outrageous £8 million just months after he paid £2.3 million for it and while it remained un-zoned for residential development. 'I threw out a figure of £8 million to see would I catch a sprat and if I caught a sprat, well and good, he may turn into a fish,' he explained, much to the amusement of the crowd.

Further insights into the relationship between Bailey, Burke and George Redmond emerged when an 'index of files' seized by the CAB at the former planning official's home in February 1999 were provided to the *Post*. The files were released by the CAB following a successful court application for them by the tribunal. They showed that Redmond had accounts in 'a large number of financial institutions over many years, at various times [and] had deposits of up to £200,000 in the Isle of Man'. The files also contained a series of photographs of Redmond with Burke.

Another person mentioned in the index was Redmond's friend Jim Kennedy, whose name appeared alongside an amount of £110,000. Redmond claimed the money was an investment he made in gaming machines.

The files contained details of planning issues dating back to the 1970s. These showed that 'Redmond appeared to retain a great interest in property development, particularly in west Dublin, well after his retirement.' Among them were extensive files relating to Gilmartin's Quarryvale project, 'with correspondence relating to the development from 1988 to 1993,' the *Post* reported.

This latest treasure trove of information revealed a thread of connections between a number of individuals central to both the Gogarty and Gilmartin modules of the inquiry. It was suspected that the CAB may previously have withheld the information in order to establish what, if any, potential damage the contents of the files posed to the Garda Síochána and how to mitigate this.

When the Flood Tribunal hearings resumed after a summer break to hear the evidence of Joe Murphy senior, they were forced to relocate to Guernsey, as the elderly businessman was not well enough to travel to Dublin. The eighty-two-year-old said he would only engage in private with Judge Flood and his team, due to what his psychiatrist called an 'irrational' fear of the media. This did not, however, stop the reclusive Murphy from posing for press photographers when he arrived for his hearing at the Les Cotils Christian Centre in St Peter Port in early October 1999.

Over his four days of direct, *in camera* evidence, later read publicly into the record in Dublin Castle, Murphy senior confirmed his reputation as a tough, shrewd and uncompromising operator. Born in Caherciveen, he and his brother John were known respectively as 'the Grey' and 'the Green' Murphy, for the distinctive colour of their vans, which were a familiar sight in London and other cities across England. The brothers made vast fortunes in the post-war reconstruction of Britain and employed many thousands of Irish navvies in road building, cable laying and tunnelling projects from the 1950s on.

The tribunal heard the controversial claims made by deceased former JMSE managing director, Liam Conroy, who described how Joe Murphy moved to Guernsey in 1976 and evaded UK income tax and exchange control regulations by depositing large sums of undeclared income in Switzerland and Ireland. These, and other allegations involving the use of false invoices and trusts in the Bahamas, the Cayman Islands and Liechtenstein to avoid tax, were made by Conroy in the affidavit he signed in 1990 as part of his High Court action against Murphy senior.

Gogarty had submitted that the decision to sell the JMSE lands in north Dublin was motivated by Murphy senior's fear that Conroy's allegations would emerge and that he would be subject to unwelcome scrutiny from the Revenue Commissioners and possibly worse. The payment to Burke was made to ensure that the lands were rezoned in order to maximise their value before being sold off. Murphy senior dismissed Conroy as a 'fantasist' and Gogarty as a 'deceitful liar', even though he had appointed both men to run the Irish part of his business empire at different times. He claimed to know nothing about the sale of land in north Dublin or much else about the activities of JMSE since 1982. He said he had never heard of Burke or Bailey 'until the tribunal started' and had no knowledge of any payment by his company to the former minister. When the tribunal presented him with letters showing contacts between him and JMSE executives since 1982, including in relation to the sale of the land in north Dublin, he claimed that he had never seen them before.[5]

Murphy had difficulty explaining two accounts he controlled in Ireland in the late 1980s, having previously stated that he'd had none in the country since 1976. His plausibility was further eroded when an old schoolfriend, Batt O'Shea, took to the stand and explained how he purchased a family home in Dublin for Murphy and his second wife, Una, in Fitzwilliam Place in Dublin in 1968. This was despite Murphy telling the tribunal that he was a tax exile at the time. O'Shea and his partner, Tom Shanahan, were among the biggest house builders in Dublin between the 1950s and 1970s, and they had extensive dealings with Redmond when he was a senior planning official during those years.

O'Shea, with a wit as sharp as Gogarty's, regaled the audience in Dublin Castle with his description of the day he gave Redmond £200 to buy golf balls. A regular golfing partner of the planning official, O'Shea explained, 'I gave him £200 to buy golf balls because when I was playing golf with him, Jesus, if his ball went into the rough, he would give the day looking for it. You would think it was gold. And I gave him £200 like, to buy golf balls and thanks for the advice you gave us in Portmarnock.'

When O'Shea was asked about a record in Redmond's diary of an appointment with him at 4 p.m. on Christmas Eve, 1989, he gave the audience another laugh: '"It could have been for a game of golf with Redmond," he agreed with Redmond's solicitor, Anthony Harris. He said Redmond was keen to play at Elm Park where O'Shea was a member. Even in the dark, it seemed.'[6]

Thirty-two-year-old Joseph Murphy junior was as vague as his father when it came to his knowledge of the JMSE payment to Burke. He insisted that he was not present in the politician's home with Gogarty and did not know of his company's involvement until reports appeared in the *Post* in March 1996. He said that Gogarty had, since 1992, been intent on 'destroying the Murphy's [*sic*] and their extensive business interests by using the triple force of the Revenue Commissioners, the Garda and the media.'

Gogarty believed that Murphy junior was angry at the manner in which he obtained his pension entitlements. Before he left the company Murphy senior had asked Gogarty to finalise a payment owed to JMSE by the ESB and agreed to pay him 50 per cent of any amount over £40,000 that he negotiated. Gogarty obtained a cheque for £750,000 from the ESB, which he gave to his solicitor, Gerry Sheedy, who lodged it in an escrow account. After protracted discussions, JMSE agreed to pay Gogarty £355,000.

Murphy junior apologised for the abusive and threatening phone calls he made to Gogarty in June 1994, saying they were prompted by a suspicion that Revenue was given false information by the disgruntled former company chairman. He claimed that when he asked about the

March 1996 story in the *Post*, his father and company chief executive, Frank Reynolds, denied that any payments were made to Burke. They and financial controller, Roger Copsey, repeated their denial when another article appeared in the newspaper in May 1997. Murphy junior could not explain why Copsey made a request for £30,000 to the company solicitor, Denis McArdle, on 8 June 1989 (the date of the letter sent by Mick Bailey to Gogarty offering to develop the JMSE lands in north Dublin in a joint venture), which the legal adviser noted as 'a political contribution'. Neither could he account for the fact that his co-directors were openly discussing the JMSE payment to Burke in June 1997, nor that it was reimbursed by other companies in the group in late 1996. The tribunal confirmed that Murphy junior certainly knew about the payment soon after he met Dermot Ahern in London, when Copsey told him just days later that he recalled a 'political contribution involving Jim Gogarty'.[7]

In mid-December 1999, George Redmond pleaded guilty to ten charges of failing to submit tax returns, a significant vindication of the tribunal's investigation into planning corruption. This was before the tribunal began its hearings into the allegations by Tom Gilmartin against the former planner and his 'double act' partner Lawlor, as well as a host of other senior political and business figures. Redmond subsequently agreed to pay £800,000 in outstanding tax to the Revenue Commissioners, reportedly raising the funds from the sale of his home in Castleknock. He admitted to accepting large amounts from builders and developers during his employment as a senior planner but insisted that his only mistake was to offer his advice to those in need.

In early 2000, the Flood Tribunal opened the preliminary Quarryvale module of its public hearings to examine Gilmartin's claims about the deep corruption he experienced at the hands of crooked politicians, planners, businessmen and their advisers. First up was the PR consultant and former Fianna Fáil press officer Frank Dunlop, who faced a barrage of questions about his dealings with his wealthy client Owen O'Callaghan.

In his early evidence, Dunlop recounted how he obtained £175,000 from O'Callaghan for work on the Quarryvale project between 1991 and 1993, and that it was paid to Shefran. Some £80,000 of these 'fees' were diverted from Barkhill Ltd without the knowledge of Gilmartin, who had established the company to develop the retail centre at Quarryvale. The Barkhill accounts showed that O'Callaghan's company, Riga Ltd, paid out £1 million in Quarryvale-related payments from February to August 1991, before O'Callaghan became a director of Barkhill. This was subsequently repaid to Riga by Barkhill without authorisation from Gilmartin.

Dunlop admitted that most of his work for O'Callaghan during this period was lobbying elected members of Dublin County Council to support crucial motions for rezoning and planning for the retail development. He claimed that he spent the £175,000 on house refurbishment, ponies for his children, family holidays and an insurance policy. However, he admitted that he withdrew large amounts of cash at the time of a crucial vote on Quarryvale in May, as well as ahead of local government elections in June 1991. The tribunal believed that this money was spent on greasing the palms of councillors and candidates who voted as Dunlop directed.

Public attention was diverted from this evidence by a story from Dunlop about how a Fine Gael councillor had asked him for an incredible £250,000 to be lodged in an offshore account in return for his support for Quarryvale motions at the council. He wrote the name of the councillor who asked him for money on a piece of paper and gave the note to the tribunal chairman. The councillor was Tom Hand (by then deceased), who seconded the motion by Colm McGrath to rezone the Quarryvale lands in May 1991. His name was revealed by Sam Smyth in the *Irish Independent* the day after Dunlop disclosed it at the tribunal. It did not go unnoticed that this dramatic corruption claim by Dunlop concerned a dead Fine Gael councillor, while his illicit dealings with members of Fianna Fáil, for which he had served as a press officer and election organiser, did not feature as prominently.[8] The well-timed leak led to a panicked response by the Fine Gael leader, John Bruton, who denied Dunlop's claim that he had been told by the PR man about the bribery demand from his party colleague.

Dunlop confirmed to the tribunal that he never informed the gardaí about Hand's extortionate demand and insisted that this was the only politician who ever asked him for money in return for a rezoning vote. He also denied giving the story to Smyth but agreed the reporter had contacted him about it. Smyth confirmed that he tried, but failed, to contact Dunlop for a comment. The source of the story was not revealed, but there was only one suspect, as I pointed out:

> The story was nicely timed in public relations terms to swing media coverage away from Dunlop's risible performance at the tribunal last week, when he was unable to recall matters of fact on a large number of occasions. The Hand story is also likely to distract from a number of questions germane to the Quarryvale controversy itself. Above all, it removed attention from several key questions surrounding Dunlop's relationship with O'Callaghan and the Shefran payments. Why did O'Callaghan employ Dunlop on the Quarryvale project in January 1991, when the developer was not a director or shareholder in Barkhill, the company developing the retail project until September 1991?[9]

With Gilmartin's help, it would not take long for the tribunal and the media to tear Dunlop's veneer of innocence to shreds. Nor would this be the last attempt to use the media to muddy the waters and to undermine Judge Flood's efforts to uncover the scale of corruption in the Dublin planning system.

Chapter Eighteen

Fingers and Floods

ON EASTER SUNDAY 2000, THE MOST explosive and contentious story related to the planning inquiry up to that point was published in the *Post*. It originated with the claims brought to me by businessman Denis 'Starry' O'Brien over twelve months earlier. Headlined 'New FF bribes probe could lead to election', the front-page lead described how the tribunal was investigating a claim that two senior Fianna Fáil politicians had 'received £50,000 each in 1989 in return for assistance with the development of a major retail project in Dublin'. Without naming our source, the politicians or the property developer whom, O'Brien claimed, provided him with the money to bribe them, the story was run when the tribunal decided to call evidence on the allegations.

O'Brien claimed that he received an AIB cheque for £100,000 from Owen O'Callaghan and lodged it in his INBS account, before distributing the two payments to the politicians in September 1989. Despite a promise to me and orders from the tribunal to provide copies of the cheques and other incriminatory documents, O'Brien failed to do so. He did provide a deposit book for an account in the building society, which, he said, he opened in 1987 and used to hold the money for the payments. This recorded a sum of £50,000 which, he told me, was the balance in the account after he paid one of the politicians a cheque for the same amount in the Silver Springs Hotel in Cork, in September 1989. He claimed that the second payment was made to the still-serving politician in the

Burlington Hotel car park on the night of the all-Ireland GAA football final in September 1989. The only way to prove whether the entries in the deposit book were authentic was to obtain the cheque journal and records of the relevant branch from June to September 1989, when he claimed to have drawn the cheques, as well as details of lodgements between 1987 and 1989.

The tribunal ordered INBS to submit its records on the account opened by O'Brien, and, when these were not produced, called on its managing director, Michael Fingleton, to explain why. When he arrived on Good Friday, Fingleton, known as 'Fingers' in media and other circles, told Flood that floods at the INBS offices in Grafton Street in Dublin destroyed many of the building society's records. He did, however, produce boxes of what he described as summaries of transactions at the Cork branch between 1987 and 1989, covering the period when O'Brien said he opened his account, lodged and withdrew the £100,000. Following his appearance, Fingleton also signed a letter on behalf of INBS authorising the tribunal to access the back records for copies of a £100,000 cheque drawn on AIB South Mall in Cork, and to obtain details of how the two building society cheques were cashed. AIB was the clearing bank for INBS.

The stakes were raised for all concerned by the headline of the *Post* article, and the insertion, during the editing of the piece, of a line which suggested that 'the allegations are of such a serious nature that a general election is inevitable if they are proved'. This line, which was not in my original copy, was added during the production process and implied that a senior member of Cabinet must have been one of the two alleged recipients. Starry O'Brien was not named in the story – at his request – and neither were the two politicians nor O'Callaghan.

The article explained how I had been researching the story since March 1999, when O'Brien first approached me, but that I had not obtained the promised copies of the actual cheques. The two politicians had denied the allegations when I first contacted them in May 1999 and 'threatened to sue the newspaper if their names were printed in connection with corrupt payments'. O'Callaghan denied that he ever provided the businessman with any such monies.[1]

When O'Brien first contacted me, his central claim was that he had acted as a bagman for O'Callaghan for payments related to the Quarryvale/Liffey Valley scheme. He acknowledged that what he did was illegal and that he had previously been accused of forgery and perjury by a judge in the High Court in November 1989. For this, and other reasons, I had thought it prudent to obtain a signed affidavit setting out the details of his allegations, which was taken by Dublin solicitor Padraic Ferry, and later passed to the tribunal.

O'Brien told both myself and the tribunal lawyers that he left copies of the cheques, made out to the named politicians, with a Christian Brother in Ennis for safekeeping and that he would provide these and other documents to the inquiry, when appropriate. However, during my initial year of investigation, no information was provided by him to prove his claims or legally permit the newspaper to publish the story. For months after our first encounter, O'Brien contacted me weekly to ask about when his story would be published, while declining to provide the necessary documents to back it up. During visits to Dublin, he would meet with me and tribunal lawyer John Gallagher, who gave him the pseudonym John Maughan, the name of the Mayo football manager, when they spoke on the phone. Despite their reservations about his story, Gallagher and his colleague Patrick Hanratty diligently followed the trail of evidence laid out by O'Brien, but, like me, they met a brick wall at every turn.

In May 1999, the *Post* was served with an order by the tribunal preventing it from publishing details of the story in the context of my investigation, and a further order preventing us from disclosing the existence of that first order. These were served on Post Publications, Damien Kiberd and myself, and directed that we would not report that

O'Brien had met or spoken with members of the tribunal, provided information to it, or been introduced to the inquiry by me, or link the tribunal to any allegations made by the Cork businessman.

As there was no reason to believe that the allegations would stand up to legal scrutiny or that the story could be published anytime soon, we did not challenge it. The orders were lifted in October 1999, following a ruling by the Supreme Court in an unrelated case brought by Liam Lawlor against the Flood Tribunal. Even then, extreme caution was required, not least because at every turn we met with denials from those accused of giving and taking bribes, from the man whom O'Brien claimed had introduced him to the former politician, and from the former manager of the building society in Cork, who said he had no knowledge of the lodgements. One of the men named as an account holder in the deposit book said he was unaware that his name had been used by O'Brien. The Christian Brother told me, and the tribunal lawyer who visited Ennis separately, that although he had once stored some documents for a time for O'Brien, a former pupil of his, he had no idea of their contents.

The unexpected arrival of Fingleton at the tribunal during Easter week 2000 altered the situation with regard to publishing the story, as we were the only media outlet with knowledge of the background to his appearance and felt obliged to explain the context in which the building society boss had been called to explain his delay in handing over financial records that might support the sensational allegations. We were also fearful that other media might publish carefully tailored elements of the story, as there was already intense speculation in political circles that the *Post* was once again involved in a potentially major exposé. In short, without the tribunal calling evidence on the matter, the story would never have run.

I filed the story from west Cork, where I was spending the bank holiday weekend with my family. Following its publication, with the added spicy and unnecessary ingredient of how it could lead to a general election if proven, I was immediately asked to do an interview on RTÉ *News at One* from their Cork studio that Sunday. I set out the background to the story and how we published it following Fingleton's hesitant and somewhat confused evidence, and his subsequent admission to me, before it went to print, that he did not know what information the tribunal was seeking. It was in the public interest to set out the facts without naming anyone involved in the alleged bribery or accepting the authenticity of the allegations, but just a day later, all hell broke loose.

On the morning of Monday 24 April, Bertie Ahern was at Arbour Hill commemorating the eighty-fourth anniversary of the Easter Rising at the graveside of the executed leaders. Earlier that day, the *Irish Examiner*, apparently ignoring all risks of a defamation action against it, published a story naming the Taoiseach as the politician paid in the Burlington's car park. Katie Hannon, their political correspondent, confirmed later that she felt that the Fianna Fáil advisers to whom she spoke regarding the *Post*'s exclusive were 'relaxed' about naming Ahern as one of the recipients of the alleged payments. 'I think they thought it was helpful and allowed them to deal with it the next day when he was due to participate in the annual Arbour Hill commemoration,' she told me.[2]

At Arbour Hill, when Ahern was asked about the sensational claims, he stated that the paper had got it badly wrong and there was no truth in the allegations. 'I can say I never received one penny from Owen O'Callaghan, for myself, for the party, or for anyone else … I never met Owen O'Callaghan, as far as I know, until 1993, and I think he would say that too. I don't know him particularly well,' the Taoiseach told the assembled media, continuing:

> I didn't get money from anyone else either in the car park in the Burlington. Or in any other car park in 1979, '89, '99 or at any other time. So with the same gusto that everybody ran around the place since Frank Connolly's article, and he's usually a fairly good

> journalist, though he's been talking about this for a long time and he now picked this period to write it, but I deny it categorically ... I was the Taoiseach who set up these tribunals, along with our colleagues, Progressive Democrats and Mary Harney, and we'll co-operate with everything.

He repeated, 'Owen O'Callaghan has given me nothing, he's given the party money ... The details of how much he has given the party are all in the public domain.'

In radio interviews the following day, I responded that Ahern 'was a fairly good politician' and reiterated that the story was published in the public interest and because of Fingleton's appearance at the tribunal. Inevitably, the story dominated the news agenda for a few days, with particularly aggressive attacks on the *Post* and the tribunal from media organs that had spared no opportunity to undermine the corruption inquiry over the previous three years. There was also internal criticism by some *Post* reporters, who questioned why we had published allegations provided by such a dubious source.

Newspapers were provided with salacious details of Starry O'Brien's previous unsavoury history by the Fianna Fáil press office, which had plenty of time to prepare its response, having been informed a year earlier of the allegations by the Cork businessman. O'Brien claimed that he fell out with O'Callaghan after his company, Edenfell Holdings, was forced out of a housing project in Carrigaline, and that he was mistreated by the prominent Cork developer. He claimed to be involved in various construction projects, none of which he could identify when probed. He had what appeared to be a letter of comfort written by Haughey in the 1980s, which he, strangely, brandished as evidence of his credibility. A former business partner later told me that it was widely suspected that O'Brien was a scam artist and was most likely paid to bring forward his fabricated claims.

But O'Brien's description of the alleged payment of £50,000 to Ahern after the all-Ireland GAA football final of 1989 had also set alarm bells ringing. When Gilmartin and I spoke about it, he recalled a boast that O'Callaghan had made of giving Ahern £50,000 in return for his and Joe Burke's assistance with securing the purchase of lands owned by Dublin County Council at Quarryvale in 1989. O'Callaghan described how he paid the cash to the politician during an international soccer game at Lansdowne Road in autumn 1989. He told Gilmartin that he paid the money directly and did not use a go-between. The stories were strangely similar.

As for O'Brien's motivation in all this, Gilmartin had been warned by a friend, Peter Kearns, long before the story was published in the *Post*, that the Cork man was involved in an effort to discredit him; he received a tip-off from an anonymous source to the same effect. Kearns lived in Crosshaven, County Cork, close to where O'Brien sometimes stayed in a cottage owned by relatives. Gilmartin believed the story 'was hatched in order to damage my credibility and the tribunal's investigation. You and the *Sunday Business Post* were used to achieve that end because you were seen as sympathetic to my position.'[3] The invented allegation was a less than subtle attempt to muddy the waters by providing details that were similar to those Gilmartin had given to me and the tribunal, but with significant differences, such as the location of the alleged payment to Ahern, raising questions about the truth of both versions.

Following the Arbour Hill intervention by Ahern, Gilmartin told me how he had witnessed the politician in deep discussion with O'Callaghan in the late spring of 1989, when he visited Leinster House. Ahern was minister for labour at the time, and when he arrived in the self-service restaurant in Leinster House, where Gilmartin and O'Callaghan were sitting with some other politicians, he greeted the Cork developer. 'O'Callaghan and Ahern were on first name terms. They had a long discussion at the door of the room. There was a vote on that night and a lot of political tension. I remember it well as there was an election called soon after,' Gilmartin said.[4] The story was significant in that Ahern had told reporters only days earlier at Arbour Hill that he had never met Owen O'Callaghan before 1993. Whatever his motivation for this, Ahern's attempt to distance himself from O'Callaghan backfired and only added to the confusion that was sown by the latest bizarre turn in the payments saga.

O'Brien persisted with his claims, despite the denials by Ahern, O'Callaghan and the other former politician who was not publicly named. Fianna Fáil demanded a front-page apology from the *Post*, with my name prominently attached, which the newspaper refused. However, a front-page apology to Ahern and O'Callaghan was subsequently made, without damages or other conditions, and life moved on. Ahern also took a successful defamation action against Starry O'Brien in the Circuit Court.

Some months after the story was published, I met Ahern in July 2000, when he formally opened the renovated family home of Patrick Pearse at 27 Pearse Street in Dublin as the headquarters for the newly established Ireland Institute. I was at the foot of the stairs when the Taoiseach descended with his minders. He approached me, smiling, and struck me hard on the arm. I did not return the blow.

In an interesting postscript to this story, in March 2026, during research for this book, I visited Starry O'Brien at his home in Cork. He was friendly and talkative, although he would not explain why he had made up the elaborate story about bribing politicians. However, he claimed that he was not the only person involved in the affair but refused to identify the others. 'There were people behind me,' he said.

Chapter Nineteen

Lawlor's Last Stand

THE UNEXPECTED APPEARANCE OF MICHAEL FINGLETON that prompted the publication of the controversial *Post* exclusive overshadowed the more dramatic performance by Frank Dunlop at the tribunal on the appropriately named Spy Wednesday, two days earlier. Indeed, the now infamous spin-doctor Dunlop could not have orchestrated a more effective distraction from what amounted to a public confession of guilt, albeit an unwilling one. During several hours of questioning, he provided a list of fifteen named members of Dublin County Council whom he said he had bribed in connection with the Quarryvale rezoning. He confirmed that he received over £1.3 million from O'Callaghan between 1991 and 1998, a significant amount of which went into his own pocket.

Dunlop's epiphany was induced by the tribunal's discovery of a bank account he controlled at AIB's Terenure branch in Dublin, through which monies were siphoned to politicians, whose names he scribbled on a piece of paper that was handed to the tribunal chairman. The tribunal heard how the payments were made by the PR man in pubs, in the Dáil and at the homes of politicians. As well as Tom Hand, he named Pat Dunne of Fianna Fáil (also deceased) and a 'powerful individual', later identified as Liam Lawlor, among those who collectively received £112,000 in payments in return for their support for Quarryvale in 1991 and 1992. There was no immediate explanation for the balance of the

£240,000 lodged in the account during this period, but Dunlop agreed that it was set up for the 'concealment of monies' that came from Shefran. In addition, the *Post* reported:

> On top of this Dunlop told the tribunal that he received a further £400,000 from O'Callaghan in the late 1990s. He said he was on a monthly retainer of £5,000 a month plus VAT for these services. He said that he obtained £300,000 as a success fee from the developer when the cap of 220,000 square feet on Quarryvale was lifted by Fingal County Council 18 months ago. A further £100,000 was paid for PR services provided by Dunlop in relation to the controversy over the Horgan's Quay site in Cork in which O'Callaghan was implicated …[1]

These revelations prompted an angry editorial in the *Post*:

> As for Dunlop, well, he has done the state some service even if he cuts a sad figure at present. We recall that when *The Sunday Business Post* wrote some years ago about the company called Shefran and the extraordinary sums flowing through it and around it, Dunlop hired one of Dublin's highest and mightiest solicitors to pursue the newspaper. He, in the sort of understatement one normally associates with lawyers, described the behaviour of this newspaper and its journalists as 'scabrous'.
>
> Mr Dunlop, of course, could not be described as 'scabrous'. Far from being rough and uneven, his well-washed and manicured exterior gives him the appearance of a fairly successful Bible salesman. Even late at night when he is running around with bags of cash belonging to companies that don't pay their taxes and don't put their receipts through their books or bank accounts.[2]

Frank Dunlop & Associates, one of the city's most successful PR practitioners, lost its sheen following his public defenestration, and a succession of high-profile public and private companies terminated their contracts with the firm. These included prestigious State bodies, the Electricity Supply Board and the National Treasury Management Agency, as well as the Construction Industry Federation and Woodchester Bank in the private sector. Dunlop had provided services to the government departments of Defence, Health and Transport, and semi-state bodies, Aer Lingus, the Spencer Dock Development Company and Irish Sugar, as well as a host of other private companies over the previous decade and more. His client list reflected the deeply embedded and influential role the former Fianna Fáil and government press officer enjoyed in the ranks of corporate and public life in the capital.

In late 1998, following revelations published in the *Post* from Tom Gilmartin, Dunlop had been forced to declare more of his earnings under pressure from the Revenue Commissioners. There was a fourfold increase in the income declared by his PR firm to over €500,000 in that year, but the tribunal suspected that he had much more stashed away. In his 2000 appearance at the tribunal, he admitted to bribing councillors in relation to land deals and rezonings across County Dublin, from Carrickmines and Monkstown in the southside to Swords, Baldoyle and Portmarnock in the north of the city, over many years.

Before his evidence finished, a mentally and physically diminished Dunlop tarred thirty councillors across the two largest parties and the Progressive Democrats, the Labour Party, and some independents, with his dirty strokes. Among those he implicated were 'Mr Big' (soon identified as Liam Lawlor) and 'Mr Insatiable', who repeatedly came back looking for more (Colm McGrath). He paid monies to a clatter of Fianna Fáil councillors, among them Senator Don Lydon, Tony Fox, Marian McGennis, Finbarr Hanrahan, G.V. Wright and the late Sean Gilbride. Fine Gael councillors Liam T. Cosgrave, Therese Ridge and Michael Joe

Cosgrave were named, along with the Progressive Democrats' Colm Tyndall, who secured a lucrative insurance contract from O'Callaghan for the Quarryvale development.

It was evident that Dunlop's malign influence reached across the political, professional and administrative elite of the country, and that many powerful people were tainted. However, there remained a deep suspicion that 'lots of small fish and a few big ones were being sacrificed in order to save a shoal of sharks'.[3]

Despite his apparent mental and physical collapse, Dunlop continued to insist that O'Callaghan did not know of his network of corrupt councillors, even when it was confirmed that he received £300,000 (ostensibly to help with his legal costs) from the Cork developer after he confessed to the tribunal in April 2000 about the extent of his bribery. It later emerged that Dunlop met with O'Callaghan on two occasions while he was appearing before the tribunal during April and May 2000, despite warnings by Judge Flood to all who appeared before him not to converse with other witnesses during their evidence. The meetings took place in the County Club in Dunshaughlin, near Dunlop's home in County Meath.[4] According to Dunlop's diary, he also met Taoiseach Bertie Ahern in the weeks after he admitted to multiple acts of corruption of public representatives.

Like Dunlop, George Redmond had also had problems with Revenue after he was convicted for failing to make returns on his income for ten years since his retirement from the council. In April 2000, he agreed to pay almost £800,000 in outstanding tax to the Revenue Commissioners. When he returned to the tribunal the following month, Redmond found it hard to recall how he had acquired the now estimated £1.05 million that was found travelling through a myriad of his accounts between 1965 and 1998, on top of his modest salary, and he continued to evade and obfuscate in his replies. 'As an exasperated Judge Flood said on Friday, for a man who calculated his finances down to the last penny at monthly intervals, it is unbelievable that he could not remember the sources of his wealth,'[5] the *Post* noted.

Redmond eventually admitted to accepting what he described as an 'unsolicited cheque' from Brendan Fassnidge, the garage owner in Palmerstown. The senior planner had signed off on the sale of a ransom strip giving the businessman access to the Lucan bypass at Palmerstown, even though Fassnidge did not own the land in question. Fassnidge recalled giving him a bundle of cash in return for the lucrative access.

Reeling from the combined attentions of the tribunal, the CAB and the Revenue Commissioners, Redmond would only admit to accepting payments of about £350,000, of which the builder Tom Brennan contributed a quarter of a million, which, he continued to insist, was in return for his legitimate 'advice' on planning matters. As was pointed out in the *Post* that May:

> What Redmond has not explained is the motivation for such extraordinary generosity on Brennan's part. As an executive in Dublin County Council, Redmond knew a lot about property. He had a role in decisions on zoning and planning permissions and enjoyed reserved powers which allowed him to overrule the views of planners, architects and engineers. He could influence the size of the contributions sought from builders in return for the council's provision of roads, sewerage and water services to new estates. He could decide on whether to take enforcement proceedings against errant builders who failed to complete houses and estates as promised to the council and home buyers. If we were to believe Redmond, he was berating Brennan on the golf course to finish estates or face enforcement proceedings issued by Redmond, while pocketing his weekly consultancy fees (of £200) at the 19th hole.[6]

While the tribunal managed to make some cracks in his stone wall of refutation, it was Tom Gilmartin's testimony, and his direct experience of collusion between Redmond and Liam Lawlor in obstructing the Quarryvale project, that helped to bring down the edifice of lies and deceit that the former assistant city and county manager had constructed. Lawlor and Redmond were joined at the hip when it came to fleecing people who required rezonings, planning permissions and access to public services in order to advance their corporate and business interests. Gilmartin had told of Lawlor's demand for £100,000 each for himself and Redmond after a meeting in the Dublin City Council offices in 1988, which the developer had refused to pay. He had also outlined his discovery that Redmond had blocked his purchase of council-owned lands and had encouraged a competing developer, John Corcoran, to tender for them. In return, Corcoran had offered Redmond a consultancy with his firm, Green Properties, on his retirement from the council in 1989, a plan that was scuppered by the failed Garda investigation into Gilmartin's allegations.

In May 2000, the same week that Redmond was deflecting questions at the tribunal and just weeks after Dunlop named 'Mr Big' as the politician who took almost £50,000 in payments from him, Gilmartin weighed in with a claim that Lawlor had extracted £100,000 in so-called 'donations' and 'consultancy fees' from his two projects in Dublin. The dogs in the streets around Dublin Castle did not take long to work out that Lawlor was 'Mr Big'.

After years of skirting around corruption allegations arising from dodgy property deals and rezoning controversies, Lawlor finally met his match in Judge Feargus Flood and his tribunal team. He spent months ignoring its orders to provide details of his multiple bank accounts in a variety of jurisdictions, and the sources of more than £4.6 million it uncovered in them, until he was forced to give evidence by a High Court order obtained by the tribunal.

Over three days of ducking and diving from questions by tribunal senior counsel John Gallagher, the west Dublin TD failed to explain where up to £2.6 million of the monies found in various bank accounts in Dublin, Naas, in Liechtenstein and Jersey came from. His explanations dragged several prominent names into this financial orbit, including Larry Goodman, who, he claimed, gave him £375,000 in 1987 to develop a plant to extract blood plasma and other by-products from beef. The money went through Lawlor's company, Advance Proteins, which recorded transactions of up to £900,000 through its accounts between 1987 and 1991, although it never traded.

Lawlor could not offer an explanation as to why publican Pat Murphy, owner of the Sarsfield Bar in Inchicore, paid him over £70,000 between 1996 and 1998, in 'dribs and drabs', or why he asked another friend, Pat Long, to open an account in the name of John Long in Ulster Bank, Palmerstown, into which £25,000 was lodged in 1997. Long opened a second account for him in the Irish Permanent Building Society (IPBS) in 1998, which Lawlor failed to disclose to the tribunal until soon before the hearing.

When Lawlor finally admitted, under pressure from Gallagher, to the existence of another credit card on the IPBS account, which he had not previously explained, the chairman lost his patience and stood the witness down. Before his public dismissal, Lawlor recounted visits to Prague in the Czech Republic, where a businessman he did not wish to name generously gave him £600,000 between 1995 and 1998, and to Liechtenstein, where he lodged large amounts of money during the same period. He denied a claim published in the *Post* that he may have carried a suitcase full of cash to Vaduz in June 1995, where the Irish football team were playing a European Championship match against Liechtenstein in the country's capital. A witness saw Lawlor carry two suitcases off the plane when it landed in Vaduz, but he arrived at the hotel where he was staying with only one, an hour or so later.

Lawlor refused to provide details of the building projects he claimed to have in Prague and could not reveal the exact address on Wenceslas Square in the centre of the city where he said his lawyer, a Mr Vavalak, was based, nor did he have his phone number. He forcefully denied that he ever received money in return for planning favours during his twenty-three years as a TD and county councillor, notwithstanding Dunlop's evidence to the contrary. On the week of his dismissal by Flood, Lawlor joined the queue of politicians seeking a handshake with the US president, Bill Clinton, during his visit to Dublin. As the *Post* editorialised:

> One day you are shaking the hand of the most powerful man in the world, the next you are on the way to Mountjoy Jail. Do not pass 'Go'. Do not collect '€200,000'. That's life for Liam Lawlor the former chair of the Dáil ethics committee who gives out false invoices for his political donations and accumulated £4.569 million in his 16 bank accounts over 20 years. On Tuesday, the former Fianna Fáil TD shook hands with President Bill Clinton. On Friday, after three exhausting days of evasion and apparent falsehood, tribunal chairman Feargus Flood stood Lawlor down as a witness and said he would take High Court proceedings against him.[7]

In January 2001, the High Court imprisoned Lawlor for obstruction for seven days – the first politician to be sent to jail in connection with tribunal investigations – with the rest of his three-month sentence suspended. He was also fined £10,000 and ordered to pay legal costs of up to £100,000. Before his dramatic fall from grace, he resigned from Fianna Fáil and as chairman of the Dáil ethics committee, to which he had been appointed by Bertie Ahern some years earlier. He doggedly continued to maintain his innocence of any wrongdoing.

In February 2001, just weeks after Lawlor's seven-day imprisonment, and after several others he accused of corruption, including Dunlop and

Redmond, had been exposed and discredited, Gilmartin returned from England with Vera to his native Sligo. In May, he submitted a further statement to the tribunal in which he claimed that Bertie Ahern was on 'O'Callaghan's payroll' and had received up to £80,000 from the Cork developer, an allegation that would require years of further investigation before it became a subject for public hearings.

In July 2001, Lawlor was handed a second seven-day prison sentence and a fine of £5,000 over his refusal to comply with a High Court order obtained by the tribunal, but he appealed the conviction to the Supreme Court, delaying his incarceration for several months. During the same month, Denis 'Starry' O'Brien appeared before the Circuit Court to face the defamation action taken against him by Ahern. O'Brien failed to produce any evidence to support the claims he had made to the *Post* and to the tribunal lawyers, while the building society documents he presented were found to be forgeries. He did not challenge any witnesses brought forward by the Taoiseach and did not submit any defence, leading to a ruling that Ahern was 'grossly defamed'. Ahern was awarded damages of £30,000 with all costs against O'Brien, who did not pay the monies until he was served with a sheriff's order several years later. When asked to make a comment after the case, a smiling O'Brien told reporters: 'Sin a bhfuil [That's it]'.

In December 2001, the Supreme Court upheld the prison sentence and fine imposed on Lawlor six months earlier but deferred the order until January to allow the now disgraced politician to visit his son in New York over Christmas. He went back to Mountjoy Jail in January 2002 and just weeks later was given another one-month prison term, again for failing to comply with a High Court order. During this time, he was released from jail to attend a Dáil debate and speak against a motion calling for him to resign his seat before being promptly sent back to the 'Joy to complete his sentence.

Chapter Twenty

Bare Feet and Bad Trousers

BY THE TIME LIAM LAWLOR WAS sent to jail for the third time, in February 2002, the tribunal had traced the origin of some £2 million of the more than £4.6 million moving through hundreds of accounts he operated across Ireland, Liechtenstein and the US. The payments were tied to a multitude of land deals, rezonings and other developments in which he provided assistance. The tribunal uncovered paperwork relating to payments amounting to £50,000 by Ballymore Homes to Lawlor between 1994 and 1998. Ballymore, owned by Sean Mulryan, paid £10,000 in 1994 to a company called King and Co. International, through which Lawlor operated businesses in Prague, and a further £40,000 to another company, Long Consultants, which the politician controlled.

If the lawyers acting for Lawlor, Frank Dunlop and Owen O'Callaghan, who berated Judge Feargus Flood in autumn 1998 over what they claimed were overly extensive and unnecessary orders for financial discovery by the tribunal following Gilmartin's allegations, had prevailed, the scale of self-enrichment by political insiders would never have emerged. It took time but, three years later, the same orders helped to establish that Lawlor had obtained payments from more than fifty companies or individuals during his time in politics and had amassed a large fortune.

In early 2002, the government appointed two lawyers, Alan Mahon SC and Mary Faherty SC, as judges of the Circuit Court and asked them to assist Judge Flood, while another barrister, Gerald Keyes, was made a reserve member of the tribunal team. The tribunal lawyers received increases of up to €800 per diem, with some getting up to €2,250 for a day's work. At the same time as the appointments were announced, the public hearings of the tribunal were suspended until after the May 2002 general election, so that the inquiry would not influence voters. Flood's report into payments to Ray Burke was also delayed until after the election, much to the relief of a number of serving politicians entangled in the investigation. Bertie Ahern duly survived the political storms brewing around himself and his party and formed a second administration with the Progressive Democrats, after both parties increased their support in the election. He was not known as the 'Teflon Taoiseach' for nothing.

The 150-page, second interim report of the Flood Tribunal, published in September 2002, was a public event, as hundreds of people queued to purchase it from the Government Publications Office in Dublin. It sold an unprecedented 25,000 copies for just €1 each. The report found that, as well as obtaining £125,000 in payments from the builders Brennan & McGowan, Burke acquired his home, Briargate in Swords, corruptly as the price of the property did not reflect its market value. It concluded that the payments Burke received from JMSE and Oliver Barry were also improper and related to the former minister advancing the business interests of the companies involved. The report contained a list of fourteen people it said obstructed the tribunal during its first module into Gogarty's allegations, including the Bailey brothers, Joseph Murphy junior and senior, Oliver Barry and James Stafford of Century, Joseph McGowan, John Finnegan and Frank Reynolds. Judge Flood said that the cost of the inquiry amounted to €21 million, but that the Revenue Commissioners and the CAB retrieved over €34 million from some of those cited in the report.[1]

Another name that came up in the report was that of P.J. Mara, who, when asked to provide the tribunal with details of an account he had opened in the name of Pullman Limited at Royal Bank of Scotland in the Isle of Man, failed to do so. The immediate political effect of the report was the resignation of Mara, who, at the time of its release, was director of the campaign by Fianna Fáil to have the Nice Treaty ratified. This was particularly embarrassing for the Taoiseach, who welcomed the Flood report as 'profoundly significant' but was forced to watch his, and Haughey's, long-serving confidante walk the plank.

Ahern must also have found it difficult to swallow Flood's devastating findings about Burke. The former minister was facing further scrutiny over the vast amounts he accrued, in addition to his salary, during his three decades in politics. At 2002 values, Burke and his companies took in over €2.4 million between 1972 and 1991.

Concerning the report, Ahern said, 'It sends out a clear message. Those who acted improperly and illegally while engaged in public life can be assured that their actions will be exposed.'[2] For some who recalled his comments to RTÉ in 1993, when, as minister for finance, he announced a tax amnesty for the wealthy, inevitably including many of his party's supporters and donors, the irony was particularly rich. 'It would actually give me the greatest of pleasure watching non-compliant taxpayers going to jail,' he had said at the time.[3] Early that year, he also devalued the Irish punt against sterling by 10 per cent. A number of political and business insiders had enriched themselves by purchasing large volumes of the UK currency ahead of the finance minister's anticipated decision on this.

Ahern had more to worry about than the integrity of his public statements when *Ireland on Sunday* (*IOS*) published my story exposing details of the tribunal investigation into an £80,000 payment to 'a serving Fianna Fáil minister'. Tom Gilmartin, in a new statement to the Flood Tribunal, had claimed that a senior politician allegedly received £50,000 in 1989 'in return for assistance with a major development in Dublin' and £30,000 in 1992 in relation to a tax designation on another Dublin site. After investigating this claim, the tribunal was expected to call evidence from politicians and others in early 2003, when public hearings into Gilmartin's claims would be opened. As the newspaper reported, it was 'almost certain' that Ahern would be one of those summoned to give evidence.[4] This was the same story Gilmartin had previously told me, of O'Callaghan telling him he had paid £50,000 to Ahern in return for the politician's help in ensuring that council land at Quarryvale was sold to Barkhill and did not fall into the hands of Green Property. The Cork developer also told him that a further £30,000 was paid to Ahern in return for a commitment by the minister for finance that Green Property would not get the benefit of a lucrative tax designation for its retail centre in Blanchardstown.

The names and details were not included in the *IOS* story for legal reasons, and, unlike the almost hysterical reaction provoked by the O'Brien fairy tale of Easter 2000, the Taoiseach's response to this latest dramatic tribunal revelation was initially muted. It would take a few days and a row on the radio before Ahern confirmed that he was the politician concerned.

The morning after the *IOS* story, a swift and negative reaction came from the recently installed Minister for Justice Michael McDowell, who spoke on RTÉ Radio with presenter Pat Kenny to dismiss the newspaper report as absolutely 'without foundation'. He said that it was not the first time I had concocted a story about bribes to a senior politician – a reference to the 'Starry' O'Brien story – over which the person accused was vindicated and awarded damages. I was listening, so I called the station and was immediately put on air. I asked McDowell to specify which line or paragraph in the *IOS* story was inaccurate and reminded listeners that only a few years previously the minister had, as a barrister, represented the businessman at the centre of the corruption allegations, a comment that McDowell protested was 'below the belt'.

I refused to comply with McDowell's request to identify the politician who was the subject of the article, on the grounds that, as the minister well knew, it could expose me and the newspaper to a libel action. During the heated exchanges, I wrongly referred to the 'Starry' O'Brien case as having 'collapsed' rather than explaining that his false claims were disproved and rejected by the court. This prompted the Taoiseach, a few days later, to respond to my ill-chosen words and insist that he was vindicated in the Circuit Court when it ruled that he had been the victim of completely unsubstantiated and untrue allegations. 'I have never taken a bribe from anyone in my life,' he stated. 'I succeeded in my Circuit Court case for one reason and one reason only, that is, that I was defamed and lies were told about me. It is wrong for Frank Connolly to say that the case "collapsed", because Denis "Starry" O'Brien decided not to contest the charge.'[5]

If Ahern thought he could deflect attention from the thrust of the latest disclosures, he was badly mistaken. The similarity of Gilmartin's latest allegations to O'Brien's fabricated account of handing over £50,000 to Ahern after the 1989 All-Ireland football final was intriguing. In the early 1990s, O'Callaghan had told Gilmartin that he directly paid Ahern a sum of £50,000 at a soccer match at Lansdowne Road in autumn 1989. O'Callaghan had stated to Gilmartin that he and Ahern had tickets for a soccer game during which the money changed hands. The resemblance between the two stories was no coincidence. Close observers of the tribunal and its legal team knew that the Starry O'Brien story had been a deliberately weaponised concoction to damage Flood's inquiry and the *Post*'s journalism, and to shield O'Callaghan and Ahern from, arguably, Gilmartin's most damaging allegation.

For the next four years, Ahern and his lawyers spent a lot of time trying to avoid the tribunal's unrelenting efforts to examine his finances during his time as a Cabinet minister between 1988 and 1994. For a lengthy period, he obstructed the discovery process by refusing to provide details of his income over and above his salary as a politician;

he then came up with patently false explanations for large amounts, including in sterling and US dollars, which were lodged in various bank accounts under his control during that period.

This was not the only way Ahern managed to postpone his day of reckoning at the tribunal. By delaying the appointment of new members to the tribunal for months, Ahern was accused of adopting 'a deliberate strategy to delay the Flood Tribunal's investigations and ensure that controversial evidence would not be heard before the 2002 general election', as claimed by Green Party TD Dan Boyle.[6] When Feargus Flood announced that he intended to resign with effect on 27 June 2003, following what he believed was a deliberate attempt to smear his reputation, the government held up the appointment of Alan Mahon to replace him until the last sitting day of the Dáil before the summer recess. Flood resigned after he was subjected to a false allegation that he promised Ray Burke's barrister, Joe Finnegan, that his client's legal costs would be paid in full by the tribunal. This assertion deeply wounded the judge, as it implied he had engaged in an improper and secret deal with the lawyer. Finnegan denied that any such deal had been made, but the damage was done and Flood chose to step down. It is almost certainly the case that Finnegan, who examined me on behalf of Burke at the tribunal, was not party to the spurious allegation.

By the time hearings resumed into what was expected to be even more dramatic evidence of corruption at the highest level of government, relations between it and the tribunal were fractious to say the least. When Gilmartin travelled from Cork to give evidence in March 2004, he was greeted with a massive media presence, an excited audience and a barrage of insults from Liam Lawlor. The former politician ranted for half an hour about the Sligo man who 'left the west of Ireland in proverbial bare feet and trousers in a bad condition' and then came back to save the country 'by driving a coach and four through the 1972 development plan'.[7]

Lawlor, shouting from the body of the hall, described his perceived adversary as a man 'in the middle of a glasshouse, and by the time myself and others are finished dealing with Mr Gilmartin's lies I respectfully suggest that there won't be too many panes of glass left, and I hope as it splinters it doesn't inflict too many deserved wounds on him'. Gilmartin recalled:

> On the first day I did not know what to expect going into the tribunal. Lawlor opened up about me leaving Sligo with no arse in my trousers and in my bare feet. He accused me of throwing stones even though I lived in a bigger glass house. I had no feeling of animosity towards Lawlor. I actually enjoyed it. He wanted to discredit me, bring me down a peg or two and unnerve me. All I did was smile, and actually it steeled me for what was to come.[8]

As he entered the witness box and took the oath, the packed hall was silent, as the crowd waited to hear directly from Gilmartin, following the years of statements from the great and good of Irish politics, who denied having ever met him, never mind taking bribes to shaft the Sligo man and destroy his business. During his early evidence, Gilmartin noted how many people, including fellow Sligo man Ray MacSharry, could not remember their meetings with him. At a private session with the tribunal team in 1999, MacSharry had denied meeting with Gilmartin, and Gilmartin described how he had even gone to the trouble of trying to get his fellow county man to confirm, in writing, that they had never met. Asked by tribunal counsel, John Gallagher, whether he could recall anything that might jog MacSharry's memory, Gilmartin replied, 'All I know is I was there. And I seemed to have an awful problem with being invisible or some sort of ghost that turns up.'

In fact, the tribunal had evidence of the meeting between the two men in the former minister's constituency office in Sligo in August 1987 and again in Government Buildings in December of that year. An unexpected witness also emerged to confirm the Sligo meeting. Pádraig Leonard was listening to the tribunal evidence being replayed on the radio, as he sat in the home of one the former minister's relatives. He immediately contacted the tribunal to confirm that he had met Gilmartin in MacSharry's constituency office on the day in question in August 1987. The school principal from Grange, where Gilmartin's sister Una lived, later gave credible evidence at a public hearing of the tribunal.

Similarly, when asked about his first meeting with Minister for Labour Bertie Ahern in the Mespil Road office in October 1987, Gilmartin could not understand why the Taoiseach could not find any record of the engagement. He said that although he did not ask for any particular assistance at that time, Ahern was supportive of his plans for Bachelors Walk, which was located in the politician's north Dublin constituency.

When the meeting in Leinster House with Charles Haughey and other members of his Cabinet in February 1989 came up, Gilmartin provided a graphic description of the discussion, with Haughey and assorted members of Cabinet standing and sitting around a long table in the room. Ahern said, 'Hello, Tom,' when they met in the room in Leinster House, while Pádraig Flynn and Seamus Brennan also acknowledged him before Haughey entered with Ray Burke. Gilmartin recited the approach by the £5 million man with 'salt and pepper' hair after the meeting with Haughey, with the crowd in Dublin Castle becoming visibly agitated as the witness described in angry tones being handed the piece of paper with the number of a bank account in the Isle of Man. 'I could not believe what I was hearing, and I did not respond to the man until the piece of paper was put into my hand,' Gilmartin continued:

> Bearing in mind that I had just left a meeting with Mr Haughey and ministers of the Government, and that Lawlor was waiting outside the room and witnessed the encounter, I assumed that this approach must, in some way, have been connected with Mr Lawlor

> and Mr Haughey. So all in all I could only come to one conclusion: that the place was totally corrupt. And I had good reason for it.

When he told the unidentified man 'You make the fucking Mafia look like monks', the man replied that he 'could wind up in the Liffey' for saying this. He then recounted his meeting with Flynn a couple of months later, when the minister for the environment asked him to leave the £50,000 donation to Fianna Fáil on the desk in the Custom House office without putting any recipient's name on the cheque. Asked whether this could have been interpreted as a bribe, he responded:

> I would not bribe anybody. I felt it despicable that you could come into a country that was on its knees, and there's queues down at the American embassy and elsewhere with the kids leaving and walking the streets of London and on the underground begging when they couldn't get a job – absolutely despicable that the people who run this country have no interest whatsoever in those people other than feathering their own nest.

This drew loud applause from the crowd, which had to be silenced by the chairman, Alan Mahon. Gilmartin then outlined how he was told to 'fuck off back to England' during the flawed Garda investigation into his complaints of corruption involving Lawlor and Redmond, and how he received death threats over the phone after he first spoke to the *Post* and other media in the summer of 1998:

> The first one said that if I turned up in Dublin for me to remember Veronica Guerin. The second phone call that came, my son answered the phone, and he was told in no uncertain terms to tell me if I gave evidence to the tribunal or turn up that I wouldn't be coming back. And the third one, I picked up the phone and

> it was much on the same lines. I asked them who they were, but they wouldn't tell me but they said, 'Just remember what we are telling you.' I said, 'You remember one thing, you'll definitely have to make a good job of me ...'

Gilmartin was no stranger to anonymous phone calls and had previously faced down far more sinister threats than those from the 'mini mafia' he confronted in Cork and Dublin. In the 1970s, he was targeted by the English Special Branch because he assisted the son of an Irish foreman at his factory in Luton, who was wrongly arrested and accused of trying to help three Irish men escape from jail. The three members of Sinn Féin had been jailed after an informant claimed to police that they were planning a robbery, which never happened. The informant, Kenneth Lennon, was later found dead, after seeking help from a civil liberties group in London. The killing was blamed on the IRA, but it was later alleged to be the work of the English police, who did not want Lennon to disclose how he had been used by the Special Branch to set up innocent men for a crime they did not commit.

An anonymous caller told Gilmartin that under no circumstances should he provide bail money for the young man as requested by his father, as the kid would be in even greater danger if let out of custody. Subsequently, the same caller, who had a posh English accent, warned Gilmartin that a local Scotsman widely known as a police informant would visit his factory and ask for permission to shoot pheasants in the grounds. He was told that the hunter would ask to leave his weapons there overnight. The anonymous caller warned Gilmartin that there would be an attempt to set him up and have him arrested for the illegal possession of weapons.

Sure enough, Hughie the Scot called one evening and asked could he hunt in the grouse land around the factory. It was getting dark and Hughie suggested he might leave his rifles in the factory overnight, a request which Gilmartin politely refused. He suspected his anonymous and friendly caller worked for the UK security services and, for some reason, was hostile to the Special Branch. From contacts in the Catholic clergy, Gilmartin later received information about high-level collusion by the British establishment with the Dublin and Monaghan bombings in 1974 and the Enniskillen bombing in 1987. The shadowy people he dealt with in Ireland paled in comparison to the Brits when it came to dirty tricks and threats.

The Flood Tribunal itself would see its work impeded by a tragic incident involving people with criminal connections, this time in eastern Europe, that would rock the establishment in Ireland.

Chapter Twenty-One

Death in Moscow

WHEN GILMARTIN'S CROSS-EXAMINATION BY THE BARRISTER representing Bertie Ahern began, it was evident that his legal strategy was to aggressively seek to undermine the character and credibility of the Sligo man. Conor Maguire SC was a formidable barrister and was clearly instructed to throw as much mud as possible at the tribunal's star witness. Ahern's legal team vigorously disputed Gilmartin's evidence that the Taoiseach was present at the now infamous encounter with Charles Haughey and 'the £5 million man' in Leinster House, pulling out diary details showing that their client had attended a function in Glasnevin on that afternoon of 1 February 1989.

'Well it's not entirely Hong Kong, is it?' Gilmartin replied. Asked what he meant by that, Gilmartin responded, 'I'm just saying Glasnevin … Leinster House is not a thousand miles away.'[1]

Maguire then dragged up details of a court case in Cavan in 1978, during which a district court judge described Gilmartin as 'shifty and dishonest' according to a local newspaper report from the time. It was a bad move by the lawyer, and it quickly rebounded when Gilmartin explained how a land dispute had ended up in court. He described how he bought four acres to build a house when he and Vera were thinking of returning to Ireland. He was asked to let some of the land, for grazing, to a neighbouring farmer:

> I bought the piece of land. An agent approached me to see if I'd let the meadow on it, so I did. I told him to go ahead – I told him actually that I didn't want money for it, they could have the meadow. So he said, 'You can't do that, because they may get a claim on your land.' So I charged some minimal figure. Some time later the same agent rang me to see if I'd sell it. And I says, 'No, I was not selling it.' A few days later I got a contract from a solicitor agreeing to the sale of my land. I refused to go along with it, because I had not sold it and I had stated categorically, and with witnesses, that I was not selling that piece of land. But I was sued for specific performance, on the grounds that if an agent proved that he acted for me he could sell my land. He sold the land for a pittance, an absolute pittance, to a cousin of his.
>
> I went to court. The judge wouldn't hear my evidence or any witness on my behalf. As it happened, I was there sullying the names of decent local people. That's right, I was a shifty person, all right, and he didn't even hear my evidence. He didn't allow me to talk in the box. That is a fact, and I will prove it. It was an absolute scandal and typical of this country.

The Cavan judge wrongly sided with the land agent in making the judgment against Gilmartin. On appeal, Gilmartin was awarded damages and the land was returned to him. He later sold it to the same people for three times the amount they had initially offered.

'So that is what that is about: another attempt to steal my property,' Gilmartin concluded, to another eruption of applause and laughter, which led to the suspension of proceedings and a warning from the chairman that he would restrict public access if order was not preserved.

A key plank of Ahern's defence, and of others who denied attending the Leinster House meeting with Haughey in February 1989, collapsed when Mary O'Rourke confirmed that she was present on the occasion.

O'Rourke displayed a clear and detailed memory of being invited by Pádraig Flynn to meet Gilmartin and shake his hand at the Leinster House meeting, after he visited her office across the corridor on the same floor as the meeting room. As well as Flynn, the then minister for education recalled that Ray Burke, her brother Brian Lenihan, Ahern and Haughey were all present at what was an informal gathering, with no one sitting down and no 'agenda or printed papers of any kind'. O'Rourke told the tribunal:

> Well as far as I can remember, Mr Flynn knocked on the door and said, 'I'd like you to meet a man … who was going to provide thousands of jobs for Dublin.' Flynn said, 'This is a man, Mr Gilmartin, who is from your mother's own county'. My mother was from County Sligo. My mother had died at the very end of November, and he actually, Mr Flynn, said a kind comment as we crossed, about my mother's demise. That's how it sort of etched in my mind.

O'Rourke's evidence greatly enhanced Gilmartin's credibility, while also exposing the litany of untruths advanced by some of the country's most powerful politicians, who spent months distancing themselves from the infamous meeting. O'Rourke's brother and Tánaiste in 1989, Brian Lenihan, later recalled meeting Gilmartin at the Leinster House meeting. He told Freda Kelly, the editor of a local newspaper in west Dublin at the time of the Quarryvale development, that he was with other ministers who met Gilmartin in Leinster House. She informed the tribunal that Lenihan said to her that among the ministers present was Séamus Brennan, who consistently denied his attendance in his evidence to the inquiry.

In April 2004, Ahern arrived to give his direct evidence to the tribunal, with a large crowd of his supporters in train who, to the annoyance of regular attendees, occupied many of their seats in the Printworks. The Taoiseach was forced to dissociate himself from the description of Gilmartin as 'shifty and dishonest', and to concede that, based on O'Rourke's convincing account, he may have attended a 'chit-chat' type of encounter in Leinster House as she described, even if he could not recall it.

In contrast to his statement to the Dáil in January 1999, he agreed that his friend Joe Burke may have spoken to Gilmartin about the lands at Quarryvale. He now accepted that he spoke on the phone to the Luton developer in June 1989 but denied that he was told about the 'donation' to Pádraig Flynn or that he invited Gilmartin to attend a fundraiser and make a contribution to the party.

When he emerged several hours later, after a lengthy grilling by lawyers for the tribunal and Gilmartin, Ahern put his best face on it and told the waiting media:

> I said in the Dáil on the 27 January 1999 … that I would fully comply with the tribunal and I would put up with whatever cross-examination. I've done that for 5 hours and 25 minutes. That's the way it should be, and needless to say I enjoyed putting my story, because it was a long time to wait for that.

In reality, the Taoiseach was unable to dispute Gilmartin's clear recollections of the three meetings they had before the engagement with Haughey, all of which he had, for so long, denied ever happened. As Gilmartin asked, when faced with the refusal of Cabinet members to acknowledge the Leinster House meeting in February 1989, 'what was wrong with that meeting … when they feel it necessary to lie?' No allegations of wrongdoing or of inappropriate behaviour were put to the Taoiseach, and it would be some time before the tribunal was ready to ask about payments he received from Owen O'Callaghan. However, it was obvious that Ahern was distinctly uncomfortable with his gruelling ordeal in the witness box and relieved that it was over, for now.

A few weeks later, in July 2004, Ray Burke pleaded guilty to tax offences and admitted that he furnished incorrect information to the Revenue when he availed of the tax amnesty introduced by Ahern in 1993. He received a six-month prison sentence and made a settlement of €600,000 to the CAB arising from the findings of the tribunal that he had acquired his house in Swords from Brennan & McGowan for below market value and received illicit payments of almost £250,000. A day after Burke's court appearance, George Redmond admitted that he received huge amounts of money from benefactors during his long career as a planner at Dublin City Council and hid it in accounts in England and Spain, among other locations, and that he sometimes used an Irish version of his name.

Meanwhile, the tribunal met further determined resistance as it continued to serve discovery and production orders on Bertie Ahern, seeking to uncover details of his bank accounts and finances, with correspondence stretching for more than a year before it yielded any significant results. Legal battles over discovery orders on Owen O'Callaghan and others also delayed the planned public hearings of the Quarryvale 2 module, which did not open until late November 2005, without the participation of one of its most important witnesses.

In a tragedy that shocked the country, Liam Lawlor was killed in a car crash in Moscow in October 2005 along with businessman Ruslan Suliamanov, as they travelled from the airport to the city centre of the Russian capital. Lawlor had arrived from Prague with Julia Kushnir, a twenty-nine-year-old legal assistant from Ukraine who was acting as his interpreter. Suliamanov collected them at the airport and, as they drove into the city centre, he swerved to avoid two people who stepped onto the motorway. He and Lawlor, who was sitting in the rear seat, suffered fatal injuries when the car hit a concrete bollard, while Kushnir survived.

The former politician's sudden death on Saturday 22 October was front page news the following day, but several Irish and UK newspapers published entirely inaccurate and defamatory reports in which Kushnir was described as a prostitute. In a statement issued some days after the accident, Kushnir explained, 'I came into contact with Mr Lawlor about three months ago and I have, as with other business people here in Prague, acted on occasions as a translator and intermediator. Mr Ruslan Suliamanov had earlier business dealings with Mr Lawlor here in Prague and is a highly respected CEO of a Russian company.'

She said that Suliamanov was the husband of a 'dear friend' and she was going to stay in their family home after they dropped Lawlor off at his hotel. She was sitting in the front seat so she could translate for the two men when '[a] man and a woman ran out in front of the car. We swerved and I have no memory of what followed the crash. The only thing I remember was waking up in a disoriented state in the ambulance and learning that I was the sole survivor of the accident.'

Twelve years later, in November 2017, Kushnir described, in more detail, to Tom Lyons of *The Sunday Business Post* how she met Suliamanov and Lawlor, and what happened on the day of the accident. She also provided some intriguing insight into some of the people she and Lawlor encountered in eastern Europe.

Kushnir said she was previously in a relationship with a nephew of Suliamanov, a Chechan with the same name. Several years earlier, the nephew had been injured in a shooting incident in Prague, in which a number of others were killed. 'He'd been shot by a gang with pistols. Some guys died who I knew. Only Ruslan was alive. He was in a coma. I went to the hospital. I took care of him. My husband was very unhappy with this situation. He was jealous,' she told the *Post*.[2] A row ensued and Kushnir left her husband to live with Suliamanov.

When they arrived at Moscow airport in October 2005, they were met by Suliamanov senior and she interpreted as the businessman outlined the programme for Lawlor's two-day visit, during which the men would be viewing potential properties for purchase. 'A lot of property, because Liam was always interested in property. It was 2005, a very good time. Today, in Russia, it's a very high price for everything. But in 2005, it was very good for investing money,' she explained to Lyons.

She recalled how they had not been in the car long when the crash happened. 'I don't know how far we were from the airport, but for me it felt like only five minutes.' She said she was lucky, that if she had been in the back she might have died like Lawlor. In the aftermath of the crash she heard that Suliamanov had had a lot of money with him 'but it was "stolen, all stolen"' by the police. With regards to Lawlor she said, 'I don't know if Liam had money, but Hazel [Lawlor's wife] said that he had a ring and they didn't find it.'

Lawlor's son, Niall, went to Moscow with businessman Mick Quinn, a long-time friend of the dead politician and a former showband promoter and manager of The Dubliners folk group, to identify and return his father's body to Dublin. Friends said that Lawlor had suffered appalling injuries to his head and body and was apparently not wearing a seat belt when the car crashed. Questions later arose as to why Lawlor was discussing property investments in Moscow at a time when many Russians were moving money out of the economically ravaged country to Prague, London and other cities.

Lawlor had been due to appear again before the tribunal, which wanted to know more about the money they found in his plethora of accounts. At the time of his death, he had only accounted for the source of about 53 per cent of lodgements over £1,000, totalling £1.4 million, some of which came from his business activities in the Czech capital. Among those who employed him in Prague was Dublin architect Ambrose Kelly, who was also involved with O'Callaghan, Frank Dunlop and Lawlor on the project to build a multi-purpose national stadium in Neilstown. Lawlor worked in Prague for builder Sean Mulryan, who made large payments to the politician. Likewise, he acted for businessman Declan Ganley in Albania, and for Larry Goodman in Iraq, presenting himself on occasion as a representative of the Irish government.

It was not a surprise that Lawlor turned up in Moscow, but the circumstances of his death sent a shockwave through the political establishment and among delegates at the Fianna Fáil Ard-Fheis as they gathered in the conference hall, pubs and restaurants of Killarney, County Kerry, on Saturday, 22 October 2005. There were almost certainly some people who breathed a deep sigh of relief on hearing of Lawlor's sudden death, which shut down potentially embarrassing lines of inquiry by the tribunal. His untimely departure meant that those in politics and business with whom he engaged, and gardaí who covered up his corrupt activities, would not be held to account.

One subject the tribunal continued to probe was the proposal for a national stadium, for which Lawlor claimed credit. Originally conceived by him as a ruse to placate local people who were angered by the transfer of the town centre zoning to Quarryvale, it had become a more realistic commercial project with the election of Albert Reynolds as taoiseach in February 1992. Owen O'Callaghan, who controlled the Neilstown land through his ownership of Merrygrove Ltd, did not disguise his political preference for Reynolds in conversations with Gilmartin, or his role in the successful campaign to oust Haughey following the litany of scandals surrounding the former party leader. He set up Leisure Ireland Ltd to develop the Neilstown project, with the Cork man taking a 25 per cent stake in the company; equal amounts were allocated to Lawlor, Kelly and Dunlop. Merrygrove was ultimately part of Barkhill Ltd, in which Gilmartin retained a 40 per cent share, but he was not informed about the stadium plan or, indeed, about Lawlor and Dunlop's involvement in his company's affairs. The PR man described the ambitious, and potentially lucrative, project as 'the Big One' in his diary.

The plan for the 40,000-capacity stadium, costing up to £35 million, was revealed in September 1992, with an anticipated injection by the government of up to £15 million. The new taoiseach introduced Los Angeles finance brokers Chilton & O'Connor to O'Callaghan to help generate funding from the US, while Dunlop embarked on the intense lobbying of other senior political figures to enlist their support, with a focus on Minister for Finance Bertie Ahern.

Following the November election and the formation of a Fianna Fáil–Labour Party coalition, the agreed 'Programme for Government' included support for 'the building of an indoor National Sports Stadium'. In December 1992, the Ambrose Kelly Group lodged a planning application with Dublin County Council for the project on the lands at Neilstown-Balgaddy. In March 1993, Reynolds met with Bill O'Connor at an event at the Irish Consulate in Los Angeles, during the taoiseach's annual St Patrick's Day visit to the US. The invitation to the principal of Chilton & O'Connor was arranged by Lawlor's son, Niall, who was employed by the firm, while Reynolds also attended a further meeting at the brokerage in August that year.

On 24 August 1993, planning permission for the project was granted, and Chilton & O'Connor advised potential investors that the government was fully committed to supporting the development with tax designation, lottery funds and other initiatives that would allow for debt servicing and repayment to be managed over a fifteen-year period. During the last months of 1993, O'Callaghan held regular meetings with Reynolds on the stadium project, while Dunlop was in contact with Ahern to ensure it was advanced at discussions that took place in the absence of senior officials or documented minutes. During this period, there was also intense party fundraising to clear the huge £3.5 million debt it had accumulated. Ahern's close friend, Des Richardson, was appointed to oversee that money-gathering operation.

A fundraising dinner in Cork on 11 March 1994 was examined by the tribunal, after Gilmartin claimed he was told by O'Callaghan that the latter paid £150,000 to Reynolds in the early hours of the morning following the event. The function, which took place in the home of Cork businessman Niall Welch, was attended by several individuals from the property and construction industry in the city, some of whom donated sums of up to £10,000 each. Richardson collected the envelopes in which the monies, including £10,000 from O'Callaghan, were placed, and he later lodged £50,000 to the party's bank account.

Among the guests at the dinner were property developers Michael O'Flynn, who said later he did not make a donation, Ed McNamara John McCarthy and John Fleming from Bandon.[3] Party stalwart, Noel C. Duggan, the man who denied receiving the Sheik's money from the passport for investment deal in late 1990, was also present. O'Callaghan told Gilmartin that he made the further contribution of £150,000 to Reynolds, who stayed in his home after the dinner party, just hours before the Taoiseach was collected by helicopter in Cork. The Taoiseach was then brought to Dublin, from where he travelled to the US for the annual St Patrick's Day celebrations and meeting in the White House. When I spoke to Reynolds in August 1999 about this claim, the former taoiseach said that he 'probably had attended the Cork dinner' but denied receiving any contribution from O'Callaghan 'at any time'. Fianna Fáil sources said that O'Callaghan did make a 'sizeable donation to the party in 1994' but that it was 'considerably less than £100,000'.[4]

O'Callaghan subsequently confirmed in a letter to the party, which emerged at the tribunal, that he contributed £10,000 at the dinner as part of his commitment to pay the party a total of £100,000 to support its fundraising drive. The promise was made in response to a request from Ray MacSharry to several wealthy Fianna Fáil supporters. On the same day as the fundraising dinner attended by Reynolds in Cork, Ahern was in Los Angeles meeting with Chilton & O'Connor in relation to the stadium project during his own excursion to the US to mark the St Patrick's Day celebrations. On his return, he informed the Dáil of this meeting with the US brokers. During this time, O'Callaghan delivered the balance of the £100,000 he had promised to the party to top up the £10,000 placed in an envelope at the Cork dinner in early March.

Bill O'Connor, along with Dunlop and O'Callaghan, had a further meeting with Reynolds in May 1994, while his partner in Chilton & O'Connor, Kevin Burke, met with the Taoiseach again in Galway. This took place during the annual horse racing week in July, when the party hosted benefactors in the infamous Fianna Fáil tent at Ballybrit Race Track. At the meeting, held in the Connemara Coast Hotel, Reynolds was presented with an updated feasibility plan for the stadium, which projected a total cost of just under £60 million, with an annual subvention for twenty years from the National Lottery of £4.4 million, or £2.7 million if a certain tax designation was granted by the government, which would reduce the outlay. Within days, the proposal was sent to Ahern by Dunlop in a letter marked 'Strictly private and confidential', with a request for a meeting to discuss the matter further. Following a meeting with the minister for finance in the Davenport Hotel in Dublin in late October, Dunlop hopped on a plane to New York for another rendezvous with O'Connor who, in turn, arrived back in Dublin for a meeting with Ahern on 10 November, at which O'Callaghan was also present.

This flurry of engagements on the stadium project came against the background of heightened tensions within the Fianna Fáil–Labour coalition, caused by the controversy surrounding the extradition of child-abusing priest Brendan Smyth. Reynolds was forced to resign in November 1994, after he misled the Dáil in his statements on the issue. It was a particularly sensitive time for such unwelcome and unnecessary political instability as, just three months earlier, Reynolds had helped broker an IRA ceasefire and a potential settlement of the thirty-year conflict in the North. This followed successful negotiations with British Prime Minister John Major and US President Bill Clinton, and private and protracted discussions between the SDLP leader, John Hume, and Sinn Féin president, Gerry Adams.

The main beneficiary of the political debacle was Ahern, who became taoiseach and party leader. On 28 November Bill O'Connor wrote to Ahern to congratulate him on 'your recent unanimous election as leader of Fianna Fáil' and also to 'thank you for allocating time to meet Mr Owen O'Callaghan, Frank Dunlop and myself on the financing of the National All-Purpose Stadium. We wish you every success in the crucial talks you are embarking upon [to form a Government] and we hope to be in contact with you in the near future to progress the subject.'

In the event, Ahern failed to persuade the Labour Party to remain in government and was forced into opposition. Before the collapse of the administration in December, however, in the final days of the outgoing Cabinet, O'Callaghan visited Leinster House for urgent discussions with Reynolds and Ahern over his concerns that the promised inclusion of the Golden Island retail centre in Athlone in the urban renewal tax relief scheme had not been formally and officially signed off. After some fraught discussions between the three, Ahern delivered on the commitment.

The Flood Tribunal took evidence from Ahern on all these issues but could not establish whether large payments to accounts he controlled were related to the stadium issue. It concluded that O'Callaghan and the US brokers had lobbied Ahern intensely in 1993 and 1994, during which time significant round sum amounts were lodged into the accounts of his daughters and his partner, Celia Larkin. Ahern failed to explain the true source of the lodgements, but in his private correspondence with the tribunal decided to throw himself on the mercy of public opinion with a version of events that would challenge the credulity of even his most fervent supporters.

Chapter Twenty-Two

Dig-outs and Dinners

WHEN THE SECOND QUARRYVALE MODULE OPENED at Dublin Castle in late November 2005, Gilmartin was living in Cork, where his wife, Vera, was in a nursing home. With his son, Thomas, he spent days and nights preparing more statements for the tribunal and for his long-delayed reappearance in the witness box. Given the gravity of the allegations he had made against the Taoiseach, he was anticipating another assault on his character by Ahern's lawyers and sections of the media.

Top of the list of his claims presented in the opening statement by Patricia Dillon SC for the tribunal, was the suggestion that Bertie Ahern had received payments of £80,000 from Owen O'Callaghan, including £30,000 in respect of the tax designation withheld from the Blanchardstown retail centre. Dillon did not reveal the circumstances surrounding the alleged £50,000 payment, but Ahern was well aware that they concerned the purchase of the Dublin County Council lands at Quarryvale. The reference to the £80,000 he got from O'Callaghan mirrored the details of the story I published in *IOS* three years earlier, which had provoked such hostile denials from Ahern and Minister for Justice Michael McDowell at the time.[1]

In response to Dillon's opening statement the Taoiseach once again insisted that he never received a penny from O'Callaghan and had been vindicated in the Circuit Court in his case against 'Starry' O'Brien.

Ahern said he had 'lately become aware that Mr Tom Gilmartin made very similar allegations to those disproved in court. Like Mr O'Brien, Mr Gilmartin has alleged that the Taoiseach received a large amount of money from Mr O'Callaghan. Like Mr O'Brien, Mr Gilmartin made these allegations in the period 1998–2000. Like Mr O'Brien, Mr Gilmartin's allegations are utterly false.'

For Gilmartin, the Taoiseach's remarks only confirmed what he and many others suspected, which was that the Starry O'Brien fabrication was a blatant attempt to sully and damage his character by associating him with the flawed, self-confessed fraudster from Cork. Gilmartin had informed the tribunal about the alleged payment of £50,000 by O'Callaghan at a football match in September 1989 before Starry O'Brien came forward in 1999. He had included the allegation in a formal statement. He suspected that O'Callaghan was behind the Starry O'Brien 'set-up' that attempted to disguise his payments to senior Fianna Fáil politicians, and dismissed Ahern's remarks as a futile effort by the Taoiseach to undermine the tribunal. He believed these remarks were almost certainly linked to yet another order for discovery it had served months earlier on the politician seeking details of his financial records and bank accounts. The order expired on the same day that the second Quarryvale module of the tribunal began.

O'Callaghan's reaction to the opening statement was to take judicial review proceedings against the tribunal in the High Court, postponing the hearings until after the case was heard in March 2006. The legal team for O'Callaghan, led by Paul Gallagher SC, based its High Court action on the alleged 'glaringly and significantly inconsistent statements' given by Gilmartin to the tribunal in his private and public evidence sessions. Gallagher further claimed that the tribunal was 'biased' against his client and had wrongly given immunity from prosecution to Gilmartin as an inducement to him to give evidence. It took over six months for Judge Thomas Smyth to produce a ruling, which rejected the arguments of bias against the tribunal and ruled that any inconsistencies in Gilmartin's statements could be tested in cross-examination at a public hearing of the inquiry.

Gilmartin, now facing another protracted delay while Smyth's ruling was challenged in the Supreme Court, was angry and frustrated at how his name was being abused:

> Anything I said to the tribunal was based on what O'Callaghan told me or what I heard from others. I knew nothing of Ahern's finances, for example, and had only told the tribunal that O'Callaghan said he gave him money for various reasons. Over the years different people told me different things … and I informed the tribunal about them as I had promised to do, no matter how incredible they seemed. Some things that did seem incredible turned out to be true, others were never proven. But to then get attacked and vilified in court because I repeated details in confidence to a tribunal was not one bit fair, especially as I was not there to defend myself.[2]

The appeal to the Supreme Court led to a welcome reprieve for Ahern and others accused of wrongdoing and corruption, but it also provided them with an opportunity to fill the vacuum left by the suspension of public tribunal hearings with another sequence of carefully contrived misinformation.

The elaborate deception was orchestrated with the anonymous delivery of a letter in September 2006 to *Irish Times* journalist Colm Keena, which contained details of statements people made to the tribunal about financial contributions they claimed to have given Ahern in December 1993. The monies, amounting in total to between £50,000 and £100,000, were ostensibly given to the then minister for finance to help with the legal bills arising from his marital separation. Among the donors was businessman David McKenna, the owner of Marlborough Recruitment and former employer of Des Richardson. In 1993, McKenna used his private jet to bring Ahern to Manchester United games, and he regularly attended the fundraisers for Fianna Fáil organised by Richardson during the Galway races. Marlborough Recruitment, which generated an estimated £60 million for McKenna, collapsed dramatically in 2002.

Following publication by *The Irish Times* of these alleged payments to Ahern, the Taoiseach attacked what he described as a leak of his personal financial information from the tribunal, while at the same time accepting that 'a lot of what is on the front of the paper is absolutely correct'. However, the reference to payments amounting to £100,000 described in the article were 'off the wall', he said.[3] Once again, he pointed to previous 'false allegations' against him but confirmed that he had provided details of his finances to the tribunal, including those concerning payments received from McKenna and others in 1993. He agreed that he appointed McKenna to the board of Enterprise Ireland, a State agency, but insisted this had nothing to do with any money he received from the businessman. He said he had no intention of providing information about his personal finances to anyone else and, when pressed further on the *Irish Times* story, replied:

> I'm not answering what I got for my Holy Communion money, my Confirmation money, what I got for my birthday, what I got for anything else. I'm not into that. I gave all the details of everything to do with my life to the tribunal, but I'm not under investigation for any of these things, including the unjust leak that's in the papers this morning.[4]

The political stakes were high as the Taoiseach was facing a general election by June 2007 at the latest, and he was now dealing with further questions from the tribunal about the significant sums it had found as it went through various bank accounts under his control in the early

1990s. Although this trawl was not known beyond his own circle and the tribunal lawyers, it was clear that Ahern's strategy was to put a narrative into the public mind that would distract from any suggestion that the monies in the accounts were acquired corruptly.

Just months before the unexplained, and anonymous, letter was delivered to *The Irish Times*, Ahern's accountant, Des Peelo, provided a statement of the Taoiseach's financial affairs to the tribunal on foot of a court order from June 2006. In the statement, Peelo, previously an advisor to Charles Haughey, sought to explain the lodgements made to various bank and building society accounts held in the names of Ahern's daughters, partner and others. The financial information he reluctantly provided to the inquiry forced Ahern to create a legitimate explanation for the monies in the accounts and to prove that they were not illicit or corrupt payments, as the tribunal suspected. The tale was the latest ploy to distract the public from the actual source of the funds passing through the accounts. It was a risky strategy but one that, he believed, would at least buy some time.

Despite his protestations that no one was entitled to ask about his personal finances, Ahern chose to give a detailed interview to the RTÉ evening news on 26 September 2006, during which he disclosed the names of those who gave him a 'dig-out' amounting to some £50,000, in late 1993, when he was going through the legal separation from his wife, Miriam. He described the contributors as 'close friends, people who have been close to me for most of my life. They are not political friends, they are personal friends … longstanding friends.' They felt sorry for him and wanted to support him through his marital crisis, he suggested.

He claimed that eight friends gave him £22,500 in December 1993, naming David McKenna, Des Richardson, Paddy Reilly, Pádraic O'Connor, Jim Nugent, Fintan Gunne, Michael Collins and Charlie Chawke as his benefactors. A second payment, of £16,500 in 1994, came from Joe Burke, Dermot Carew, Barry English and another Paddy Reilly.

The final payment of £8,000 sterling was given to him by a group of businessmen after a function in Manchester in September 1994, the first mention he made of any sterling amount. He described the money as a debt of honour that he wanted to repay in full, but his friends would not accept. He insisted that he dealt with the tax implications of the payments. He conceded that he appointed some of these friends to State boards, but only because 'they were friends, not because of anything they had given me'.

Five of the twelve Dublin donors served on State boards. Solicitor, Gerry Brennan, whom *The Irish Times* suggested was the man who collected the 'dig-out' money, served on the board of Telecom Éireann before his death in 1997, while Richardson was a director of Aer Lingus between 1997 and 2002. Joe Burke was on the board of the Dublin Port Authority, Jim Nugent on the Central Bank and Cert boards, while Pádraic O'Connor was a director of Eircom and the State-owned bank ACC.

During the lengthy RTÉ interview with Bryan Dobson, Ahern became emotional when talking about his marriage breakdown, and then made the startling public revelation that he did not operate any bank accounts between 1987 and 1993, during which time he served as minister for finance. He railed against the claims made by 'Starry' O'Brien and others over alleged bribes he received from O'Callaghan. He dismissed these and reports about his offshore accounts in distant lands as proof of a massive conspiracy against him. He complained that he was forced to provide the tribunal with details of all his financial records and the bank accounts of Miriam, those in the names of his children and of his constituency organisation. If he wanted to distract people from what was coming down the line at the tribunal, he certainly succeeded, while also providing great entertainment for the huge audience watching the six o'clock news.

Ahern's description of his donors as 'personal friends' was somewhat tarnished when businessman Barry English later said he gave his contribution at the request of Joe Burke and that he barely knew Ahern.[5] Among the others were some colourful characters, who were indeed loyal to Ahern. Publican Dermot Carew was the owner of the Beaumont House, a regular haunt of the Taoiseach and one of the places to which Joe Burke brought Gilmartin on their search for the elusive politician in north Dublin in 1989. Fintan Gunne appeared as a witness at the Flood Tribunal over his financial dealings with builders Brennan & McGowan and was among those criticised in its interim report for non-cooperation in its investigation into Ray Burke. Paddy 'the Plasterer' Reilly was a landlord in Gardiner Street, Dublin.

The tribunal called Keena and *Irish Times* editor Geraldine Kennedy to explain how they got hold of the story of the personal contributions. Keena said it came into his hands after he received a phone call at the newspaper offices. Tribunal chairman, Alan Mahon, said that only one original copy of the letter, on which the newspaper story was based, existed, and that it was in the possession of David McKenna or his solicitor. He said there was no other copy, the implication being that the so-called 'leak' must have come from Ahern's camp rather than someone disgruntled with the Taoiseach. The tribunal carefully indented copies of its correspondence with individual witnesses with a special mark, in order to track their origin in the event of any such attempt to misuse them.

Ahern was pursued around the country by reporters, who wanted to know more about his generous friends, forcing him to provide more embarrassing details about the gifts he accepted while in Cabinet. Asked in Ballyjamesduff in Cavan to explain the function in Manchester, Ahern said that he had spoken at a dinner involving twenty-five Irish emigrant businessmen some of whom did a whip-around, and he believed the £8000 sterling raised was not taxable as it was given to him outside the State. He was in the city for a Manchester United game, so, in his words, 'no official script, not an official function, not in my capacity as minister, paid my own way, spoke at the function'.[6]

With a general election only months away, the opposition parties smelled blood, while his government partners in the Progressive Democrats became nervous, with their recently chosen leader and tánaiste, Michael McDowell, suspecting, rightly, that his party might be tainted by the latest revelations of sleaze embroiling Ahern.

In early October 2006, Ahern protested in a statement to the Dáil that he had 'produced all of my records going back for a long number of years which show I have not enriched myself through politics and have not abused public office. I disclosed my financial records to the tribunal and it is deeply regrettable that these confidential records appeared in a newspaper.'[7]

He was reluctant to identify any of those who contributed to the Manchester whip-around, with the exception of Tim Kilroe, who owned the hotel where the suggested event took place, who had presented the monies in cash to him and since died. Another businessman, John Kennedy, later confirmed that he was present at an event with Ahern in the English city but did not provide further details. A friend of Kennedy told me that the late and successful Manchester businessman had been generous when certain visiting politicians from Dublin 'put their hands out' during those years. Ahern said he did not want 'to name anyone by mistake and then be accused of misleading the house'.

Michael Wall, the man who drove Ahern and his friend, Senator Tony Kett, in the bus to the hotel, came forward to confirm his role. Wall owned a bus hire company in Manchester, and, in an interview with *The Irish Times*, said that he believed the cash collection was made in the context of the Taoiseach's marital problems. 'If I was him, I would have found it awfully embarrassing to refuse to accept it. Most people there didn't know that he had matrimonial problems at the time. I didn't know he had matrimonial problems.'[8]

Wall confirmed he attended the dinner but did not partake of it, and neither did he contribute to the spontaneous collection, but his relationship with Ahern was much deeper than it seemed at first. Indeed, it was 'awfully embarrassing' for the Taoiseach when it was disclosed that Wall owned the house where he had lived since 1995, following years of bunking in other people's homes or above his constituency office, St Luke's, in Drumcondra. This raised uncomfortable questions about the circumstances in which Ahern acquired his home and revived memories of Ray Burke's convoluted and tearful explanations of the house acquired and built for him by his friends in Swords.

Ahern tripped himself up by claiming that he accumulated cash savings of £50,000 in late 1993, during the period with no bank account to his name. At the same time, he claimed to have used the £22,500 dig-out money from December 1993 to pay off a bank loan he had taken out with AIB to cover legal and other costs arising from his marital separation. This raised a question as to whether Gerry Brennan, the solicitor who collected the loans from his friends, knew of the cash Ahern had saved at a time when his client was claiming to have no money. If so, it would presumably have been declared as part of the required affidavit of means to the High Court as part of the separation agreement. And, while bemoaning the fact that he had to give the tribunal details of the accounts of his daughters, partner and constituency, Ahern did not explain that the tribunal sought this information because he had no bank account in his own name for the years in question. As Labour Party leader Pat Rabbitte observed during the Dáil debate on Ahern's statement on the Manchester and other donations:

> In normal life one gets gifts from one's friends and one takes loans from strangers. Yet Mr Ahern says he got loans from his friends and took gifts from strangers … Where was the £50,000 resting, since the then Minister, Deputy Bertie Ahern, did not have a bank account? Was it resting in a sock or in the hot press? … he enjoyed a ministerial and Deputy's salary and the use of a premises bought

> for him by friends of Fianna Fáil ... If he had £50,000 in savings, why was it necessary to raise a bank loan? If a bank loan was in place, why was it necessary to have a whip-around to replace the bank loan?[9]

In March, four of the five Supreme Court judges upheld the High Court decision in the case brought by O'Callaghan against the tribunal, with Judge Adrian Hardiman the only dissenting voice. Hardiman, who had acted as a senior counsel for Liam Lawlor, was among the lawyers who clashed with former tribunal chairman Feargus Flood about the extent of the orders for discovery served on their clients in autumn 1998, following the publication of Gilmartin's allegations. His close friend Michael McDowell, who represented O'Callaghan at the time, was also in the room in Dublin Castle when they made their fruitless demand to Flood to back off. Now Hardiman issued a lengthy judgement accusing the tribunal of allowing Gilmartin free rein in his private statements to the inquiry, some of which had been disproven and others of which were inconsistent with his public evidence, which was unfair to O'Callaghan. His stinging criticism did not prevent the tribunal from resuming its public hearings into the Quarryvale 2 module, but it left a sour taste in Gilmartin's mouth:

> The other four judges disagreed with his opinion on the day and the tribunal continued. But I was not happy at the way I was depicted as some kind of crazy fantasist that made outrageous allegations against people. Some of the allegations which people thought were fantastic were later proven to be true. That did not stop sections of the media from attacking my credibility, week in and week out. At some points I wondered, 'What is the point of it all?' Vera is lying in a hospital bed. I'm not getting any younger. The kids were alright, but I was like a fish out of water in a place where I hardly knew a soul. As the time approached for my next appearance in

> the witness box, the personal attacks got worse, but we decided that I should continue my evidence and get it over with.[10]

In 2007, I was working with *The Irish Mail on Sunday* (*IMOS*), produced by the owners of the renamed *Ireland on Sunday*, when I wrote another bizarre story on Ahern just weeks before the resumption of the tribunal's public hearings. The story, also published by the *Sunday Independent*, involved a claim by a former garda, who served as the official driver on a temporary basis for the then minister for finance in 1994.

Martin Fallon claimed that he drove Ahern to Dublin Airport for a flight to Manchester on one occasion with a case full of cash in the boot of the car. A day earlier, he accompanied Ahern's partner, Celia Larkin, to the AIB in O'Connell Street, where she collected a briefcase. She asked him to hold onto the briefcase and to collect Ahern in Drumcondra the following morning and bring him to the airport. Later that evening, after he went home, he decided to open the case and found it was full of banknotes. Worried that the car might be stolen from outside his house, he drove to Garda HQ in Phoenix Park, where he left the car with the briefcase in it overnight. The next morning, he collected the car and went to Drumcondra, picked up Ahern and took him to the airport for his flight to Manchester, briefcase in hand.

Fine Gael TD Jim Higgins confirmed for my article that he and fellow Mayo party colleague, Enda Kenny TD, had been told the same story by Fallon several years previously. Higgins said that he brought it to the attention of the tribunal, but it did not obtain a direct and sworn account from the now retired Fallon. He was in bad health when I contacted his wife, who said that her husband did not wish to comment further on the matter.

The story, published on Sunday, 15 April 2007, was immediately described as 'untrue' by a spokesperson for the Taoiseach, who said that Ahern was not 'aware of the allegations being put before the tribunal'.[11] Its effect was to heighten the tensions between the leader of the government and the inquiry, which contributed to Ahern's surprise decision to announce the general election two months before it was due. On 29 April 2007, it was confirmed that the election would be held less than a month later and that the Taoiseach had visited Áras an Uachtaráin before most people woke up that morning, to ask President Mary McAleese to dissolve the Dáil. It then emerged that a small number of journalists had been contacted the previous night and told to attend the Áras between 7 and 7.30 a.m. to witness the Taoiseach's arrival. He declared an election for 24 May in front of the selected media as he emerged from his hastily arranged meeting with the president.

Ahern did not inform senior colleagues, including deputy leader Brian Cowen, of his intention, nor did he follow precedent and inform the Dáil in advance of his trip to the Áras that he was going to the country. Senior Fianna Fáil minister Micheál Martin later disclosed that: 'Most ministers found out about one o'clock in the morning that an election was being called at six.'[12] Cowen, who led the party's election strategy committee, was incensed at the surprise announcement. He was also angered that, three days earlier, Ahern had given an interview to Aengus Fanning, editor of the *Sunday Independent*, who got the inside track and a front-page story on the Taoiseach's election plans. The newspaper was on the streets announcing a general election hours before it was officially called.

In the 'exclusive' with the *Sunday Independent*, Ahern expressed concern about his forthcoming appearance before what was now known as the Mahon Tribunal to explain his personal finances and answer questions about the source of monies in various accounts he controlled. It was widely reported that he later met with the newspaper's owner, Tony O'Reilly, who offered his unambiguous support to the Fianna Fáil leader in his campaign for re-election.[13]

Chapter Twenty-Three

A Stash in the Wardrobe

ON THE DAY OF HIS VISIT to the Áras to shut down parliament, Ahern's lawyers wrote to the tribunal seeking to postpone the planned hearings into the Taoiseach's financial affairs until after the election. His announcement coincided with the publication in the *IMOS* of sensational details concerning his finances. He may have been hoping that the front-page story he fed to the *Sunday Independent* announcing the election would divert attention from these, and that the tribunal's intention to reveal new and damaging information about his financial affairs the following day would be delayed by his election plan. Micheál Martin suggested that 'he may have been playing cat and mouse with the *Mail*. Maybe he wanted them to throw everything at him and then he would go to war.'[1] It was a massive gamble on Ahern's part, but it succeeded and gave him the vital breathing space he needed to survive perhaps the greatest challenge of his political career.

Before publication, the *IMOS* contacted Ahern's press office with a series of questions that arose from private interviews that he, his former partner Celia Larkin and the Manchester bus driver Michael Wall had with the tribunal. We were in possession of the transcripts of their interviews with tribunal lawyers over previous weeks. It was ironic, to say the least, that the information we obtained was circulated as a consequence of Owen O'Callaghan's successful legal action to ensure that the tribunal provided documents to all interested parties in advance of their being disclosed at its public hearings.

In one of several exclusives run by the *IMOS* over the following months, it was reported that Ahern had provided extraordinary details of his financial and personal affairs in a private interview with tribunal lawyers earlier in April. The documents I obtained confidentially exposed major flaws and inconsistencies in explanations provided by the Taoiseach in his television interview and other statements given only a few months previously. When people read the litany of ludicrous and freshly minted tales from the mouth of the country's most powerful politician, they understood more clearly why he had called the election early.

Among the details reported was what the Taoiseach told the tribunal lawyers about the proposed purchase of his home in Dublin from Michael Wall and the comical sequence of events surrounding the proposed deal. Remarkably, it was claimed that Wall travelled from England to Dublin with a briefcase filled with £30,000 sterling in cash, which was to be spent on doing up the house and which he gave to Larkin in St Luke's in early December 1994. Ahern said he put a further £50,000 into the refurbishment of the house, even though the sale was not completed and Wall was still the owner. Larkin opened two bank accounts to lodge the money on behalf of Wall and Ahern. Ahern explained to the lawyers that this was during the dramatic period when he hoped to succeed Albert Reynolds as taoiseach and he needed a permanent address. Quoting directly from the documents: 'He said he did not want questions about his living arrangements. He said he wanted to be able to inform the Garda authorities as to where his personal security should be located in the event of his being appointed Taoiseach.'[2] He also claimed to have purchased large sums of sterling during the mid-1990s, some of it to repay Mr Wall, but he never actually did. He did not finalise the purchase of the house in the upmarket Beresford estate in Drumcondra, and claimed to have been amazed to discover that, while still a tenant of Wall in 1996, his landlord made a will leaving him the house.

Ahern told the lawyers that he had a habit of storing large sums of cash in his safe in St Luke's and in the Department of Finance during his term as minister. Equally staggering was the revelation that a number of lodgements by Ahern and Larkin to various accounts in 1994 and 1995 matched foreign currency amounts. One, the tribunal established, was equal to an exact round figure amount of $45,000 on that day's trading. The lodgement to the bank, made by Larkin on 5 December 1994, was explained by Ahern as the money given to him by Wall for the refurbishment of the Beresford house. The tribunal asked Ahern about the fact that the lodgement made by Larkin of £28,772.90 at the AIB bank in O'Connell Street Dublin, just days after Wall's visit, happened to amount to the exact equivalent of $45,000. The Taoiseach replied that he had not received any dollar payments. The tribunal rejected Ahern's assertion that this lodgement was the £30,000 from Wall, but because of Ahern's failure to explain the true source of the foreign currency, the tribunal 'was unable to determine the source of these funds'.[3]

Another hole was blown in Ahern's account of the circumstances of his financial 'dig-outs' when we reported how one of those he named as a donor from December 1993, Pádraic O'Connor, told the tribunal that he was never a personal friend of Ahern. The former managing director of National City Brokers, a stockbroking company founded by Dermot Desmond, made a contribution of £5,000 to Fianna Fáil, not to Ahern. In return, he said, the company received an invoice for consultancy work from Des Richardson that had never been carried out. It transpired that Richardson had made a £2,500 'dig-out' contribution to Ahern from a company account through which Fianna Fáil paid him for work. The Fianna Fáil-issued cheques were co-signed by Ahern.

The sensational *IMOS* report on the Taoiseach's convoluted admissions was largely ignored by other print and broadcast media, which did not have the details I had obtained. However, we anticipated a reaction when the tribunal resumed the following day, Monday 30 April. Instead, chairman, Alan Mahon announced that he intended to suspend public hearings until the week after the May election.

One of the few to raise questions about Ahern's strange financial arrangements was Green Party TD John Gormley, who said that the Taoiseach should 'clarify matters before the public cast their votes'.[4] He was responding to a comment made by Ahern when asked about the £30,000 cash payment given by Wall to Celia Larkin. Ahern had said that 'any money that Ms Larkin received was towards – it was a stamp duty issue and was towards the refurbishment of the house. So, it was entirely appropriate – entirely appropriate'.[5] Gormley was not impressed with the answer and suggested that the stamp duty story was 'not credible': 'Perhaps on Planet Bertie landlords give their tenants £30,000 to pay stamp duty, but in the real world this is difficult to believe.'[6]

As the election campaign progressed, both Ahern's Fianna Fáil colleagues and his coalition partners sought to mitigate the political damage without dissociating themselves from the leader of the government. Progressive Democrat leader Michael McDowell came under particular attack after he said that he had a friendly chat with the Taoiseach, suggesting that relations were calm. This was just days after McDowell claimed that he was previously misled by Ahern in relation to the latter's financial affairs and hinted that he may have to withdraw his party's support for the outgoing government. *Irish Times* columnist Vincent Browne accused McDowell of 'cynical opportunism', which, he wrote, was 'all the more odious by its presentation as principled, wrapped in intellectual and moral conceit'. Browne pointed out that McDowell had apparently initially seen

> no reason to be concerned at all over the revelations of Frank Connolly of two days previously in the *Mail on Sunday* (29th

> April). McDowell, on Tuesday of last week, found nothing at all peculiar about this, but on Sunday it had blown up into a major crisis. It isn't remotely believable he found out anything of any consequence in the days between Tuesday and Friday, when the PDs first went into a crisis of conscience over continuance in government with Ahern over and above what Connolly had revealed the previous Sunday.[7]

I published a further story in the *IMOS* which exposed deep contradictions between Ahern's claim that the Wall money was given to Larkin for the renovation of the house and his private statement to the tribunal in which he said he was given the money by the Manchester businessman.[8] In response to the flow of negative revelations, Ahern, on Sunday 13 May, issued a 5,000-word statement in which he again asserted that the claim that he had received £80,000 from Owen O'Callaghan, as alleged by Tom Gilmartin, 'was baseless and borne out of spite and malice'. He rejected the allegation that O'Callaghan gave him £50,000 in 1989 and falsely stated that this was the same claim as that made by the discredited Starry O'Brien: 'This changing and unreliable story is essentially the same as the story which was written by Mr Frank Connolly in 2000 and was proved to be a lie in the Circuit Court.' He continued, 'I have been in political life for 30 years and I have held government office for eighteen of those years. The only transactions being examined by the Mahon tribunal cover a period of 24 months immediately following the resolution of my matrimonial difficulties and during a period of great flux in my life.'

What he failed to add is that the tribunal could only examine his finances for the years covered by its terms of reference, which were set by the government of which Ahern was taoiseach and specifically limited to the years to which Gilmartin's allegations related. He denied being the beneficial owner of the Beresford house since March 1995 and repeated that he was 'surprised' Wall left him the house in his will, which his landlord made when he thought he might die following a traffic accident. He notably did not refer to the lodgements that went into the various accounts under his control between 1993 and 1996 or explain why one amounted to the exact equivalent of $45,000. In an interview with *Sky News* on 6 May 2007 during the election campaign, Ahern denied suggestions by Fine Gael leader, Enda Kenny, in an RTÉ leader's debate that he was 'a crook' and insisted, 'I did not receive a glass of water from Owen O'Callaghan.'

Following the election, a victorious Fianna Fáil returned to government, with 41.5 per cent of the vote, but this time with the Green Party as coalition partners. The Progressive Democrats were annihilated, losing six of their eight seats, including McDowell's. Mary Harney, one of its two surviving TDs, retained her position as minister for health.

When the tribunal resumed a few days later, Des O'Neill SC delivered an opening statement that added to the scepticism many people felt over Ahern's explanations of his unusual finances. O'Neill said that, as part of its remit, the tribunal had examined the allegation by Gilmartin that Ahern received £80,000 from Owen O'Callaghan during the time the Taoiseach said he had no bank account. In the course of its investigation, it had also identified four transactions between 1993 and 1995 involving Ahern and Larkin that were preceded by sterling, and in one case dollar, amounts totalling more than £175,000.

In order to set out the background to the Quarryvale 2 module, Gilmartin was called to resume his evidence concerning his attempts to get the retail development, now the Liffey Valley Shopping Centre, off the ground between 1990 and 1993. Over a number of days in the witness box, Gilmartin described in shocking detail how Joe Burke asked him, in the late summer of 1990, for £500,000 in return for assistance from Bertie Ahern. He became emotional when he described how Frank Dunlop and others conspired to have the Inland Revenue in England hit him with a demand for almost £7 million sterling that he did not owe.

He became more upset when he recalled how Vera was knocked to the ground in the hallway of their home in Luton by a group of journalists and photographers seeking to ask him about his tax affairs.

He also referred to monies which O'Callaghan told him he had paid to Ahern and other politicians, including Micheál Martin. Martin later confirmed to the tribunal that he received more than £10,000 from the Cork developer over the years, including £3,500, which was lodged in his wife Mary's bank account. He had previously told me, after the Gilmartin allegations first surfaced in 1998, that he received less than half this amount from O'Callaghan during the late 1980s and early 1990s. I had arranged a meeting with him in Jury's Hotel in Ballsbridge, where, accompanied by his advisor, Deirdre Gillane, he assured me that he was given just a few thousand pounds in donations from the developer. His later statement showed this was untrue and that he had accepted over twice the amount he had claimed to me.

For the first time in his public evidence, Gilmartin claimed that both Ahern and Reynolds received monies in connection with the designation of the Golden Island retail development in Athlone in late 1994. The tribunal audience, which had returned in large numbers for the long-delayed return of Gilmartin to Dublin Castle, listened intently as he brought O'Neill through the circumstances of the alleged £50,000 payment at a football match by O'Callaghan to Ahern in autumn 1989 to ensure that Green Property did not get its hands on the council-owned lands at Quarryvale. He described how he had initially assumed that O'Callaghan was referring to a GAA football final in Croke Park, but that he had since recalled that it more likely happened during the soccer international between the Republic and Northern Ireland teams in Lansdowne Road in early October 1989 for which O'Callaghan told him he was getting tickets.

It was a significant distinction, given that Ahern had repeatedly, in the course of his denials of such a payment, made reference to the fabricated claim by Denis 'Starry' O'Brien about handing a cheque to him for £50,000 in the car park of the Burlington Hotel following a GAA football final. Gilmartin said that he was warned not to get involved in the Starry O'Brien claims and had, over the years, refused to comment on the matter.

'I am not alleging that Mr Ahern was paid anything. I was told by Owen O'Callaghan,' Gilmartin insisted. He recalled how O'Callaghan told him how he got zoning for the lands at Golden Island in Athlone, and how pressure was put on local Fianna Fáil TD Mary O'Rourke, who was opposed to the 'out of town' development along with other traders in the town. O'Rourke had previously complained about intimidation and a physical assault on her by a local businessman, Tom Diskin, who sought her backing for the Golden Island scheme. Gilmartin said he was told by O'Callaghan that he paid £25,000 to £30,000 to Ahern for the tax designation of Golden Island, which was agreed just before the collapse of the Fianna Fáil–Labour administration in late 1994.

He also outlined how O'Callaghan predicted that the cap on the size of Quarryvale to half the scale envisaged by Gilmartin would be lifted, based on a commitment given to the Cork developer by a senior local government official. Lawyers for O'Callaghan questioned this claim that a public servant could be compromised in such a manner, but the tribunal lawyers were able to produce a letter to AIB in which the Cork man assured his bankers of the guarantee he had received that the cap would be lifted. When Gilmartin went through the details of the dinner party in Cork in March 1994, and how Reynolds was collected by helicopter to catch a flight on the government jet from Dublin to the US, the tribunal produced Air Corps records to show how that was the precise manner in which the then Taoiseach was transported on the morning in question.

Gilmartin went on to claim that not all of the hundreds of thousands of dollars raised by Fianna Fáil in the US between 1993 and 1996, on the back of Reynold's role in achieving the historic IRA ceasefire and promise of peace negotiations in the North, were sent back to Ireland. Instead, he said, he learned from relations in America that some of the funds raised found their way 'floating to the Bahamas and the Cayman Islands'. Air Corps records confirmed that Reynolds and his cortege had made a stoppage at Freeport in the Bahamas on their return from the US in March 1994, which was not on the original itinerary for the trip. During the three-day official visit, they enjoyed dinner with Tony O'Reilly and members of the Bahamas government at the publisher's home in Lyford Cay. Albert Reynolds was unable to give evidence at the tribunal during 2007 due to ill health, but he later denied that he ever personally benefited from money collected at party fundraising events in the US or anywhere else.

Gilmartin concluded his direct evidence in the summer of 2007, following a break due to a serious chest infection. On his return, he explained that, in December 1995, with his solicitor, Noel Smyth, he had negotiated a settlement with AIB, which paid him £8.7 million. This included damages of £1 million and another £150,000 in compensation for political donations made, without his consent, in relation to the Quarryvale project. The bank agreed to the settlement following threats by Smyth that he would take legal proceedings against AIB for its role in facilitating the corruption of politicians by its client O'Callaghan, as well as other breaches of corporate law.

As Gilmartin underwent an intense and at times brutal cross-examination by lawyers for Ahern, O'Callaghan, Redmond, AIB and others, the tribunal continued to gather evidence to support his claims and to interrogate the extraordinary explanations it received from the Taoiseach, Larkin and Wall. Before Ahern arrived to give evidence in September 2007, the tribunal heard from a string of bank witnesses, including officials who, as recently as the previous January, had dealt with queries from the Taoiseach about his sterling lodgements in advance of their discovery by the tribunal. A currency service operations manager with AIB, Rosemary Murtagh, confirmed that it was 'most probable' that the December 1994 lodgement of £28,772.90 at its O'Connell Street branch was the result of a $45,000 transaction.

Ahern never mentioned any foreign exchange transactions to the tribunal until April 2007, when he referred only to large sums in sterling. He refused to concede any lodgement was based on a $45,000 transaction and continued to insist that it came from the sterling cash given to him by Wall. Wall described how he carried the briefcase containing £30,000 sterling in cash to Dublin by boat and left it in the unlocked wardrobe of his hotel room while he attended the annual constituency fundraiser for Fianna Fáil in the Clontarf Castle Hotel in December 1994. Ahern said that the lodgement came after the sterling was converted to punts, even though the bank records showed that only £2,000 sterling was transacted in the branch on that day, 5 December 1994, while there were unusually large dollar exchanges.

The tribunal estimated that Ahern had lodgements under his control of more than £80,000, which was almost twice his annual salary of £42,000. When it came to the sterling amounts, it turned out they were lodged in large round figures, in contrast to Ahern's 'dig-out' story and other explanations to the tribunal over the previous three years. The question now was whether the inquiry could unearth any other probable narrative as to the source of the monies resting in his various accounts. The evidence presented, including by Ahern himself, begged the question as to why he did not buy his own house, given that he clearly had the resources and income to do so as a highly paid politician, minister and leader of the opposition. It also explained why Ahern, several years earlier, had sought to limit, through his lawyers, the discovery sought by the tribunal to transactions of less than £30,000. This suggested that he had clear knowledge of the origins of the larger lodgements. He also called AIB in January 2007 to ask whether any of the lodgements to his accounts in 1994 and 1995 were preceded by foreign exchange transactions. This was before the bank or the tribunal knew anything about lodgements that involved sterling cash amounts. In November 1993, Ahern had opposed a proposal by his government partners in the Labour Party to set up the Standards in Public Office Commission, which would oblige members of the Oireachtas to declare the interests of their spouses and children.

It was apparent that Ahern's strategy over a long period was to design and manage his delayed responses to the tribunal's queries to what he believed was its level of knowledge of his financial affairs. When it discovered the foreign currency transactions, he created a narrative to explain them, including the tales of dig-outs and the landlord who left him a house in his will. In short, Ahern spent years obstructing and abusing the inquiry he created, in the hope that it would fail before it brought him down.

Chapter Twenty-Four

It All Came Out in the Washing

DUE TO HIS POOR HEALTH, GILMARTIN continued his cross-examination with curtailed hearings held in the mornings at Dublin Castle. As he anticipated, lawyers for O'Callaghan and Ahern sought to denigrate his character and, on one occasion, his mental health, but he gave as good as he got.

Citing evidence from a bank memo from 1994 that recorded Paul Sheeran describing his friend Gilmartin as 'incoherent and paranoid', Colm Ó hOisín, senior counsel for Ahern, asked him whether he ever received 'psychological or psychiatric treatment'. Gilmartin replied that, like many people, Sheeran found it hard to believe what he was hearing about the number of high-ranking politicians and public servants who were trying to squeeze money out of him. He told the tribunal that he never needed any such treatment and then launched a sustained assault on Ahern, whom he described as a liar, the 'biggest conman this country has ever seen' and a man who 'pales Charlie Haughey into the ha'penny place'. He spoke about Ahern meeting Tony O'Reilly during the election campaign, and how, since then, 'all we are reading are the thoughts of Chairman Mao', in reference to the uncritical coverage of the politician in the *Sunday Independent* over the previous months.

When he completed his evidence in late October 2007, the tribunal called a number of witnesses who corroborated some of the more damaging claims that Gilmartin made about the Taoiseach. Among them was former international soccer player turned journalist Eamon Dunphy, who had previously worked for O'Reilly's newspaper and more recently hosted *The Last Word* on Today FM, to which I was a regular contributor. After a show one evening in February 2007, Dunphy informed me that he had met Owen O'Callaghan in the mid-1990s to discuss a proposal to bring the London-based soccer club Wimbledon FC to Dublin and set up shop at the developer's planned stadium in Neilstown. They met socially, and, on more than one occasion, the Cork developer talked about the problems he encountered in his dealings with politicians in the capital. In his statement, which we published in the *Irish Daily Mail* just weeks before he gave evidence to the tribunal, Dunphy described how O'Callaghan complained that he paid money to Ahern in connection with some of his business projects. He told Dunphy that Ahern was slow to deliver on promises he made, even when he was 'looked after'.[1]

'The thing about Bertie is that he takes the money and he doesn't do the business,' Dunphy said:

> He (O'Callaghan) told me a story over a meal about Bertie, when Albert [Reynolds] had to put a gun to his head to get tax designation [for Golden Island]. And he said he was wary of Bertie, he didn't trust Bertie. Owen O'Callaghan told me that there was panic the night before the Government fell (in December 1994). He had to put a gun to Bertie's head. Money was paid to Bertie Ahern, and Albert had to intervene.[2]

He described how O'Callaghan said, 'Albert had to get the gun out at quarter to twelve,' and that 'Bertie had been bought, had taken money'. The amount was unspecified.

Dunphy continued, 'This thing about Bertie recurred a number of times over a couple of years, but he made no bones about him, saying to me, "You can't rely on Bertie" and that "he would take money, all right, but won't deliver". Describing the Cork developer as a 'thoroughly decent man', Dunphy said that O'Callaghan complained that, in order to do business, it was necessary to bribe politicians.

Although Dunphy had previously told me about some of his discussions with O'Callaghan, he was reluctant to come forward to the tribunal on the basis that they were private and confidential. However, he said that 'iron entered his soul' because of the manner in which I was treated by Ahern and Michael McDowell when I was executive director of the Centre for Public Inquiry (CPI) in Dublin from 2004 to 2006. The agency was funded by Irish-American Chuck Feeney, who asked me to head up an organisation to expose political corruption, including the abuse of public monies in Ireland, through investigative journalism. The retired judge and former tribunal chairman, Feargus Flood, chaired the board of the CPI.

The CPI produced two reports in 2005: an investigation into the role of public officials and politicians who allowed the development of a hotel within the curtilage of Trim Castle, a significant national monument in County Meath, and a report called the 'Great Corrib Gas Controversy', which forced the re-routing of a pipeline from an offshore natural gas field to Ballinaboy in north Mayo that was the subject of a long-running protest by the local community. The board of Feeney's charity, Atlantic Philanthropies, withdrew its funding from the organisation, following allegations made against me in the Dáil by Minister for Justice McDowell under Dáil privilege in late 2005, including that I had travelled to Colombia using a false passport in 2001, which I denied. No charges were made against me, but a worthwhile anti-corruption body was shut down. One of the conditions of ensuring that the outstanding debts to staff and other creditors of the agency would be covered following its closure was a commitment that we would not publish any further reports.

At the time, in early 2006, we had been investigating conflicts of interest between Anglo Irish Bank and its chairman and former chief executive Seán Fitzpatrick, due to his other role as a board member of the Dublin Docklands Development Authority. The Authority provided lucrative, publicly owned sites along the city quays to developers who borrowed millions from Anglo Irish to finance their construction projects. Two years later, Anglo Irish contributed significantly to the banking and financial collapse that destroyed the lives and livelihoods of hundreds of thousands of people and contributed to a housing crisis that still persists.

O'Callaghan's counsel, Paul Sreenan, accused Dunphy of inventing the allegation against Ahern at my instigation, which the broadcaster vehemently denied:

> If you are suggesting for one minute that I would come to this tribunal and perjure myself and damage the Taoiseach of this country and a businessman for whom I have the highest regard in order to wreak revenge, as you put it, for what was done to Frank Connolly, I don't want to be in any way bad-mannered, but that is outrageous. It is a preposterous allegation to make. And if that is what you are suggesting, well, then you must be pretty short of material.[3]

Another witness, a former executive with the Investment Bank of Ireland, Johnny Fortune, provided valuable testimony to support Gilmartin's extraordinary claim about being hit for a £5 million sum after his meeting with Haughey in February 1989. Fortune recalled a distressed Gilmartin calling into his office and recounting how a man approached him for 'a seven-figure sum' immediately after he left the meeting with the then Taoiseach in Leinster House. He said Gilmartin was 'ashen-faced' when he spoke to him soon after the encounter, and that he mentioned Liam Lawlor in relation to the incident. 'When he spoke to me, he was extremely angry and upset. He mentioned a seven-figure sum, using quite a number of expletives,' Fortune said. He told the tribunal that he came forward after a discussion with Paul Carroll, a friend and partner with solicitors A&L Goodbody, the firm acting for Gilmartin.

Combined with the other supportive witnesses who corroborated his evidence, his own performance in the witness box and the forensic investigation carried out by the tribunal, Gilmartin was reasonably satisfied when his cross-examination was complete.

When he returned to Cork, Gilmartin suffered further health problems, including a diagnosis of leukaemia, which set him back for several months as the tribunal trundled towards some form of conclusion at Dublin Castle. It continued to delve into Ahern's finances and his even more opaque elucidation of them, while I continued to expose stark inconsistencies in the testimonies of the country's most powerful politician and his closest allies.

As hearings resumed after the Christmas break in early 2008, I revealed how the Taoiseach did not hold a tax clearance certificate while minister for finance and provided misleading information about his dealings with the Revenue Commissioners. Pádraic O'Connor, now chairman of the Irish Stock Exchange, confirmed to the tribunal that he never gave a personal donation to Ahern in 1993, who, he added, was not a friend and was trying 'to protect his political existence'. 'I never had a pint with Mr Ahern. I never went to a football match with him. These are things I would do with my friends,' O'Connor said in a devastating blow to the 'dig-out' story.

Details further emerged about some peculiar activities in the management of funds in Ahern's constituency organisation based at St Luke's in Drumcondra, which he controlled with Des Richardson and Tim Collins, among others. A mysterious account named B/T, opened by Collins, provided a £30,000 loan to Celia Larkin, which she used to buy the house where her elderly aunts lived in Phibsborough in Dublin. The account was opened at the IPBS in Drumcondra close to St Luke's. Ahern and Collins described the B/T account (named with their initials, Bertie and Tim) as a 'sinking fund', with the monies used to shore up the building and prevent it from sliding into the adjoining Tolka river.[4]

The almost farcical explanations and attempts to shift the narrative came to an unfortunate climax when Ahern's former secretary in St Luke's broke down in the witness box after being questioned about her role in the lodgement of sterling to another account controlled by Ahern in the IPBS branch. Gráinne Carruth, who worked for Ahern for years, at first denied that she had carried out the transactions, but after constant questioning by tribunal lawyers who identified her name on the lodgement slips, and on the advice of her solicitor, accepted tearfully that she must have done so. The sight of Ahern's former secretary telling the tribunal lawyer that she was 'hurt' and pleading that she 'just wanted to go home' to her children was the final nail in the coffin of Ahern's credibility and hubris. She only admitted to making the sterling lodgements because of the pressure she came under to get her traumatic public appearance over with.

Carruth accepted that, on Ahern's instruction, she occasionally lodged monies into the accounts in the IPBS opened in the names of Ahern's two daughters. However, it emerged that she had, in fact, taken the hit for apparently making lodgements of sterling because her former employer did not want to implicate his Garda driver, who had handled the more sensitive, and larger, sums involved. Ahern, who was lacerated for unfairly placing his secretary under such duress, later told the tribunal that it was probably his 'then security officer', who carried the larger amounts, including in sterling, for lodgement. I subsequently learned that his official driver, Garda Matthew Ignatius 'Nashie' Grady, who died in 2016, would regularly carry large sums of cash from St Luke's to the nearby building society after getting the lodgement slips from Carruth, who pre-signed them. Getting Carruth to accept responsibility deflected from the optics of a serving garda depositing large sums of cash into an account controlled by the Taoiseach, which were not good from an ethical or compliance perspective.

Ahern trusted Grady, who drove the politician for many years. On one occasion, the car was stolen after Grady parked it overnight outside a house in Cabra, north Dublin. There was considerable panic in St Luke's when Ahern was told about the theft, as a case containing cash was in the vehicle, along with Grady's gun. They managed to retrieve the car by making contact, through a social worker, with prisoners in Mountjoy Prison, who facilitated its recovery before the gun or money was removed.

Ahern's appearance at the tribunal, coupled with the unfolding financial crisis in the country, with Anglo Irish Bank suffering a meltdown in its share value on St Patrick's Day 2008, led to a showdown in St Luke's on April Fool's Day. Brian Cowen made the trip to Drumcondra to hear the Taoiseach state 'his intention to announce stepping down'. Ahern had indicated during the 2007 campaign, when challenged by Cowen over the manner in which the election was called in response to the revelations in the *Mail* and the tribunal grilling he faced, that he would not be around as leader forever. Less than a year later, he was calling it a day.

On 2 April 2008, Ahern publicly announced that he would resign the following month, on 6 May, after thirty-one years in the Dáil and eleven as taoiseach. From the steps of Leinster House he declared, to an emotional response from his Cabinet colleagues, that the work of the government had been distracted by 'my life, my lifestyle and my finances'.[5] He continued to deny that he had done anything wrong and insisted that he never put his personal interest ahead of the 'public good'.

The emerging financial crisis that was, domestically, a consequence of the policies of deregulation and the promotion of reckless lending by banks to property developers pursued under his watch, overshadowed the handover to his nominated successor, Cowen. Ahern then made a final 'lap of honour' with a farewell tour, during which he addressed the UK Parliament and a Joint Meeting of the US Congress in April 2008, before he left the political stage. During his trip, I received information from his increasingly porous circle of friends that he was going to claim that monies the tribunal found in various accounts came from a streak of wins from bets he made in the bookies. *IMOS* editor, Sebastian Hamilton, reckoned that if we were to run this story, it could possibly dissuade Ahern from pursuing this line and thus discredit the newspaper.

On his return to the witness stand in early June, Ahern told the tribunal that some of the sterling lodgements were from the winnings he made on the horses, prompting much gaiety from the audience and the wider public. Other monies, he insisted, came from his late mother. He said he was shocked and surprised when his landlord Michael Wall left the house on Beresford Avenue to him in 1996. If Wall died, he would have been 'honour bound' to pay the man's widow in full, he said, to more laughs. On foot of these blatantly manufactured explanations, Hamilton ran a splash across the front page of the *IMOS* asking whether 'the Taoiseach committed perjury' – a courageous but risky headline that did not prompt any legal action from Ahern's lawyers. It was clearly the beginning of the end for the politician, even if many people were taken in by the laughable tales of 'dig-outs', lucky bets and an exceedingly generous landlord.

Ahern continued to resist the tribunal's conclusion that he purchased the house with his own money and was unwilling to disclose the details of that transaction for fear of undermining his own explanations for the sources of his income over and above his salary as a public servant. While there was no obvious trail of payments to Ahern from O'Callaghan, copious amounts of correspondence and diary entries relating to the

Cork developer and his agent, Frank Dunlop, regarding different commercial projects, pointed to, at the very least, potentially significant conflicts of interest.

The politician did admit to getting Joe Burke to help with the acquisition of the council lands at Quarryvale, and also to meeting with O'Callaghan in relation to the non-designation of the Blanchardstown shopping centre, the two issues at the heart of Gilmartin's claim that he was paid £80,000 by the Cork developer. By ensuring that Gilmartin secured the deal with the council, O'Callaghan avoided a loss of the £3 million owed to him by his reluctant partner in Barkhill for his purchase of the lands at Neilstown, while securing ownership of a strategic part of the Quarryvale site. If Blanchardstown did not get the favourable tax designation, it meant that it could not attract the anchor tenants lined up by Gilmartin for the Liffey Valley development. By any reckoning, Ahern helped to greatly enrich the Cork developer and his company through these two actions and other decisions he made while in office. Ahern also accepted that he approved the hugely beneficial tax designation for the Golden Island development in Athlone in the dying hours of the Fianna Fáil–Labour government in 1994.

Finally, Ahern agreed that he had met with O'Callaghan and Dunlop in relation to the proposed stadium project for which Albert Reynolds had promised up to £5 million a year in government support but which required the authorisation of Ahern as minister for finance to proceed. This is where the tribunal delivered its coup de grâce in its battle to uncover the relationship between Ahern, his meetings in advance of the collapse of the government in late 1994, and the deposit of what, it believed, was the $45,000 transaction on 5 December 1994.

In late October that year, Dunlop made his brief visit to New York to meet Bill O'Connor, having received £70,000 from O'Callaghan just days earlier. On 10 November, O'Callaghan and Dunlop brought O'Connor to meet Ahern in Dublin to discuss the stadium project, in the absence of department officials. Following the meeting, O'Connor wrote to Ahern to congratulate him on his accession as Fianna Fáil leader. Within days, the equivalent of $45,000 was lodged by Larkin in the AIB account he controlled. Asked whether this sum could have been related to the prospect that he was expected to become taoiseach, Ahern protested:

> Never in my forty years working in the public service, never have I taken a bribe or money from any individual, including any of the people put forward in this, whether it's Chilton O'Connor, Mr Gilmartin, Mr O'Callaghan or anyone else associated with it. I never, ever from any of those individuals, to the best of my recollection, got a cup of coffee, not to mind money.

Des O'Neill, senior counsel for the tribunal, then pointed to the other round figure sums lodged to his various accounts following meetings with O'Callaghan and Dunlop. He cited the £20,000 that was lodged to one of his daughter's accounts after Ahern's ten-minute meeting with the PR man about the stadium in August 1994. He also brought up the £30,000 transaction and lodgement to one of his accounts that took place on the same day Ahern met Dunlop in the spring of that year. The lawyer had records showing that Ahern met O'Callaghan in Government Buildings just hours before the statutory order to include Golden Island in the urban renewal incentive scheme was signed by the outgoing minister for finance and asked whether he received any consideration in return for this 'eleventh hour decision'.

Ahern replied, 'To the day I die, Mr O'Neill, I never got a penny from any of these characters. The only sad thing is that I ever met any of them.' He also had good reason to regret setting up the tribunal in the first place. He did not appoint 'a fucking Lowry' to his first Cabinet. He appointed Ray Burke instead. The rest is history, one might say, but not quite. In 2025, Fianna Fail and Fine Gael formed a government with the backing of regional independent TDs, including Michael Lowry, based on a programme for government which he negotiated. Plus ça change.

As for Ahern, he is still fanning the flames of discord. In early May 2026, he spoke to a woman about his concerns over immigration. She was secretly recording him as he canvassed for Fianna Fáil during a by-election in north Dublin. 'The ones I worry about are the Africans. We can't be taking in people from the Congo and all these places.' By chance, a few days after the tape was released, Congolese-born Yves Sakila died after he was forcibly restrained by a number of men who suspected him of stealing a bottle of perfume from the Arnotts department store in the city centre. One man had his knee pressed into Sakila's neck while the thirty-seven-year-old cried for help. The Fianna Fáil candidate lost his deposit in what was the worst by-election result suffered by the party in its hundred-year history.

Postscript

THE CORRUPTION OF SO MANY AT the highest levels of political, administrative and corporate life in Ireland from the 1970s until the end of the century, as recounted in these pages, was eventually exposed by the often dramatic revelations at public hearings of the tribunals. Protracted and costly as they were, the Moriarty, Flood/Mahon and Morris inquiries exposed extraordinary levels of illegality, graft, duplicity and the sustained and brutal abuse of power by those called to answer for their misdeeds in public view.

In December 2006, the Moriarty Tribunal found that, between 1979 and 1996, Charles Haughey

> lived a lifestyle and incurred expenditures vastly beyond the scale of the public service entitlements which were his sole apparent income for virtually the entirety of that period, and which were in any event cashed by him on a monthly basis.
>
> This was primarily enabled by the bill-paying service set in place for Mr. Haughey by Mr. Desmond Traynor. The funds provided to that bill-paying service were primarily enabled by borrowings during the first year of that period, and for some years prior to it. After Mr. Haughey first became Taoiseach at the end of 1979, the borrowings receded, and the funds were derived primarily from clandestine donations, and recourse to the Leader's Allowance Account, including not merely amounts of public monies, but money intended for the medical expenses of the late Mr. Brian Lenihan.

The tribunal calculated that Haughey accepted payments in return for favours of over £9 million during his years in public office between 1979 and 1996.[1] Despite this, when he died in 2006, he had never been held accountable for his corrupt activities.

In March 2011, the Moriarty Tribunal found that Michael Lowry provided information to businessman Denis O'Brien, which was 'of significant value and assistance to him in securing the second mobile phone licence'. Judge Moriarty described Lowry's role as 'disgraceful and insidious', and concluded that he had received over £500,000 in payments made or facilitated by O'Brien. In response, Fianna Fáil leader, Micheál Martin, called for the resignation of the TD for Tipperary North. However, Lowry has continued to represent the constituency, topping the poll in successive elections. In 2025, he represented the mainly rural independents in negotiations for the formation of a government. In March 2026, it was confirmed that no criminal charges would be brought against Lowry arising from the findings of the Moriarty Tribunal.

In March 2012, the Planning and Payments Tribunal issued its final report, which vindicated Tom Gilmartin and castigated his detractors, including Ahern, Flynn, Lawlor, O'Callaghan and Dunlop. A host of other politicians, public servants, bank officials and businessmen were criticised and accused of varying scales of wrongdoing. Again, no one was charged with criminal offences following its publication, and most of its recommendations were left on the shelf. The tribunal cost an estimated £144 million. It concluded, among other findings, that 'Much of the explanation provided by Bertie Ahern about the substantial funds identified and inquired into by the tribunal was "untrue"'. Ahern failed to account 'for over IR£165,000 which passed through bank accounts connected to him in the early and mid-1990s.' The tribunal was unable to determine if Bertie Ahern received corrupt payments from developer Owen O'Callaghan because Ahern 'did not give a true account as to the source of the money'. Judge Mahon said that corruption continued in the planning system because it 'affected every level of Irish political life' and 'those with the power to stop it were frequently implicated in it'.

The findings against Ahern by the tribunal referred only to his period as minister for labour and then finance between 1988 and 1995, and no action was taken against him. Others did face consequences as a result of this tribunal. Ray Burke was jailed for tax offences, and George Redmond and Frank Dunlop for bribery offences, while Liam Lawlor was sent to prison for three short periods for obstructing the work of the tribunal.

In his eight reports into 'Certain Gardaí in the Donegal Division', Judge Frederick Morris said that he was 'staggered' by the amount of 'indiscipline' and 'insubordination' that he found in the force. Morris noted that following the hoax bomb finds organised by Detective Garda Noel McMahon and Superintendent Kevin Lennon, no statements were taken from the gardaí involved and no forensic examination was carried out on the fertiliser and other materials 'found': 'The materials were simply gathered up and brought back to the station. They were subsequently spread on the gardens belonging to Superintendent Duffy and another officer and also on some wasteland. There was no investigation file prepared in relation to this incident. Yet again, Crime & Security Branch were not appraised of the true situation.'

In relation to the evidence heard from members of the force, Morris said:

> There was a clear failure on the part of various members of An Garda Síochána to account for their actions while on duty when appropriate enquiries were made of them by senior officers. The attitude adopted by these members ranged from an unhelpful lack of candour and detail to an absolute refusal to co-operate other than by blanket rejections of the propositions put to them. It is clear that members of An Garda Síochána adopted a thoroughly unco-operative manner with my investigators. The Tribunal has noted

> the same attitude in testimony. It is completely at variance with the minimal standards of behaviour to be expected of members of a disciplined force.

In September 2025 I revisited some of the victims of Garda corruption in Donegal, including Sheenagh McMahon O'Doherty, ex-wife of Noel McMahon, Amanda Fullerton, Jalisco Shortt and Bernie Diver. All expressed their shock that Noel McMahon had been awarded a Scott medal for bravery in 2021 in connection with his role in the rescue of Don Tidey. Despite a subsequent commitment to the Dáil by Taoiseach Micheál Martin in late 2025 to review the award, the Garda Commissioner has said that it cannot be withdrawn.

The tribunals were still under way when the financial crash of 2008 and 2009 exposed further layers of corruption, greed, incompetence and a breakdown of regulation and control of the banking and financial system fuelled by the political decisions of successive Fianna Fáil-led administrations. While the crash was global, its severity in Ireland arose from the overheating of the property market through the uncontrolled lending practices of Irish-owned banks to a relatively small group of developers. The improper, unethical and, at times, illicit relationship between developers, their lenders and the political and regulatory authorities contributed to the crash. It led to a €67.5 billion bailout and the introduction of the Troika of the European Central Bank, EU Commission and International Monetary Fund to supervise the public finances in late 2010, the enforcement of a drastic austerity programme on working people, and a savaging of public services.

Later, there was a massive transfer of assets, largely through the National Asset Management Agency (NAMA) and the Irish Bank Resolution Corporation (IBRC – formed from a merger of Anglo Irish Bank and INBS) from public to private hands as subsequent governments incentivised international investment in the property market at the expense of social and affordable housing programmes. Despite several controversies surrounding the manner in which hugely valuable assets were disposed of by NAMA, the agency has been wound down without any independent review of its operations. Similarly, the details of much of the activity surrounding the disposal of billions in public monies by the IBRC is shrouded in mystery and wrapped in a cloak of commercial sensitivity. Meanwhile, some of the largest debtors, whose reckless borrowing contributed to the collapse of the economy, have now recovered, some with the financial assistance of NAMA and other State agencies and local authorities.

The effects of the political, financial and economic strategies pursued by successive governments since the crash are still evident and have greatly contributed to the current crises in housing, health and the provision of other public services, which, in turn, have deepened inequality of income and opportunity, and worsened the quality of the lives of a vast number of citizens. The deep and sustained cost of living and accommodation crises have further widened the disparity in wealth across society.

Long before the financial and property collapse, governments ceased to build the social and affordable housing required by any decent and democratic society. It is no coincidence that the decision by the State to withdraw from the direct construction of homes was made during a time of significant corruption at the highest levels of national and local government as outlined in these pages. Delegation by the State of responsibility for house building to private interests has inevitably contributed to land speculation, greed and the corruption of elected and public officials across the globe. Ireland is no exception to this strategy, which has failed to deliver the numbers of dwellings required at accessible prices in the appropriate locations for socially mixed communities.

In more recent times, corporate interests have been allowed to dominate the housing market, at the same time capturing lucrative State contracts for the construction of public health, water, transport and other large-scale infrastructure projects. These invariably exceed the original tender price and predicted time scale. These consistent failures recur, despite the plethora of inquiries, agencies and regulators established over recent decades. The people were assured these were intended to ensure accountability from politicians and public servants, but instead they have served, in many cases, to protect them from scrutiny and have allowed them to avoid responsibility for their actions.

In 2004, the Fianna Fáil–Progressive Democrats government announced that, due to the cost and lengthy duration of tribunals, in future, commissions of inquiry to investigate matters of public importance would be held in private, unless circumstances required that they be held in public. Such commissions preclude the attendance of the media, as well as the public, and have not produced the expected co-operation of witnesses that this privacy was intended to encourage. There have been no prosecutions for criminal behaviour as a result of the work of these commissions of investigation. Moreover, in 2019, the Public Accounts Committee complained that 'there is not an effective control of costs for tribunals and commissions of investigation which take longer than anticipated or whose terms of reference are extended'.[2]

The most recent report by a commission of investigation has revealed that the activities of sexual predator Bill Kenneally were allowed to continue for many years due to the failure of two senior gardaí in Waterford to act on complaints by young men about his sexual abuse. Kenneally's uncle and cousin served as Fianna Fáil TDs for Waterford while another uncle was a prominent cleric in the Catholic Church. Kenneally was serving a lengthy jail term before his death in June 2026. In his recommendations, former High Court judge and chairperson of the Commission, Michael White, said a new law should be introduced to make misconduct in public office a criminal offence. Given the litany of wrongdoing by public servants and politicians recounted in these pages, such legislation would seem to be the very least of the sanctions required.

The most important vehicle tasked with implementing change and reform is the Department of Public Expenditure, NDP Delivery and Reform (DPENDR). It oversees The Office of the Ombudsman, which provides staffing and corporate services support for a number of statutory oversight bodies, including the Standards in Public Office Commission (SIPO).

The government has not introduced many of the recommendations made by the report of a group headed by former DPP James Hamilton in 2020 that would strengthen the powers, and increase the resources, of SIPO and other agencies charged with tackling political and corporate corruption. Over recent years SIPO investigations into alleged wrongdoing by public representatives, including a former taoiseach, junior ministers, TDs, councillors and local government officials, have not led to any criminal charges or prosecutions. Moreover, there are a considerable number of State-funded bodies which should, but do not, fall under the remit of the commission. SIPO has repeatedly called for more resources and for an extension of its powers, including that it be allowed to initiate its own inquiries. It has no policing or legal powers of enforcement and cannot sanction those against whom it makes a finding.

The Ombudsman is also limited in the range of administrative actions it can take, while the Comptroller and Auditor General does not have the power to investigate commercial semi-State bodies and local authorities or to apply sanctions where it has identified serious wrongdoing. The Public Accounts Committee can call public servants to account for their spending but cannot make findings of fact or compel witnesses to attend before it.

The DPENDR is also responsible for the Office of Government Procurement (OGP), which is tasked with ensuring the delivery of procurement solutions to public service bodies. The government's ability to control and monitor procurement across the public service and by State supported agencies is key to avoiding improper or corrupt relationships between its employees and the private and corporate sectors. However, it is unclear how the OGP can fulfil this role, as it is not directly involved in the procurement process for major infrastructural investments.[3]

In June 2022, the minister for justice announced the formation of the Advisory Council against Economic Crime and Corruption comprising chairperson, James Hamilton, and nineteen members. The council was set up to develop a multi-annual strategy to combat economic crime and corruption. It is also tasked with engaging and consulting with international agencies and bodies to monitor global trends and ensure that Ireland is at the forefront of international efforts to tackle economic crime and corruption.

The council does not have statutory powers and, by May 2026, had not produced any report or findings arising from its terms of reference. It also does not have policing or revenue powers of enforcement. The overwhelming representation of senior civil servants reinforces its lack of independence from government and the perception that its members are likely to resist exposing potentially corrupt dealings between public officials in their own departments and commercial interests.

Annual public spending by the Irish State amounted to €150 billion in 2025, yet the delivery of vital infrastructure and services lags well behind that of other similarly sized economies in Europe. The potential for corruption and waste with this scale of State expenditure is evident, and citizens have a right to expect rigorous and constant monitoring of public monies. New planning legislation forced through the Dáil in 2026, which restricts access to judicial review by citizens, threatens to weaken the safeguards against corrupt zoning and planning decisions as recommended in the reports of the Flood/Mahon Tribunal. An Taisce said of the Planning and Development Act 2024:

> One of the key concerns is that the Act centralises power in the hands of Government and relevant ministers with very few safeguards. It gives them substantial powers and new mechanisms to introduce national-level planning policies and requirements, and then to compel regional, county-level and local planning policies to comply with those Government policies.[4]

The nature of corruption in Ireland has inevitably changed since the period covered by this work and with the intensified globalisation of the economy. US tech, pharma and other multi-nationals have deepened their integration into the State's finances, with many setting up their European headquarters and tax base in the South, gifting massive annual surpluses and revenues to government. This windfall has not been matched by the infrastructural investment in housing, transport and renewable energy required by a modern economy facing existential threat from climate change.

Successive governments have also failed to build on the potential of the Good Friday Agreement to fully develop the all-Ireland economy and integrate the health, education, administrative and other sectors across the island. The pressure on government to dramatically increase spending on defence and further dilute the State's policy of military neutrality will involve the investment of public monies into the global arms industry, which has a long history of corrupt dealings and current complicity in illegal wars and genocide.

In this unstable environment, where the international, rules-based order is under threat, we face the enormous challenge of creating a society where the most basic needs of living, of health, education and financial security are provided in a clean and safe environment for all. It makes it all the more essential that those who betray the public trust for their own gain be held truly accountable for their actions. It is not too late.

ENDNOTES

1: Will We, Fuck!

1 'Serving politician linked to re-zoning reward offer', *The Sunday Business Post*, 9 July 1995, p. 1.
2 'Politicians link to property rezoning payoffs', *The Sunday Business Post*, 13 August 1995, pp. 1, 3.
3 Paul Cullen, *With a Little Help from My Friends: Planning Corruption in Ireland* (Gill & MacMillan, 2002), p. 41.
4 'Fianna Fáil politician paid off by developer' and 'Irish steel firm supplied buildings at Sellafield', *The Sunday Business Post*, 31 March 1996, p. 1.
5 'FF will deal forcefully with corruption', *The Sunday Business Post*, 7 April 1996, p. 4.
6 Cullen, *With a Little Help from My Friends*, p. 287.

2: Sheik Down!

1 '£20 million investment promised in passport deal was never made', *The Sunday Business Post*, 31 December 1995, pp. 1, 7.
2 'Passport sheik invested £3 million in Kerry Airport', *The Sunday Business Post*, 7 January 1996, pp. 1, 2.
3 Barchester Healthcare, whose subsidiary Leisure Holdings Ltd was the main beneficiary of Mahfouz's investment, was sold to US company Welltower in November 2025, netting its main shareholders, including Magnier, McManus and Desmond, over €5.2 billion.
4 'Passport holder sat on Duggan board', *The Sunday Business Post*, 28 January 1996, p. 1.
5 'Troubleshooter for north Dublin whose star seems to rise and rise', *The Sunday Business Post*, 18 February 1996, p. 8.
6 'Inquiry possible into Burke's granting of passports for investment', *The Sunday Business Post*, 4 February 1996, p. 4; 'Mahfouz passport inquiry sheik is Leisure Holdings shareholder', *The Sunday Business Post*, 11 February 1996, p. 9.
7 'FF will deal forcefully with corruption', *The Sunday Business Post*, 7 April 1996, p. 4.
8 'No one is welcome in this party if they betray the public trust', *The Sunday Business Post*, 20 April 1997, p. 4.
9 'FF politician in corruption probe', *The Sunday Business Post*, 4 May 1997, p. 1.
10 Ibid., pp. 1, 3.

3: Climbing Trees

1 'Said and done: quote unquote', *The Irish Times*, 25 January 2005, online.
2 *The Sunday Tribune*, 20 July 1997, p. 1.
3 'Burke political funding confusion remains', *The Sunday Business Post*, 27 July 1997, pp. 1, 2.
4 Tax designations for land in Ireland can involve rulings that reduce, defer or exempt the land from high rates of capital gains tax, stamp duty or residential zoned land tax. They are generally justified as being mechanisms to encourage farming, house building or consolidation of land holdings.
5 'Burke accuser denies vendetta', *The Sunday Business Post*, 10 August 1997, pp. 1, 5.
6 'Gogarty to sign Garda statement', *The Sunday Business Post*, 24 August 1997, p. 3.
7 'Life and times of the Big Fella and the Boss', *The Irish Times*, 26 April 1997, online.
8 Report of Grand Caymans Liquidators', 30 August 1991.
9 'Gogarty to sign Garda statement', *The Sunday Business Post*, 24 August 1997, p. 3.

4: Lines in the Sand

1 'Burke sought passport for investment deal for firm', *The Sunday Business Post*, 7 September 1997, p. 2.
2 Dáil Éireann debate, Wednesday, 10 September 1997, Vol. 480, No. 4: www.oireachtas.ie/en/debates/debate/dail/1997-09-10/9/.
3 'More questions than answers', *The Sunday Business Post*, 14 September 1997, p. 7.
4 'Gogarty says he gave Burke schedule of lands', *The Sunday Business Post*, 28 September 1997, p. 1.
5 'Burke home registration puzzle', *The Sunday Business Post*, 28 September 1997, p. 2.
6 'Adverse ruling for Oliver Freaney and former partner', *The Irish Times*, 29 July 2003.
7 'Standing by his man is taking its toll on the Taoiseach', *The Sunday Business Post*, 5 October 1997.
8 Ibid., p. 8.
9 'Official probe shows breach of passport regulations', *The Sunday Business Post*, 5 October 1997, pp. 1, 3, 7, 8.
10 'Brosnan backs role of passport sheik', *The Sunday Business Post*, 12 October 1997, p. 1.
11 Dáil Éireann debate, Tuesday, 7 October 1997, Vol. 481, No. 1: www.oireachtas.ie/ga/debates/debate/dail/1997-10-07/25/.
12 Dáil Éireann debate, Wednesday, 8 October 1997, Vol. 481, No. 2: www.oireachtas.ie/en/debates/debate/dail/1997-10-08/17/.

5: Out of Africa

1 'Secret trail of PD funds laid bare', *The Sunday Business Post*, 14 December 1997, pp. 1, 11, 12, 13.
2 'Gallagher gave Haughey £375K', *The Sunday Business Post*, 22 February 1998, pp. 1, 8, 9.

3 Ibid., pp. 1, 8, 9.
4 'It's Payback Time', *Irish Independent*, 5 June 1997, p. 1.
5 *The Second Interim Report of the Tribunal of Inquiry into Certain Planning Matters and Payments* (September 2002), p. 12.

6: The Gilmartin Story

1 All quotes in this chapter are taken from Frank Connolly, *Tom Gilmartin: The Man Who Brought Down a Taoiseach* (Gill & Macmillan, 2014).

7: Pub Crawl for Bertie

1 All quotes in this chapter are taken from Connolly, *Tom Gilmartin*.

8: An Oppressed Shareholder

1 All quotes up to this point in this chapter are taken from Connolly, *Tom Gilmartin*.
2 'O'Callaghan faces quiz on "six-figure" handout', *Irish Examiner*, 31 January 2008, p. 1.
3 'Charles Haughey and Othello's forgotten lines', *Irish Independent*, 21 June 2006.
4 Connolly, *Tom Gilmartin*, Appendix 1, paragraph 23.
5 Mahon Tribunal transcript, day 832, question 810.
6 Connolly, *Tom Gilmartin*, p. 78.
7 Ibid., p 283.
8 Connolly, *Tom Gilmartin*, Appendix 1, paragraph 30.

9: A Shithouse Consultant

1 'Another ex-FF minister kept £50,000 donation', *Sunday Independent*, 20 September 1998, p. 1.
2 'Developer claims he gave Flynn £50,000 for FF funds', *The Sunday Business Post*, 27 September 1998, pp. 1, 4.
3 'Lawlor fees now donations', *The Sunday Business Post*, 4 October 1998, p. 1.
4 'Angry man to put cat among the pigeons', *The Sunday Business Post*, 4 October 1998, p. 10.
5 'Gilmartin alleges £85,000 was paid to TD Liam Lawlor', *The Sunday Business Post*, 11 October 1998, p. 1.
6 For details of this meeting, see Connolly, *Tom Gilmartin*, pp. 107–8.

10: Beware of Greeks Bearing Gifts

1 'Flood ready to go to High Court over *Independent*', *The Sunday Business Post*, 20 December 1998, p. 7.
2 'An angry man heading for the Tribunal', *Irish Independent*, 23 January 1999.

3 'Gogarty wanted men to be shot', *The Sunday Times*, 14 March 1999, p. 1.

4 Not the businessman Denis O'Brien, whose dealings with Lowry were investigated in the Moriarty Tribunal.

11: Warts and All

1 'The magical mystery envelope', *The Sunday Business Post*, 24 January 1999, p. 14.

2 'Flood probes leak as Gogarty describes telephone threat', *The Sunday Business Post*, 7 February 1999, p. 14.

3 'The magical mystery envelope', *The Sunday Business Post*, 24 January 1999, p. 14.

4 'Bailey the main focus of Tribunal', *The Sunday Business Post*, 14 February 1999, p. 13.

5 'Not a normal company', *The Sunday Business Post*, 24 January 1999, p. 14.

6 'Gogarty faces quiz on £50,000 bank cash', *Irish Independent*, 3 February 1999.

7 'Bailey sought £300K from Anglo-Irish Bank', *The Sunday Business Post*, 28 February 1999, pp. 1, 4; 'Flood probes leak as Gogarty describes telephone threat', *The Sunday Business Post*, 7 February 1999, p. 14.

8 'Flood and ebb as tribunal hits stormiest waters yet', *The Sunday Business Post*, 28 February 1999, p. 13.

12: Finnegan's Wake

1 'Redmond's 14 bank and building society accounts', *The Sunday Business Post*, 28 February 1999, p. 4.

2 Connolly, *Tom Gilmartin*, pp. 28, 29.

3 'Flood of new claims: Gogarty cross-examination', *The Sunday Business Post*, 7 March 1999, p. 13.

4 'Big ambush that ended with a whimper', *The Sunday Business Post*, 28 March 1999, p. 15.

5 Cullen, *With a Little Help from My Friends*, pp. 129–30.

6 'Burke's part entrance with Finnegan's Wake', *The Sunday Business Post*, 18 April 1999, p. 17.

7 'Dermot Ahern statement is a big blow for Taoiseach', *The Sunday Business Post*, 28 March 1999, pp. 1, 15.

8 Ibid.

9 'NUJ condemns attack on Connolly', *The Sunday Business Post*, 9 May 1999, p. 15.

10 Damien Kiberd, 'Bashing the media: facts will speak for themselves', *The Sunday Business Post*, 28 February 1999, p. 39.

13: The £5 Million Man

1 'Developer told to lodge £5 million offshore', *The Sunday Business Post*, 24 January 1999, pp. 1, 3.

2 'MacSharry denies Gilmartin's claims on faxed letter', *The Sunday Business Post*, 31 January 1999, p. 1.

3 Dáil Éireann debate, Wednesday, 27 January 1999, Vol. 499, No. 1: www.oireachtas.ie/en/debates/debate/dail/1999-01-27/13/#spk_234.
4 'Gilmartin now rebuts Ahern', *The Sunday Business Post*, 31 January 1999, p. 13.
5 'Voices in the House', *The Irish Times*, 28 January 1999, online.
6 'Gilmartin diary reveals key date', *The Sunday Business Post*, 7 February 1999, p. 1.
7 'Taoiseach's friend Collins worked on Quarryvale project', *The Sunday Business Post*, 14 February 1999, pp. 1, 4.
8 'Haughey may escape tax on £75 k payment', *The Sunday Business Post*, 31 January 1999, pp. 1, 3, 11, 13, 18.

14: Who Killed Richie Barron?

1 Gerard Cunningham, *Chaos and Conspiracy: The Framing of the McBrearty Family* (Gill & MacMillan, 2009), p. 14.
2 'Garda face legal actions after Donegal murder investigation', *The Sunday Business Post*, 2 May 1999, pp. 1, 4.
3 Garda statement by John Sweeney, 18 October 1996.
4 Cunningham, *Chaos and Conspiracy*, p. 9.
5 Ibid., p. 10.
6 Ibid., pp. 182–3, photo caption.
7 'Judge expresses surprise over pub prosecutions', *The Sunday Business Post*, 19 September 1999, p. 7.
8 'Gardai face legal actions after Donegal murder investigation', *The Sunday Business Post*, 2 May 1999, p. 4.
9 'Opposition TDs meet minister over Garda corruption claims', *The Sunday Business Post*, 2 July 2000, pp. 1, 2.
10 'Four Donegal gardai face corruption charges', *The Sunday Business Post*, 23 July 2000, pp. 1, 4.
11 'Senior garda officer may face serious charges', *The Sunday Business Post*, 30 July 2000, p. 1.
12 Ibid.

15: Lawyers, Drugs and Money

1 'Gardai used bombings to get promotion', *The Sunday Business Post*, 25 April 1999, pp. 1, 4.
2 'Farmer seeks apology for armed raid', *The Sunday Business Post*, 17 September 2000, p. 8.
3 'Inquiry to re-examine explosive finds in Donegal', *The Sunday Business Post*, 2 April 2000, pp. 1, 4.
4 Cunningham, *Chaos and Conspiracy*, p. 149.
5 'Informant claims he knows who killed cattle dealer', *The Sunday Business Post*, 28 January 2001, pp. 1, 4.
6 'Gardai funded drugs found in Donegal premises', *The Sunday Business Post*, 4 February 2001, p. 1.

7 'Donegal Garda inquiry', *The Sunday Business Post*, 29 April 2001, p. 2.

8 Following the Morris Tribunal findings against him, White was sacked in 2006. He was later acquitted on charges of perverting the course of justice and of planting the firearm at the halting site. He died in 2020.

16: Courts and Tribunals

1 'McBrearty seeks senior garda testimony in Donegal case', *The Sunday Business Post*, 25 November 2001, p. 13.

2 'McBrearty case for High Court', *The Sunday Business Post*, 10 February 2002, p. 2.

3 'McBrearty calls for inclusion of Byrne, O'Donoghue in inquiry', *The Sunday Business Post*, 31 March 2002, p. 3.

4 'McBrearty takes legal battle against state to Europe', *The Sunday Business Post*, 5 May 2002, p. 6.

5 'McBrearty lawyers seek sensitive document from Minister and Commissioner', *The Sunday Business Post*, 7 April 2002, p. 3.

6 Cunningham, *Chaos and Conspiracy*, p. 10.

7 'Cocktail of alcohol and ambition', *The Sunday Business Post*, 16 June 2002, p. 12.

8 Michael Heney, *The Tallaght Two: Justice Delayed* (Gill & Macmillan, 1995), pp. 91–2.

9 Tom Inglis, *Truth, Power and Lies* (University College Dublin Press, 2003), p. 74.

10 Ibid., pp. 98, 101, 102.

11 'John Carthy death: A tale of blunder, negligence and cover-up', *Magill*, 2 August 2006, online.

17: The Pussy Book

1 The figure of £300,000 that Gallagher gave to the tribunal differed from the £375,000 that he told me he had paid.

2 Flood Tribunal, 'Opening remarks', 7 July 1999.

3 'Bullish Burke backtracking', *The Sunday Business Post*, 11 July 1999, p. 14.

4 Cullen, *With a Little Help from My Friends*, pp. 129–30.

5 'Murphy – the boss who said he knew nothing', *The Sunday Business Post*, 31 October 1999, p. 19.

6 'Evidence gives flavour of free loot', *The Sunday Business Post*, 14 November 1999, p. 16.

7 'A meeting full of contradictions', *The Sunday Business Post*, 12 December 1999, p. 16.

8 'Fine Gael TD says: I knew about £¼m "bribe" bid', *Irish Independent*, 15 April 2000, online.

9 'Dunlop's unanswered questions', *The Sunday Business Post*, 16 April 2000, p. 11.

18: Fingers and Floods

1 'New FF bribes probe could lead to election', *The Sunday Business Post*, 23 April 2000, pp. 1, 11, 13.

2 Connolly, *Tom Gilmartin*, p. 128.
3 Ibid., p. 130.
4 'Tribunal witness stands by £50,000 payments claim', *The Sunday Business Post*, 30 April 2000, pp. 1, 11, 12, 13, 14, 18.

19: Lawlor's Last Stand

1 'Digging deeper into Dunlop's can of worms', *The Sunday Business Post*, 23 April 2000, p. 13.
2 'Take the gombeen men out of planning', *The Sunday Business Post*, 23 April 2000, p. 18.
3 'Game of two halves between Dunlop and Redmond', *The Sunday Business Post*, 14 May 2000, p. 12.
4 'O'Callaghan met Dunlop twice during evidence', *The Sunday Business Post*, 20 August 2000, pp. 1, 4.
5 'Game of two halves between Dunlop and Redmond', *The Sunday Business Post*, 14 May 2000, p. 12.
6 'Redmond's circle of friends', *The Sunday Business Post*, 21 May 2000, p. 14.
7 'Lawlor's Liechtenstein money case', *The Sunday Business Post*, 17 December 2000, pp. 1, 3, 12, 13.

20: Bare Feet and Bad Trousers

1 '€34.5m collected so far thanks to inquiry … millions more in pipeline', *Irish Independent*, 27 September 2002. In 2010 Joseph Murphy senior and junior and Frank Reynolds successfully challenged the findings made against them by Flood in his second and third interim reports and the refusal of their costs. As a consequence, the adverse findings in the second and third reports were removed in relation to Oliver Barry, James Stafford, John Mulhern, Joseph Murphy Snr, Joseph Murphy Jnr, Frank Reynolds, Thomas Bailey, Michael Bailey and Caroline Bailey, among others not referred to in this book. In relation to George Redmond, adverse findings in the third interim report were removed, but a finding of corruption made against him in the fifth and final report remained.
2 'Law will take ill-gotten gains from corrupt, Ahern pledges', *Irish Independent*, 27 September 2002, online.
3 'Bertie Ahern – 1993 – Tax Evaders', YouTube: www.youtube.com/watch?v=bKztnNY1q2U&t=36s.
4 'Investigation into alleged £80,000 payment to serving FF minister', *Ireland on Sunday*, 29 September 2002.
5 'Taoiseach is furious over "bribe" remark on airwaves', *Irish Independent*, 5 October 2002, online.
6 Connolly, *Tom Gilmartin*, p. 141.
7 Ibid., p. 146.
8 Ibid., p. 147.

21: Death in Moscow

1 Unless otherwise stated, all quotes in this chapter are taken from Connolly, *Tom Gilmartin*.

2 *The Sunday Business Post*, 26 November 2017.

3 In 1999 Micheál Martin acquired a holiday home in a development in Courtmacsherry, near Bandon in Cork built by John Fleming. Fleming was among the first major debtors from Ireland to move to England and declare bankruptcy following the financial crash of 2008. On 11 March 2010, six days after Fleming's property company went into liquidation, the Irish Permanent mortgage on the Courtmacsherry holiday home purchased by Martin was cancelled, according to documents lodged with the Land Registry. In 2020, in response to queries by *Village* magazine, Martin failed to explain how he paid the Bandon-based developer for the large seaside property. A spokesperson for Martin said, 'The property was bought through an auctioneer with a mortgage in 1999. In 2010, Micheál switched mortgage provider and the loan was restructured to include the balance of this loan and refurbishment of Micheál's family home. Repayment of this mortgage is ongoing.'

4 'Mystery over size of O'Callaghan's donation to FF', *The Sunday Business Post*, 8 August 1999, p. 1.

22: Dig-outs and Dinners

1 'Investigation into alleged £80,000 payment to serving FF minister', *Ireland on Sunday*, 29 September 2002.

2 Connolly, *Tom Gilmartin*, p. 191.

3 Interview with Bertie Ahern, Clare FM, 20 September 2006.

4 Ibid.

5 'Businessman who gave £5,000 had only met Ahern a few times', *The Irish Times*, 13 December 2007, online.

6 'Home and away … more difficult questions for Bertie', *Irish Independent*, 29 September 2006, online.

7 Dáil Éireann debate, Tuesday, 3 October 2006, Vol. 624, No. 3: www.oireachtas.ie/en/debates/debate/dail/2006-10-03/16/.

8 'Names of four men present at meeting with Ahern now known', *The Irish Times*, 4 October 2006.

9 Dáil Éireann debate, Tuesday, 3 October 2006, Vol. 624, No. 3.

10 Connolly, *Tom Gilmartin*, p. 208.

11 Ibid., p. 209.

12 Colm Keena, *Bertie: Power and Money* (Gill Books, 2011), p. 193.

13 Fanning, according to his wife Anne in a 2013 interview, said that, in return for not publishing embarrassing details of Ahern's finances, the *Sunday Independent* would get exclusive stories from the Taoiseach during the election campaign. See 'Election will take place on Thurs March 24', *Sunday Independent*, 29 April 2007, p. 1; Connolly, *Tom Gilmartin*, p. 270; *Print and be Damned*, TV3, August 2013.

23: A Stash in the Wardrobe

1 Keena, *Bertie: Power and Money*, p. 193.
2 'Bertie: The Money Trail', *The Irish Mail on Sunday*, 29 April 2007, pp. 1, 2, 4, 5, 6.
3 *The Final Report of the Tribunal of Inquiry into Certain Planning Matters and Payments*, 22 March 2012, p. 2476, sections 2–3.
4 Connolly, *Tom Gilmartin*, p. 216.
5 'FF relief at postponing of hearings into Ahern finances', *The Irish Times*, 1 May 2007, p. 1.
6 'Ahern refused to elaborate on Larkin payment', *The Irish Times*, 2 May 2007, p. 13.
7 'McDowell uniquely opportunist', *The Irish Times*, 9 May 2007, p. 20.
8 'Mahon is not finished with murky deals for house in Drumcondra', *Irish Daily Mail*, 11 May 2007, p. 21.

24: It All Came Out in the Washing

1 *Irish Daily Mail*, February 2008.
2 'Albert "put a gun" to Bertie's head', *Irish Daily Mail*, 16 February 2008, pp. 7, 8.
3 Connolly, *Tom Gilmartin*, Appendix 1, paragraph 37.
4 Ibid., Appendix 1, paragraph 38.
5 'Bertie Resignation Bomb Shell', RTÉ, 2 April 2008.

Postscript

1 *The Irish Times*, 20 December 2006, online.
2 '"No effective control" of rising costs of tribunals and commissions', *The Irish Times*, 26 June 2019, online.
3 'Policy submission to the new government', 10 December 2024, Public Procurement Services, https://publicprocurement.ie.
4 'Could new Planning Act be a law of unintended consequences?', *The Irish Times*, 4 December 2024, online.

SELECT BIBLIOGRAPHY

Connolly, Frank, *Tom Gilmartin: The Man Who Brought Down a Taoiseach* (Gill & Macmillan, 2014)

Cullen, Paul, *With a Little Help from My Friends: Planning Corruption in Ireland* (Gill & Macmillan, 2002)

Cunningham, Gerard, *Chaos and Conspiracy: The Framing of the McBrearty Family* (Gill & Macmillan, 2009)

Heney, Michael, *The Tallaght Two: Justice Delayed* (Gill & Macmillan, 1995)

Inglis, Tom, *Truth, Power and Lies* (University College Dublin Press, 2003)

Keena, Colm, *The Ansbacher Conspiracy* (Gill & Macmillan, 2003)

Keena, Colm, *Bertie: Power and Money* (Gill Books, 2011)

Kerrigan, Gene, 'The Kerry Babies Case', *Magill*, 30 May 1985

McCafferty, Nell, *A Woman to Blame: The Kerry Babies Case* (Attic Press, 1985)

Shortt, Frank, *Abuse of Power* (Shortt Forefathers Publishing, 2012)

Taylor, Joe, and Douglas, Malcolm, *Trials and Tribulations: The Best of the Worst of the Tribunals* (New Island, 2005)

ACKNOWLEDGEMENTS

I am grateful to publisher Conor Graham and Síne Quinn of Merrion Press for their decision to commission this work, and to editor Wendy Logue and copy editor Heidi Houlihan for their diligent efforts to make it more accessible to readers.

Much of the work recounted here derived from my time working for *The Sunday Business Post* from 1992 to 2002 and later with *Ireland on Sunday* (2002–4), *Village* magazine (2006–7) and *The Irish Mail on Sunday* (2007–8).

During that period, I also worked on related documentaries and programmes for television and radio stations including RTÉ, TV3, TG4, Today FM and Newstalk. This work included documentaries on the Donegal Garda corruption story made with producer Garret Harte for the *20/20* series on TV3, and regular reporting on the Flood/Mahon and Morris Tribunals for *The Last Word* hosted by Eamon Dunphy on Today FM and *Tonight* with Vincent Browne on RTÉ radio.

I deeply appreciate the many colleagues with whom I have spent a very fulfilling career in investigative journalism, including publishers, editors, reporters, photographers, production and other staff, and far too many to record by name. Among those who deserve particular mention for his support and encouragement is the former editor of *The Sunday Business Post*, Damien Kiberd, who worked closely with me on the major stories recounted here. Sebastian Hamilton and the late Paul Drury at *The Irish Mail on Sunday* played a huge part in the months of exclusives that preceded the downfall of Bertie Ahern in 1998.

Sincere thanks are also due to the late Jim Gogarty and Tom Gilmartin, who trusted me with the explosive details of their harrowing dealings with corrupt politicians, planners and business people. Frank McBrearty senior and Frank junior, Mark and Róisín McConnell, and the many other Raphoe victims of the attempted framing of innocent people for the death of Richie Barron were generous with their time.

Sheenagh O'Doherty, who had to endure the physical violence of her husband, Detective Garda Noel McMahon, and the trauma of losing her children for three years due to his and the State's illegal actions, courageously shared her experiences of harassment and abuse. The late Hugh Diver and his wife, Bernie, the late Frank Shortt, his wife, Sally, son, Jalisco, and others mentioned in this book provided me with their time over the years of my investigations and since. Both the late Albert Fullerton, who fought a long battle to expose the truth about those who killed his father Councillor Eddie Fullerton in Buncrana in 1990, and his sister Amanda, who has continued this long campaign for justice, should also be commended.

The late Martin Giblin SC and solicitor David Walley did immense work in exposing the Donegal scandals and provided me with information, as did other lawyers, politicians and gardaí too numerous to name individually. Following his retirement as chairman of the Planning and Payments Tribunal I was privileged to befriend and work with the late Feargus Flood who did so much to expose corruption within Ireland's political and business elite.

Others who would not wish their identities as sources of sensitive information to be disclosed are also deserving of my gratitude. Without the courage of whistleblowers and truth-tellers, investigative journalism would not exist.

The research for this book required access to the newspaper archives of the National Library of Ireland, as some of the titles have not yet been digitised. I am extremely grateful for the generous assistance of the staff of the Library during my frequent visits. I would like to express my sincere gratitude to the generous and amiable Derek Speirs, the outstanding photo-journalist of our generation with whom I have collaborated over many years, including on this work.

I would also like to thank Ciara Mary-Alice Thompson (CMAT) for graciously allowing me to use the lyrics from her song 'Euro-Country'.

Finally, I sincerely thank my wife, Mary, for her guidance and love, as ever, during the making of this work. To our children and grandchildren, we will be eternally thankful for the joy you bring to our lives, and that sustains hope for a brighter and better future for humanity.

INDEX

La philosophie est une réflexion pour qui toute matière étrangère est bonne, et nous dirions volontiers pour qui toute bonne matière doit être étrangère.

Georges Canguilhem